ONE CHRISTMAS IN WASHINGTON

THE SECRET MEETING BETWEEN ROOSEVELT AND CHURCHILL THAT CHANGED THE WORLD

David J. Bercuson and Holger H. Herwig

McArthur & Company

Toronto

First published in Canada in 2005 by
McArthur & Company
322 King St., West, Suite 402
Toronto, Ontario
M5V 1J2
www.mcarthur-co.com

Library and Archives Canada Cataloguing in Publication

Bercuson, David Jay, 1945-
One Christmas in Washington : forging the alliance that won the
war / David Bercuson and Holger Herwig.

ISBN 1-55278-538-6

1. World War, 1939-1945--Diplomatic history. 2. Churchill,
Winston, Sir, 1874-1965. 3. Roosevelt, Franklin D. (Franklin Delano),
1882-1945. 4. Great Britain--Foreign relations--United States.
5. United States--Foreign relations--Great Britain. I. Herwig, Holger
H. II. Title.
D750.B465 2005   940.53'22'0922   C2005-904789-5

Printed in Canada by Friesens

The publisher would like to acknowledge the financial support of the Government of
Canada through the Book Publishing Industry Development Program, the Canada
Council for the Arts, and the Ontario Arts Council for our publishing activities. We also
acknowledge the Government of Ontario through the Ontario Media Development
Corporation Ontario Book Initiative.

10 9 8 7 6 5 4 3 2 1

ONE
CHRISTMAS
IN
WASHINGTON

For Barrie and Lorraine

CONTENTS

PROLOGUE

CHRISTMAS EVE 1941 BROKE CLOUDY AND RAINY IN WASHINGTON, DC. Since the dastardly Japanese surprise attack on Pearl Harbor seventeen days earlier, the provincial Southern town had begun to swell to almost a million people as a host of bureaucrats and administrators descended on it from around the country. Temporary wooden housing began to clutter the Mall, destroying the artistic beauty of the reflecting pool graced by the Washington and Lincoln monuments. For many of the newcomers, Washington seemed to have the charm of the North and the efficiency of the South. For all who came, it was a city on the move.

It was also a city gripped by fear that December—fear of imminent bombing, fear of sabotage, fear even of invasion. Newspapers ruminated about Japanese attacks on the Aleutian Islands, on Seattle, on San Francisco, and on San Diego. Civil defense spotters scanned the gray skies over the Potomac basin for any signs of German bombers or U-boats. The Secret Service suspected attacks any moment on the White House and studded it with antiaircraft guns, both real and wooden due to a shortage of these weapons. Secretary of the Treasury Henry Morgenthau, Jr., haunted by visions of the London Blitz, dispatched an army of Secret Service agents to blacken the mansion's windows, to fit bulletproof glass in the Oval Room windows, to install special General Electric outdoor floodlights, and to pour a concrete "bomb barrier" along the west wall of the Executive Office Building.

Franklin Delano Roosevelt was less than amused by Morgenthau's frenetic activities. It was, after all, Christmas. Washingtonians would be looking for signs of confidence, not fear, from their leaders. The president understood the mood well. Around dusk on December 24, as the thermometer dipped into the low 50s, between 15,000 and 20,00 Yuletide revelers gathered on the Mall, and from there sprawled onto the lawn and gardens in front of the White House. Several score of invited guests made their way through the black iron fence at the southwest and southeast gates of the mansion amidst cries of "No cameras, no packages" from the guards. The grounds were spectacular with their ancient Jackson magnolias, Hayes buckeyes, and horse chestnuts in the fading light. In fact, an eerie, reddish light set the Washington Monument aglow. What had earlier been a delightfully warm day had suddenly turned cold.

Precisely at 4:30 P.M. the Marine Band struck up "Joy to the World." Choirs from six area churches and a choral club provided the singing. Half an hour later the band played "Hail to the Chief." Across the Potomac, the sunset gun at Fort Myer boomed loudly. It was the signal for President Roosevelt and his wife, Eleanor, to move out on to the South Portico. The holiday revelers, who had been abuzz all day about the upcoming Joe Louis–Buddy Baer prizefight, turned their gaze to the portico. They quickly spied a small party behind the first family. They knew from the day's papers that Crown Prince Olaf and Crown Princess Martha of Norway had come to the White House as the president's invited guests. And then they recognized the defiant, pugnacious figure of Winston Churchill standing beside Roosevelt. The prime minister had braved raging seas and violent gales to cross the Atlantic on the brand-new, 37,000-ton battleship *Duke of York*. Now, with the onset of darkness, FDR pushed a button, which sounded the signal in a dugout on the lawn below the national Christmas tree, where an electrician lighted up the great evergreen. The red-coated Marine band struck up "Adeste Fidelis" and the throng burst into song.[1]

Still, Christmas 1941 was not a happy time. In his memoirs, Churchill would speak of it as "a strange Christmas eve."[2] The world was locked in deadly struggle. The "Axis" powers had dealt the Western leaders one blow after another. By December 2, German army detachments had reached the Khimki tram station, less than twelve miles from the Kremlin. Leningrad lay under a brutal siege. In Africa, Panzer units of General Erwin Rommel's Afrika Korps had come to rescue the beleaguered Italian ally. Five days later, 350 Japanese Val torpedo bombers and Zero fighters attacked Pearl Harbor, sinking the pride of the U.S. Navy: the battleships *Arizona*, *California*, *Nevada*, *Oklahoma*, and *West Virginia*. More than 2,400 Americans died that day. Before Churchill left London on the evening of December 12, he had received the dreadful news that Japanese Mitsubishi torpedo bombers had sunk the battleship *Prince of Wales* and the battle cruiser *Repulse* off the coast of Malaya.

The news only got worse. On December 16 the Royal Navy lost two warships off Tripoli; thereafter, Italian "human torpedo" crews penetrated Alexandria harbor in Egypt and struck the battleships *Queen Elizabeth* and *Valiant*. On December 19, Adolf Hitler assumed personal command of the Wehrmacht for the final assault on Moscow. In the Battle of the Atlantic, in 1941 the Allies had lost 1,299 ships of 4.4 million tons to Admiral Karl Dönitz's "gray sharks." And while Churchill was in Washington, Japanese forces landed in Thailand and Malaya, surrounded Hong Kong, and invaded the Philippines. On Churchill's war map, the Empire was drowning in a sea of swastikas and rising suns. It was all too much for his wife Clementine. "It's a horrible World at present," she wrote Winston, "Europe over-run by the Nazi hogs & the Far East by yellow Japanese lice."[3] Churchill admitted that he felt "numb and dull and stupid."

But for Churchill, there was also a ray of hope. The Japanese attack on Pearl Harbor had at last brought the United States into the war. He, the supplicant of the past, would now be the ally of the future. Almost as a gift from heaven, on December 11, during a speech in which he railed against the "lout" Roosevelt, Hitler foolishly had declared war on the United States. Now, America was no longer a benevolent neutral, but an active ally.

From the White House to the Federal Reserve Building, from Ottawa to Florida, in those bleak December days, Churchill, Roosevelt, and their aides went about the work of forging the Grand Alliance. ARCADIA—code word for the Washington War Conference of December 1941 to January 1942—became the central venue for shaping the future course of the Second World War. It was not easy. Although the United States and Britain shared centuries of democratic values, and loathed all that Hitler and Nazism stood for, the devil was in the details. Since the days of the Spartans and Athenians, coalitions had fought wars against each other. But never before had such a coalition fought a global conflict, and never with the close harmonization that would be required to defeat the Axis. Churchill and Roosevelt knew Allied victory would demand that their two nations fight virtually as one, that they would need to coordinate much of the planning, production, and deployment of their fighting forces as well as the actual waging of the war itself.

During that Christmas in Washington, therefore, everything was on the table and open to debate: grand strategic issues such as defeating the Axis powers and creating a successor to the League of Nations; political decisions concerning the future borders of the Soviet Union; operational decisions about where to place the emphasis on rolling back the Axis fronts; tactical considerations regarding future war production of warships, aircraft, and tanks; economic decisions about steel and ship construction, food production and distribution; and decisions about the financial affairs of war funding. In short, the men in Washington during Christmas 1941 were reshaping the course of a war and reordering a world gone awry.

At every step of the way, pride, national interests, and personality threatened the enterprise. Roosevelt was brilliant and a consummate politician. He had a good grasp of the broader strategic considerations of this global war and he greatly admired Churchill. Still, he was a patrician at the head of the largest democratic nation in the world and was far from naïve about the underlying predominance of American power in this brand-new alliance. He had to serve the vital interests of his nation, to bring it fully united onto the world stage, and to lead the Allied drive to victory while also subordinating American interests where necessary to maintain Allied unity. His most difficult challenge was where to draw the line. In deciding that he had not only Congress, the American press, and his administration's defense, foreign policy, and military leaders to cope with, but also his wife, Eleanor, who had her own view of what the United States ought to fight for and her own reservations about Churchill.

Churchill was a brilliant and much accomplished man who had never been humble about his own talents and achievements. He too had to know where to draw the line between vital British interests and the requirements of the larger alliance. In many ways he took a very different view of the world than did Roosevelt. He was far less of a democrat; he was a strong advocate of imperialism and of the destiny of the British Empire. He believed in maintaining defined spheres of interests. But most important, he had been the supplicant in his relationship with Roosevelt and was acutely aware of the power and potential of the United States. At heart he was a vain and proud man, fully believing in his own sense of destiny, who now had to swallow a subordinate relationship to an American politician from upstate New York.

Both these men brought their retinues to the Washington talks. Military leaders such as Admiral Ernest J. King, who loathed the British, and General Sir John Dill, who had recently been stood down as chief of the imperial general staff, who thought Americans terribly disorganized at the business of war. The British were often insufferably arrogant toward their new ally. Sir Charles Portal, chief of the air staff, demanded that the Americans place their air forces at the disposal of the RAF, an idea brusquely dismissed by U.S. Army Air Forces Commander in Chief General H. A. "Hap" Arnold. As the talks proceeded, the personal animosities of the top military men threatened to derail the discussions. Roosevelt and Churchill struggled as much with their own subordinates and their own domestic interests and considerations as they did with each other. Success was vital for the future of the civilized world. The frightful danger of failure dogged almost every step the Western leaders took. In the end, they succeeded—but it was never easy.

1
A MEETING AT ARGENTIA

WHEN GEORGE WASHINGTON CHOSE THE SITE OF THE NATION'S new "Federal City," he did not choose well. From out of the 100 square miles of land on both sides of the Potomac River that Maryland and Virginia offered, the first president selected a plot closest to his home at Mount Vernon—a quadrangle of pastures and malarial swamps, most of it at, and some of it below, sea level. During the summer months, the city named after its founding father was so hot, humid, and inhospitable that the British Foreign Office once classified it as a hardship post.

Though Pierre L'Enfant laid out grand avenues and designed magnificent marble temples for the capital, by 1939 Washington had miles of desolate slums inhabited by impoverished blacks. In fact, the capital was one-third black—and rigidly segregated. It was a city of 15,000 outdoor privies, where it was difficult to find food that was not deep-fried. The fortunate ate at one of the Child's restaurants, where forty cents would buy the blue plate luncheon special of string beans, mashed potatoes, and roast beef. Every workday near dusk, an army of federal bureaucrats scurried out of town on Capital Transit trolleys to their small houses bought with $5,000 mortgages at 3 percent to seek some relief from the heat via air stirred up by the brass blades of black Westinghouse fans. Those with sufficient wealth escaped Washington altogether during its torpid summers.

Sunday, August 3, 1941, found the capital in the clutches of heat, with temperatures soaring through the 90s.[1] The leaves on the elms and sycamores hung limp in the humid fog. The stench of outdoor sewage permeated the city, the tar melting on its broad boulevards. Some Washingtonians headed out to Griffith Stadium home of the American League Senators, to take in a baseball game. President Franklin D. Roosevelt, in what Secretary of the Interior Harold Ickes called "a state of innocuous desuetude," stuck to his second-floor bedroom in the White House. In May 1933, Westinghouse had installed air-conditioning units in the fireplaces of six of the rooms on the second floor. This made life almost tolerable for FDR.

A surly Congress debated the merits of extending the draft. Few "cave dwellers," as native-born, blue-blooded Washingtonians were called, took much notice of a report in their city's newspapers—*Post, Times-Herald, Evening Star,* and *Daily News*—that Roosevelt had decided to escape the summer heat and to fish off the coast of New England from his yacht, the 400-ton *Potomac*, anchored at New London, Connecticut. The sixth presidential yacht, the *Potomac* was the former U.S. Coast Guard cutter *Electra*. FDR had the steel-hulled craft outfitted because he was afraid that Herbert Hoover's wooden yacht *Sequoia* was susceptible to fire.

At 10 A.M. that muggy August 3 the president's special train, the *Ferdinand Magellan*, pulled out of Union Station. His private car, built by the Association of American Railroads, had two elevators to lift his wheelchair on and off. The windows were bulletproof, the sides were of heavy armor plate, and the floor had steel-reinforced concrete to protect against bombs placed in the rail beds. Soldiers with bayonets protected every bridgehead en route to New London. Strangely, Roosevelt had kept the fishing trip confidential from his family as well as from his White House staff. Even the Secret Service had been taken in. From New London, the *Potomac* steamed on to Point Judith, Rhode Island, and then to Martha's Vineyard Sound. There, the yacht met up with a flotilla of American warships, and Roosevelt transferred to the 11,500-ton, 8-inch heavy cruiser *Augusta*, flagship of the Atlantic fleet. The welcoming party included Admirals Ernest J. King and Harold R. Stark and Generals George C. Marshall and Henry H. "Hap" Arnold. Neither Secretary of War Henry L. Stimson, Secretary of the Navy Frank Knox, nor Secretary of State Cordell Hull had been invited on the trip. The *Potomac* returned through the Cape Cod canal. On deck, for all reporters to see, was a man dressed in white ducks with a long cigarette holder clenched between his teeth. In what has been called "one of the best-kept, most startling secret adventures in modern history,"[2] FDR had eluded his innermost entourage and was steaming to Placentia Bay, Newfoundland. The time had come to get acquainted with Winston S. Churchill—and to discuss the future of the Western world.

Though the idea of a Roosevelt–Churchill meeting had been mooted for months in both capitals, the immediate cause of the rendezvous at Placentia Bay was the German invasion of the Soviet Union in June 1941. Churchill had warned Joseph Stalin that Hitler was about to stab him in the back, but the Soviet leader had done nothing to prepare his military for the assault. The attack came as a strategic surprise. In the long northern days of late June, German aircraft virtually destroyed the Soviet air force while armored spearheads slashed deeply into Soviet territory, encircling and capturing hundreds of thousands of Russian troops. Few military observers in London or Washington thought the Soviets would hold out for longer than a month; a miracle might buy them six weeks. Churchill took no heed. Almost as soon as he learned of the attack, he took to the airwaves to offer Stalin an alliance and promises of as much aid as he could deliver. In fact, he had very little to send and only a very hazardous sea route, past Luftwaffe airfields in northern Norway, to Archangel and Murmansk, over which to send it. The first convoy would not leave for months.

Soviet entry into the war was a potential godsend to Britain, if the USSR could survive. It was a wake-up call to Roosevelt. The war had gone badly for Britain since the late spring. Efforts to bolster Greece against an Italian invasion had foundered with the intervention of Germany. Hitler's forces had chased the British and thousands of their Australian allies out of Greece while conquering Yugoslavia. Then they had invaded Crete from the air and taken that too. Churchill worried that Francisco Franco might allow German troops through southern Spain to attack Gibraltar. The war in North Africa had become a hard, seesawing battle since General Erwin Rommel's arrival; the buildup of German forces now threatened Egypt and the Suez Canal. And German submarines continued to take a heavy toll of British and Allied shipping in the Battle of the Atlantic.

Through all of this, the president had seemed lethargic, even unmoved, frozen in indecision. Harry Hopkins, confidante and presidential advisor, was "totally unable to account for this sudden reversal from a position of strength [earlier in the year] to one of apparently insouciant weakness." He chalked it up to the constant, wearing battles with the increasingly extreme isolationists.[3] Roosevelt biographer Kenneth S. Davis attributed FDR's inactivity to "his caution and suspension of judgment, which was still to some extent determined by ill health." Roosevelt was often plagued for weeks by persistent sinus problems and general lack of "pep."[4] Now, with Soviet troops in full retreat, FDR seemed to spring to life once again.

The Soviet Union's sudden entry into the war had broad implications for the United States and further complicated the already complex pattern of Anglo-American relations. There were rumors in the United States, spread by isolationists and Anglophobes, that Britain was using American-produced war supplies to make lucrative trade deals with Latin America. Roosevelt soon decided that the United States ought to aid Russia, as it was already aiding China against Japan, but he was not sure what succor the Soviets really needed, nor to what use it would be put. He worried about secret arrangements that Churchill might attempt to make with Stalin in return for a Soviet promise to stay in the war until victory or the bitter end. He was fully aware that Churchill had sent massive amounts of American-supplied munitions and tens of thousands of troops to North Africa and the Middle East. Some of his military advisors thought that was insane, given the ongoing threat to the British Isles. Roosevelt was not pessimistic about British chances in that theater, but he could not really understand why Churchill was prepared to gamble so much there. Here, no doubt, the ongoing suspicion that American aid—and, later, American troops—were underpinning British imperial aims, played a significant part in American thinking. After all, the United States had no stake "east of Suez." Roosevelt was also anxious to use the period of relative calm that his military chiefs foresaw in the Atlantic to increase the American naval role there. Roosevelt needed to learn a lot, and quickly.

Thus, on July 11, 1941, Roosevelt had summoned Hopkins to the White House. He wanted him to go directly to London to meet with Churchill to propose a meeting in the near future. Although Roosevelt had many concerns on his mind, his major objective was to pin the British prime minister down to a joint set of war aims. In part, that would allay fears of Churchill making deals with Stalin or anyone else without American participation. It would also clear up the question of exactly what America was going to fight for, in the likely event that it would fight, other than in its own defense, before it actually got dragged in to the war.

Here was another significant difference that had emerged between Churchill and Roosevelt. FDR was a progressive. A cautious one, it is true, but nevertheless a man who believed that government had a major role to play in guaranteeing a basic standard of living for all citizens. His New Deal had evolved from a largely voluntary program designed to stiffen morale into a sweeping government program of welfare legislation, Social Security, labor standards laws, and union empowerment. Now Roosevelt wanted a "New Deal" for the world. Pushed hard by his wife, Eleanor, and by other lingering New Dealers, Roosevelt had tried to convince Churchill to adopt a coherent set of war aims such as universal democracy, freedom of worship, freer trade, and self-determination, not unlike some of the "Fourteen Points" Woodrow Wilson had publicly striven for when the United States had entered the First World War.

Churchill had resisted. He was unwilling to commit Britain to principles that might undermine its imperial ties, such as self-determination for India and the elimination of the 1932 Ottawa Agreements that bestowed trade preferences among the self-governing Dominions of the British Commonwealth such as Canada, Australia, and Britain itself. But mostly, Churchill believed that Britain was still fighting for its very life and that the relief that came from the nightly German bombing raids in May 1941, when Hitler sent the Luftwaffe east to prepare for the invasion of the Soviet Union, was but a temporary reprieve. If Russia collapsed, then its tremendous reserves of oil and other raw materials would be at Hitler's disposal, as would its arms industries. Then Britain would face a second Battle of Britain—more terrible and more doubtful in its outcome than the first had been. This was not the time for fancy thoughts about building a better world after victory; victory was still very much in doubt.

But Churchill was eager to meet Roosevelt when Hopkins proposed it one warm afternoon in the garden of No. 10 Downing Street shortly after his arrival. A face-to-face encounter would give him an

additional opportunity to woo Roosevelt and to discuss issues of pressing concern to Britain. Foremost among these, of course, was America's
entry into the war—which FDR most decidedly did not want to talk
about. But there was also the looming issue of American-Japanese relations, which had been growing steadily worse since the Japanese invasion of China in 1937. Churchill feared a Japanese attack on British
possessions in Southeast Asia. If that should happen, and if the United
States continued to stay aloof from the war, another nail would be driven
into Britain's coffin. Churchill wanted some assurances from Roosevelt
that he would not weaken in his stance against Japanese expansion, or,
better, a commitment to declare war on Japan if it attacked British possessions. Finally, he too had concerns about American aid to Russia, and
how such aid might impact American deliveries of war materials to the
United Kingdom.

At noon on August 3, 1941, Churchill boarded a special train that
took him and his retinue north, toward Scapa Flow, where the battleship *Prince of Wales* awaited its important passengers. Churchill took a
large group with him. He insisted Hopkins come along, giving the
American a long sea voyage in which to recover from his recent quick
and very wearing trip to visit Stalin. Chief of the Imperial General Staff
General Sir John Dill and the First Sea Lord Sir Dudley Pound represented the army and the navy, respectively. Air Vice Marshal Sir Wilfred
Freeman represented the RAF. Sir Charles Portal, RAF Chief, and
Major General Hastings "Pug" Ismay, Churchill's principal military
advisor, stayed home to assist Deputy Prime Minister Clement Attlee
and the War Cabinet in the prime minister's absence. Churchill
arranged for Lord Beaverbrook, Minister of War Production, to travel by
air to Newfoundland to meet the party on arrival. Also on the sea voyage
were Sir Alexander Cadogan, undersecretary of state for foreign affairs,
Churchill's friend and scientific advisor, Professor Fred Lindemann
(known as "the Prof"), assistant secretary to the War Cabinet L. C.
Hollis, and a number of other personal staff. He also invited two journalists, even though he and Roosevelt had agreed that the press would
be kept far from this secret meeting.

Prince of Wales departed Scapa Flow on August 4, heading west
into heavy weather. It soon left its escort destroyers behind. One of the
British journalists, H. V. Morton, later recalled:

The monstrous plunges of a great battleship are so deliberate and slow as to be unlike the movement of any other ship, indeed they are not like the movement of a ship at all: it is as though some vast steel works, or some factory . . . were flying unsteadily through the air. Almost as alarming as the movement are the sounds of a battleship in a storm . . . sudden bumps and bangs of ferocious power, as if the ship had struck a rock or had been kicked by a passing leviathan, followed by an uneasy silence in which metallic objects fall with a crash and men are heard far away running in heavy boots on steel decks.[5]

On the morning of August 9, three U.S. Navy destroyers pulled into view to escort *Prince of Wales* into Placentia Bay. At 9:00 A.M. local time the battleship glided to a halt. Churchill wired King George VI: "With humble duty, I have arrived safely, and am visiting the President this morning."[6]

The newly leased American base on the shore of Placentia Bay, on the southeast tip of Newfoundland, was a beehive of activity. Civilians had been evacuated from the town of Argentia, and now thousands of American workers and soldiers labored around the clock to construct an airfield, hangars, and a naval yard. Eventually, Washington would pour $45 million into the site. The rocky hills ringing Ship Harbour were graced with misty green forests.

The work crews were astounded when at 9:24 A.M. on Thursday, August 7, an American naval flotilla consisting of two heavy cruisers and five destroyers hove into sight in and dropped anchor at the head of the harbor. They were even more startled when two days later, precisely at 9 A.M., there appeared another flotilla of four warships: a U.S. Navy destroyer division escorting the dazzle-painted battleship *Prince of Wales*. It was a gray, drizzling morning with much fog and cold wind as the battleship dropped anchor near the *Augusta*, the ship upon which FDR was traveling. Despite all the secrecy, German agents in Lisbon had caught word of the impending meeting; German radio had announced it to the world on the night of August 4.

The Americans were the official hosts and turned to the task at once. Roosevelt was well aware from Hopkins' visit to Britain earlier that year that the British were on reduced rations and lacked sweets and tobacco; hence he handed out 1,950 gift boxes containing cigarettes, fresh fruit, and cheese. U.S. Navy crews passed out vast amounts of cigarettes and candy. Royal Navy and Royal Canadian Navy crews knew that American warships had been "dry" since the days of President Wilson, and thus responded with liquor. Yet, despite this open friendliness, many Royal Navy hands were appalled at the Americans' naïvete about the war in general and Britain's dire predicament in particular. Group Captain (later Vice Air Marshal) W. M. Yool leafed through a stack of recent American magazines and was shocked to discover that the "main preoccupations" of the American public seemed to be "1) the elimination of B.O.; 2) keeping the bowels open; and 3) lying on a beach with a blonde."[7] He failed to notice that the nation was more riveted on Joe DiMaggio's fifty-six-consecutive-game hitting streak than on the European war.

Shortly before noon on Saturday, August 9, Churchill, dressed in the blue uniform of an Elder Brother of Trinity House (the body which ran the lighthouses and Britain's coasts), boarded the *Augusta* to the strains of "God Save the King." He was ebullient about the opportunity to plead his case with Roosevelt one-on-one, away from the glare of public circumspection. "You'd have thought," Hopkins later recalled, "Winston was being carried up into the heavens to meet God!"[8] FDR, dressed in a tan Palm Beach suit, led off with a cheerful, "At last we've gotten together." But then relations quickly deteriorated. The Americans were not pleased that Churchill had brought two journalists with him, even though both were prohibited from leaving the British battleship.[9] "Isn't that just like the British," Admiral King tartly noted.[10] Roosevelt, fearing what the White House press corps would do to him if he allowed Fleet Street to scoop the story, immediately dispatched a Grumman aircraft to Gander Lake to bring in several Army photographers. Then Churchill committed a major gaffe when he stated how delighted he was to meet FDR for the first time person to person. In fact, the two had met at a dinner at Gray's Inn in London in 1918; Roosevelt was less than pleased that he had apparently left no impression on the prime minister that long-ago evening. Then it was discovered that the visitors had brought a staff of twenty-one, and the hosts only had fifteen. But soon tempers calmed and it was "Winston" and "Franklin."

Even the crusty Anglophobe Admiral Ernest J. King, commander of the U.S. Atlantic Fleet, played the role of gracious host. Nine years earlier in his Naval War College thesis, King had depicted the Royal Navy as a potential enemy. "In the future the question of trade, of shipping, and of naval strength may lead to war,"[11] he had written. Now, at Argentia, he grew to like Admiral Pound. Both shared a common view of the centrality of the Atlantic theater.

That night, Roosevelt hosted a formal dinner in the captain's salon of the *Augusta*. FDR, who was exempted from the Navy's no-alcohol rule, impressed the guests by mixing martinis, using a special dry gin and potent Argentine vermouth. Thereafter, the visitors were treated to a sumptuous banquet amidst candlelight glowing on silver. The main course consisted of broiled chicken, buttered sweet peas, spinach omelet, and candied sweet potatoes; next came a sliced tomato salad, assorted cheeses, and crackers; dessert included chocolate ice cream, cookies, and cupcakes.

After dinner, Roosevelt asked Churchill for an appraisal of the current situation. With the customary eight-inch Corona cigar firmly clenched between his teeth, the prime minister dazzled his hosts with an impromptu and lengthy review of the war. Unaccustomed to not being center stage, FDR nervously twiddled with his pince-nez, doodled on the tablecloth with a burnt match, and rubbed his eyes from all the smoke. He had lost the first round to Churchill.

Roosevelt had no less an ego than Churchill. His strong sense of self-confidence, his belief in his ability to get things done, his desire to leave a mark on the world, had helped him overcome personal and political crises. It had driven him to the head of his country through the worst economic depression in its history and in to a second world war. Now, he was being upstaged by Churchill on his own cruiser—as he had been, in a sense, in the world at large since Churchill had taken over as prime minister. Churchill's speeches thrilled the free world. His image—defiant, steady, determined—stared from covers of *Time, Life, Colliers,* and *Newsweek,* from the front pages of the *Washington Post* and the *New York Times.* Churchill's image flickered on newsreel screens across the world, surveying bomb damage, greeting British fliers, being cheered by the British people. Churchill was flamboyant, erudite, a leader of a nation at war while he—the president of the United States—

trod cautiously between the needs of his country's military, the growing calls for intervention in the war, and the still-shrill plaints of the isolationists and the Anglophobes. Many years after the war Lord Halifax, the British ambassador to Washington during most of the war, recalled: "I'm sure he [Roosevelt] was jealous [of Churchill]. Marshall told me that the President did not look forward to Winston's visits. He knew too much about military matters; besides, he kept such shocking hours."[12]

Behind the scenes, British and American military planners huddled in groups to grapple with potential future strategies. The British, from Churchill to Pound to Dill, had come ready to discuss the specifics of war strategy. The Americans had not. As General Marshall would later recall:

> The British would like to have gone much further. They were at this business every day—all day—on a very definite warmaking basis. We were in a position of mobilizing and equipping an Army. Just how this was to be handled on our side largely remained to be determined. Therefore we were not prepared to give them any fixed advice.[13]

A second major difference revealed itself even more glaringly. British strategy seemed to the Americans to be shaped by the Somme in 1916, by the memory of millions of young men led to their slaughter in a giant, bloody stalemate of trenches, barbed wire, machine guns, and gas. The British wished to avoid the horrendous slaughter of the Western Front at all cost, and thus laid out an "indirect" strategy, one whereby Germany would be defeated not by direct invasion, but rather by aerial bombardment, blockade, propaganda, fomenting of dissident or resistance groups, and only eventually by hit-and-run operations on its periphery. This "Fabian strategy" appalled the Americans, especially George Marshall. The lesson of the First World War was simple and obvious to him: the war yet again would have to be won by a massive land offensive through German-occupied Europe and into Berlin.

Part of Marshall's reticence was grounded in the fact that U.S. forces were in no position to intervene in European affairs. In 1939 he had inherited an army and air corps strength of just 225,000; and although he had raised that figure to around 1.5 million by the time of Argentia, this was still inadequate even for the defense of the Western

Hemisphere. Thus, in Washington, one of Marshall's planners, Major Albert C. Wedemeyer, was just then putting the finishing touches on what would become the "Victory Program" of September 1941: the standing up of an army of some 215 divisions of 8.8 million men, of whom 5 million would be moved overseas.[14] L. C. Hollis later recalled: "American ideas were running at this time towards an army of about four million men, a figure which we urged was too large and would involve a waste of manpower and of factory capability."[15] Agreement at this stage was beyond hope.

Moreover, Congress in these hectic times had forced on Marshall yet another onerous task: as chief of staff of the U.S. Army, it became his sole responsibility to decide on what military equipment—Army and Army Air Forces—might be spared stateside and sent abroad to aid the Allies, and what was vital at home to build American defenses. It was a Hobbesian choice. No matter what Roosevelt wanted to do, no matter what Churchill asked for, Marshall was the man who had to sign off on military aid. He was responsible both to the president, his commander in chief, and to the Congress. And he stood between two stools in the public eye: while the interventionists wanted to ship as much American military hardware as possible to the United Kingdom, the isolationists, within the army and without, demanded the defense of the Americas take priority. By and large, the British were unsympathetic to Marshall's plight.

Sunday morning, August 9, proved to be the climax of the historic meeting—officially code-named RIVIERA. Almost on cue, a soft breeze parted the wet and leaden skies, letting sunshine through. The destroyer *McDougal* took Roosevelt, hatless and attired in a blue double-breasted suit, across the shimmering bay to the *Prince of Wales*. Mustering all the strength in his feeble lower extremities, FDR walked the entire length of the battleship's deck to meet his host, who was dressed in the uniform of the Royal Yacht Squadron.

What followed was a veritable love feast of Christian solidarity. In the best tradition of the Royal Navy, Captain J. C. Leach read the lesson, from Joshua 1:1–9: "There shall not any man be able to stand before thee all the days of thy life; as I was with Moses, so I will be with thee: I will not fail thee, nor forsake thee. Be strong and of good courage. . . ." Words aimed directly at Roosevelt. Then came a host of hymns, all selected by Churchill: "O God, Our Help in Ages Past"; "Onward, Christian Soldiers"; and "Eternal Father, Strong to Save." Did Churchill know that the latter was Roosevelt's own hymn? Or was he simply appealing to the U.S. Navy by singing its hymn? Many in the huge throng were moved. Hollis would later recall: "British and American Marine personnel intermingled in one mass on the huge quarter deck. It was noticeable that we all seemed to know the words of the hymns. . . ." The journalist H. V. Morton

> watched the two men in the seats of honour, the tall man and the smaller man in blue, who together represented the people of Britain and the United States; and I wondered what was passing through their minds at that moment. Churchill was affected emotionally, as I knew he would be. His handkerchief stole from its pocket. . . .[16]

Lunch, what Admiral King called "a simple meal," was served in the officers' wardroom of the *Prince of Wales*. The menu, printed with Churchill's crest in the header, was sumptuous by any standard: smoked salmon and caviar, roasted grouse, dessert, champagne, wines, and brandy. The highly emotional day ended with a light dinner on the *Augusta*. Thereafter, as Roosevelt and Churchill drained their brandy snifters and consumed their Camels and Coronas, the subject turned to empire. Elliott Roosevelt, who served at Argentia as a special presidential aide, recalled that earlier his father had stated that he did not "intend to be simply a good-time Charlie" to be used to "help the British Empire out of a tight spot." Now, the president calmly reminded the prime minister that America stood for freedom of trade. "No artificial barriers. . . . Markets open for healthy competition."[17] Churchill responded that Britain had no intention of giving up the favored trading position among the Dominions that the Ottawa Agreements had given her. Light banter ranged from the British role in India to that of the Americans in the Philippines. The sparring match completed, Roosevelt saw what he called the "real old Tory, of the old school" off for the night. All that time, their respective staffs had been working on a common communiqué. It would be known to history as the Atlantic Charter.

The historian Theodore A. Wilson has described the Atlantic Charter as "the longest-lived result" of "the first summit"; it "turned up like a copper penny throughout the war—alternately embarrassing and pleasing its designers."[18] The two sides quickly reached agreement on seven matters: that they sought "no aggrandizement, territorial or other"; that they desired to see "no territorial changes that do not accord with the freely expressed wishes of the people concerned"; that they would "respect the rights of all peoples to choose the form of government under which they will live"; that they would "bring about the fullest collaboration between all nations in the economic field"; that after the destruction of the "Nazi tyranny," they would strive to create a world free "from fear and want"; that they would guarantee freedom of "the high seas and oceans"; and that they would create a "wider and permanent system of general security" through general disarmament. On an eighth point, however, the one pertaining to free trade, there was strong disagreement.

While Roosevelt and Churchill discussed grand strategy on a global scale, Under Secretary of State Sumner Welles closeted himself with Sir Alexander Cadogan of the British Foreign Office to tackle the one issue that threatened to torpedo the Argentia talks: the Americans' demand that the delivery of war supplies be coupled with an end to the Ottawa Agreements of 1932. The talks were hard and direct. Welles had no desire to head back to Washington and face the wrath of Secretary of State Hull—whom Cadogan saw as a "pig-headed" and "dreadful old man"—without winning on the Ottawa accords. The Ottawa accords were important because Hull and other Americans wanted Lend-Lease linked to their demise.

Everything Britain had acquired from the United States in the first 18 months of the war had been bought and paid for. But British resources were limited; in the fall of 1940 the United Kingdom had begun to run out of money. The matter had been discussed at a Cabinet meeting in Washington in mid-December. Roosevelt and Henry Morgenthau, Jr., his secretary of the treasury, had wanted to be certain that the British liquidated all their American holdings, about $2 billion, before the United States moved to outright assistance of the United Kingdom. When that time came, however, one option discussed was to supply munitions to the British "under leasing arrangements . . . [of]

ships or any other property that was loanable, returnable or insurable."[19] Roosevelt had decided to proceed along this line. He would ask the Congress to approve sweeping new "Lend-Lease" legislation that would give him the power to lend or lease American-built munitions to any nation that, in using them, was contributing directly to the defense of the United States.

One way Roosevelt explained Lend-Lease was that the United States simply could not allow the "silly, foolish, old dollar sign" to restrict its desire to help the democracies. And with a homely analogy—that in case of fire one lent his neighbor a garden hose without payment and asked only that the hose be returned after the fire had been put out— he tried to convince the press that Britain ought simply to "borrow" what she needed and return it after the war.[20] To Senator Robert A. Taft of Ohio, who refused to accept FDR's reasoning that the survival of Britain was vital for the defense of the United States, this was like asking someone to return used chewing gum! But out of this grew the $7 billion Lend-Lease Act of March 1941, dramatically labeled House Bill 1776. Churchill deemed it "The Third Climacteric" of the war, after the fall of France and the German attack on the Soviet Union.

More than any other measure Roosevelt devised to keep Britain afloat, the Lend-Lease Act exposed the raw nerves that lay at the root of Anglo-American relations. At stake was money, billions and billions of dollars, and most likely the future balance of power in the Anglo-Saxon world. By all accounts, FDR had no illusion that Britain's defeat would be anything other than a disaster for the United States. Nonetheless, he approached the Lend-Lease negotiations with a sharp eye on his political opponents in Congress and the nation, and a strong sense of America's national interest. Thus, he issued Morgenthau clear marching orders: in return for the proposed virtually unlimited aid, the British were to be squeezed until they popped and divested of just about everything they had left in America and elsewhere. While he was prepared to extend an immediate credit of $1 billion, FDR insisted that Britain "must put a couple of billion" up front "as collateral." Morgenthau, for his part, demanded "a hundred cents on the dollar" for every item "lent" Britain.[21] His Majesty's government would first have to provide the U.S. Treasury with full revelation of its financial position, then sell its securities and investments in the United States at whatever price they brought, and finally pledge South African gold production to cover deficits. In an attempt to defang the president's opponents in the Congress, Morgenthau promised the Republican-dominated Senate Foreign Relations Committee, "Every dollar of property, real property or securities that any English citizen owns in the United States" would have to be sold off to pay for war goods, "every dollar of it." The treasury secretary then informed the House Foreign Affairs Committee that he would demand any South African gold that London received in 1941 to pay for war material. To make Lend-Lease still more palatable to Americans, Morgenthau had Irving Berlin compose a song for the Treasury, "Any Bonds Today?" It became the theme for the CBS weekly broadcast, *Treasury Hour*, starring the likes of Fred Allen, Mickey Rooney, and Judy Garland. To show the British that he meant business, FDR in late December dispatched a ship to collect $120 million of South African specie.[22]

Churchill was angry, but he was also the beggar. His personal reaction to the dispatch of Roosevelt's gold ship was that it was like the "sheriff collecting the last assets of a helpless debtor."[23] But worse was yet to come. Secretary of State Hull spied in Lend-Lease a God-given opportunity at last, in the words of historian Warren F. Kimball, "to open that oyster shell, the empire." Specifically, Lend-Lease could be applied to dismantle the system of imperial preferences established at Ottawa in 1932. Tormented by diabetes and tuberculosis, the crotchety secretary was adamant that the United States, in order to avoid the war debts problem of the First World War, simply ask for the return of undamaged ships and planes after the war, and "forgive" the rest of Lend-Lease supplies in return for an end to the Ottawa accords. Moreover, Hull was convinced that the British were cooking the books and hiding their global assets, which he estimated at $18 billion.

In the end, what John Maynard Keynes called Hull's "lunatic proposals" carried the day. Morgenthau simply was unwilling to fight both Hitler and the State Department. "Every time the President asks me to do something, Mr. Hull goes into a sulk and gets mad," Morgenthau moaned. "I am through being the President's whipping boy on the foreign affairs stuff."[24] Roosevelt put Harry Hopkins on the White House payroll as a $10,000-a-year special assistant for Lend-Lease. By the time of Pearl Harbor, the United States had appropriated about $13 billion for Lend-Lease, but had only sent Britain some $1 billion in equipment.

Given the origins of Lend Lease, Sumner Welles had little room to maneuver at Argentia. He could hardly return to Washington with anything less than what Hull had formally demanded. Welles insisted that the words—"[to enjoy] the freest possible economic interchange without discriminations, without exchange controls, without economic preference utilized for political purposes"—stay in the Argentia communiqué. Cold and self-righteous as ever, he lectured Cadogan that this was not "a question of phraseology," but rather "a question of a vital principle."

When Churchill heard this he ranted that Roosevelt was "trying to do away with the British Empire." FDR, relaxed in a gray suit and open shirt, sat comfortably in the admiral's cabin of the *Augusta* and stood his ground. Churchill, angered by Welles' intractable position, threw up a constitutional roadblock—the Dominions would each have to be consulted. He knew that Roosevelt desperately wanted a ringing proclamation to be issued from Argentia, and so with the help of Hopkins, whom he once jokingly vowed to raise to the peerage as "Lord Root of the Matter," Churchill came up with a disarming clause: "with due regard for their existing obligations."[25] This, of course, gave away the American bargaining position and infuriated Welles, but FDR agreed.

The prime minister could now assure the War Cabinet in London that he had held his ground on the Ottawa treaties; FDR could assure Hull that all trade matters would be regulated at the final grand summit after the defeat of the Axis powers. But the Foreign Office in London saw the Atlantic Charter as little more than a grandiose statement of vague American principles. "A terribly wooly document," Oliver Harvey termed it, "full of all the old clichés of the League of Nations period." Roosevelt, in the cricket terminology of Secretary of State for Foreign Affairs Anthony Eden, had "bowled the P.M. a very quick one."[26] Many of Roosevelt's supporters were astonished that he had not included "freedom of religion" in the document. Others were disappointed that FDR, perhaps remembering Wilson's debacle with the League of Nations and as ever keenly aware of isolationist sentiment back home, had vetoed the inclusion of any reference to a future "international organization." In the end, the document was simply mimeographed and released. No signatures were appended to it as that might make it seem a "treaty"—which, of course, would require Senate ratification.

Roosevelt had his declaration of war aims, his principal reason for the meeting, and British acquiescence on a joint mission to Moscow by Averell Harriman and Lord Beaverbrook to determine firsthand what Hopkins had not been able to discover—just exactly what the Russians needed and how long they might last. Churchill got a less than ringing endorsement of his Middle East strategy, but no solid assurances from Roosevelt that Japan would be duly and clearly warned about a possible attack on British possessions. He did get a firm commitment for more additional supplies and assurances that the U.S. Navy's presence in the central North Atlantic would be greatly strengthened. From now on, American ships would play the predominant role in escorting convoys from the east coast of North America to the waters off Iceland. Yet, he got no American declaration of war, just an enigmatic nod from Roosevelt that although the United States would not declare war, it would wage it, and become "more and more provocative. If the Germans did not like it, they could attack American forces."[27]

What, then, had taken place at Argentia? Churchill left a detailed record of the meeting, but only as *he* saw it. Like so many summits since, this "first summit" is important more for style than for substance. The two leaders had taken the measure of one another. Each had a better understanding of what motivated the other. The various staffs had begun to probe their concerns and needs in case of common war. While General "Hap" Arnold, upon hearing the British request for 6,000 more heavy bombers than the Republic was currently producing, felt lucky to have escaped with his pants, the British came away with some appreciation of just how bare the American cupboard was. Specifically, Roosevelt had gained a better impression of Churchill's persuasiveness and perseverance, but also of his commitment to preserving the Empire. Churchill had experienced firsthand Roosevelt's disinclination to take a firm stand when circuitousness would better serve. He now knew what an "artful dodger" the president was; Roosevelt had kept from Churchill what he most desperately wanted to take home with him: an American promise to enter the war. The "inscrutable mystery man of

American politics" remained inscrutable. The "juggler" had once again kept all the balls in the air.

One of Roosevelt's most capable biographers, James MacGregor Burns, concluded: "The two had amused, propagandized, flattered, annoyed, upstaged, and yielded to each other; their friendship had survived intact, deepened, and was ready for the heavier pressures to come."[28] Supreme Court Justice Felix Frankfurter, well known for his sycophantic letters to FDR, for once was realistic: "And like all truly great historic events, it wasn't what was said or done that define the scope of the achievement. It's always the forces—the impalpable, the spiritual forces, the hopes, the purposes, the dreams and the endeavors—that are released that matter."[29]

The most important result of the conference as far as Churchill was concerned was an intangible one, as he later reported to the War Cabinet. "The Prime Minister said that he had got on intimate terms with the President. Of the six meals they had had together, five had been on the President's ship."[30] The conference was thus one more step in a relationship that Churchill would later describe as having been "most carefully fostered by me."[31] But in private, Churchill despaired over the results of the meeting. No joint declaration of war aims was worth the paper it was written on when the United States was still not a belligerent and showed no signs of becoming one. At the end of August he wrote Hopkins a private letter:

> I ought to tell you that there has been a wave of depression through Cabinet and other informed circles here about the President's many assurances about no commitments and no closer to war, &c. I fear this will be reflected in Parliament. If 1942 opens with Russia knocked out and Britain left alone again, all kinds of dangers may arise. I do not think Hitler will help in any way. . . . You will know best whether anything more can be done. Should be grateful if you can give me any sort of hope.[32]

Of course, Hopkins could not.

At 4:47 P.M. on Tuesday, August 12, *Prince of Wales* slipped anchor in a gray drizzle. The ominous heavy clouds had closed in again. As the mighty battleship passed by, the *Augusta*'s band struck up "Auld Lang

Syne." Admiral King had three destroyers discreetly escort the British to Iceland. Beaverbrook had brought along for the home journey several films, including, mischievously, the Laurel and Hardy comedy *Saps At Sea*.

The same day that Churchill left Argentia, Roosevelt received a stunning reminder of how isolationist America still was: the House passed the extension of the Service Training and Selection Act by a single vote, 203 to 202. The America First Committee had bombarded the Hill with a million "keep out" postcards. Women in black dresses and black veils had taken over a bench in a reception room near the Senate chamber, weeping and wailing against the proposed extension of the draft. Robert Sherwood, FDR's speechwriter, recalled that the news of the close vote "dropped like enemy bombs on the decks of the *Augusta* and the *Prince of Wales*."[33] On a personal level, FDR was furious when he discovered that his Scottish terrier Fala looked like a plucked chicken, as many sailors had snipped off locks for souvenirs.

Once back in Washington, on Navy Day, October 27, 1941, Franklin Roosevelt shocked the nation with a startling announcement: "America has been attacked, the shooting has started." Before his listeners could take in the magnitude of that statement, Roosevelt continued, "I have in my possession a secret map, made in Germany by Hitler's govern-ment—by planners of the new world order."[34] The map showed South and Central America divided into five German vassal states, including the Panama Canal. More, the document revealed sinister German plans to abolish all religions and to replace them with a single Nazi creed. Congress at once amended the Neutrality Act to allow American ships to carry arms directly to Britain. Official secrecy, the president informed the press the next day, kept him from showing them the map.

The "sly squire of Hyde Park" had, in fact, played a dangerous hand. He was well aware that London had established a special dirty-tricks office in New York, the British Security Co-ordination Office under Sir William Stephenson. A flying ace in the First World War, Stephenson, whose code name was "Intrepid," had purloined the map from a German courier who had met with a mysterious "accident" in Buenos Aires. Stephenson had handed the map to the American Colonel William "Wild Bill" Donovan, who had passed it on to the White House. We know today that the map had been produced by German intelligence in Argentina, and after its capture had been "touched up" by Stephenson's forgery factory, "Station M" in Canada. Roosevelt, rather than being duped by British intelligence, had used this British "dirty trick" to further his own ends.[35]

Out on the Atlantic, the "shooting war" had already begun. American destroyers were the first targets. In September 1941 a German U-boat attacked the *Greer*. In October another "gray shark" drew first blood during an attack on the *Kearny*. And on the last day of the month, the *Reuben James* became the Navy's first casualty of the war. Still, Americans seemed more interested in the Army–Notre Dame football game than in the German U-boat attack on the *Reuben James*. For all too many, who well remembered the *Lusitania*, this seemed to be history repeating itself. For Admiral King, it was a reminder of both the closeness of the war and how unpreparedness of the United States. "I'm afraid the citizenry will have to learn the bitter truth," he wrote a friend, "that war is not waged with words or promises or vituperation but with the realities of peril, hardships, and killing."[36]

Adolf Hitler flew into a rage when he received news about the Argentia meeting. Already in June 1941 he had poured out his bile to Benito Mussolini concerning Roosevelt. The American president, the Führer had informed the Duce, was envious of the Fascists' success in overcoming their economic problems and filled with hate over their accomplishments. Roosevelt's only recourse was to try to aggrandize his nation at the expense of the British Empire.[37] Now, on August 14, Hitler was the one filled with rage and envy over the Anglo-Saxon summit. He arranged yet another conference with Mussolini, and on August 29 issued a venomous communiqué, in which he vowed "to destroy the Bolshevik danger" as well as the "plutocratic exploitation" of the Anglo-Saxons.[38]

Across town, Hitler's propaganda minister, Joseph Goebbels, recognized the potential danger of the Atlantic Charter. Its eight points smacked all too much of President Wilson's Fourteen Points of 1918, and they might resonate among the German people. He used three pages of his diary to denounce the Charter as "a typical propaganda product," a "propaganda bluff," and a "totally stupid propaganda maneuver."[39] But a secret report of the *Schutzstaffel* (SS) on the mood of the

German populace concluded that the meeting at Argentia had caused no great concern among the masses. This gave him comfort. So did the close vote in the U.S. Congress on the extension of the draft. Goebbels was certain that Washington was weighing any eventual entry into the European war against the outcome of the war in the East.[40] He was not wrong. But he could not know that even as he recorded those thoughts, Japanese aviators were practicing for the audacious strike at Pearl Harbor that would shock America and energize Roosevelt as no single event in his life had ever done.

2

THE SPHINX OF PENNSYLVANIA AVENUE

FRANKLIN DELANO ROOSEVELT REMAINS AN ENIGMA. FOR contemporaries and subsequent scholars alike, he defies easy explanation. Political scientists have resorted to buzzwords such as "practical idealist" and "idealistic realist" to portray him. Historians have sought refuge in literary metaphors such as "the sphinx of Pennsylvania Avenue" and "the sly squire of Hyde Park." His coworkers simply called him "the Boss." Roosevelt readily admitted to being deceptive, devious, and disingenuous. His adversaries added sobriquets such as dishonest, deceitful, and dictatorial. The more mean-spirited among them referred to him only as "That Man"; the most mean-spirited as "that megalomaniac cripple in the White House."[1]

And adversaries there were aplenty. On the far left, the Communist leader Earl Browder accused FDR of carrying out "more thoroughly and brutally" than even his predecessor, Herbert C. Hoover, "the capitalist attack against the masses." On the far right, the Fascist William Dudley Pelley called Roosevelt the "lowest form of human worm—according to Gentile standards." J. P. Morgan's family kept newspapers with pictures of "That Man" out of sight. H. L. Mencken, the Sage of Baltimore, uncharitably said of FDR's political ambitions: "If he became convinced tomorrow that coming out for cannibalism would get him the votes he so sorely needs, he would begin fattening a missionary in the White House backyard come Wednesday." One of

Roosevelt's Hudson Valley neighbors denounced him as "a swollen headed nit-wit," and promptly exiled himself to the Bahamas until Roosevelt was no longer in the White House. Another critic savaged him with the comment, "If you were a good honest man, Jesus Christ would not have crippled you." A Connecticut country club forbade mention of his name "as a health measure against apoplexy." And a man in Kansas went down into his cyclone cellar, vowing not to re-emerge until Roosevelt was out of office. While he was there, his wife ran away with a traveling salesman.

Roosevelt took even the most bilious attacks in stride. He liked to think that the means eventually justified the ends, that he could separate tactics from strategy. During a candid moment with fellow Hudson Valley squire Henry Morgenthau, Jr., in May 1942, FDR confessed, "You know I am a juggler, and I never let my right hand know what my left hand does." Yet Roosevelt maintained that all his actions, however devious, had a deeper purpose. "I may be entirely inconsistent, and furthermore I am perfectly willing to mislead and tell untruths," he informed his secretary of the treasury, "if it will help win the war."[2] Little wonder that British ambassador Lord Halifax claimed that dealing with the Roosevelt White House was "like hitting wads of cotton wool."[3] Halifax's boss, Secretary of State for Foreign Affairs Anthony Eden, was less charitable. After a particularly frustrating meeting with FDR at the White House during the war, Eden saw in the president a "conjuror, skillfully juggling with balls of dynamite, whose nature he failed to understand."[4] Roosevelt's Republican presidential opponent in 1932, Herbert Hoover, labeled him a "chameleon on plaid." Sir Isaiah Berlin called him simply "one of the few statesmen in the twentieth or any other century who seemed to have no fear at all of the future."[5]

Given the lack of agreement on the thirty-second president, it is perhaps surprising that the documentary record on Roosevelt is so enormous. Samuel Rosenman edited thirteen volumes of Roosevelt's *Public Papers* and twenty-five volumes of his *Press Conferences*. Elliott Roosevelt produced two volumes of his father's *Personal Letters*, and Warren F. Kimball three volumes of the *Complete Correspondence* between Roosevelt and Winston S. Churchill. And on thirty-three acres high above the Hudson River near Hyde Park, New York, stands the major monument to Roosevelt and his works: his presidential library. Housed in Springwood, the mansion that his father James had purchased in 1867, the Franklin Delano Roosevelt Library and Museum contains more than 10,000 digitized documents. Yet the serious scholar comes away disappointed, overcome by the sheer volume of documents abundantly well known but decidedly less than candid. Above all, that scholar gains virtually no insight into FDR the man and his relations with others, for the letters and messages are cold and informational. Indeed, one is struck by the great dearth of detailed personal letters of any kind; the man prided himself on committing as little as possible to paper. In January 1942, for example, he proudly informed Lord Beaverbrook during the ARCADIA conference that he did "not write over a dozen long-hand letters in a year—and even then they do not average a page and a half apiece."[6] Roosevelt would not even allow notes to be taken at Cabinet meetings.

The president from the start had an intimate knowledge of what he did *not* commit to his Library. At the dedication of its Museum Section on 30 June 1941, a mere eight days after Adolf Hitler's stunningly successful invasion of the Soviet Union, Roosevelt seemed in unusually good spirits. When asked the reason for this high dudgeon, he reportedly replied: "I am thinking of all the historians who will come here thinking that they'll find the answers to their questions."[7] It was vintage FDR. And he apparently had ample help in keeping critical materials from public inspection. The historian who wades through the more than four hundred pages of the volume of *The Foreign Relations of the United States* dealing with the Washington Conference 1941-42 is exasperated by the steady diet of "No official record of this discussion has been found" annotated to British documents by the American editors.[8] It is hard to escape the conclusion that "the sly squire of Hyde Park" had a hand in this selective selection process.

The public Roosevelt, of course, is well known. He was born in Hyde Park, New York, on January 30, 1882, the only child of James and Sara Delano Roosevelt. The Roosevelts were members of the landed gentry and the old mercantile class, involved in commerce, banking, railroads, seafaring, and real estate. Claes Martenszen van Rosenvelt, the first of the clan, had come to New Amsterdam in the seventeenth century. The Delanos likewise were a seafaring and mercantile family, at times not above engaging in privateering and in the nefarious "China trade." Franklin's academic career included all the "right" schools but was hardly distinguished: after Groton School and Harvard College, he attended Columbia University School of Law and passed the New York bar examination, but never bothered to complete his law degree. On St. Patrick's Day 1905 former president Theodore Roosevelt—of the Oyster Bay branch of the family—gave his niece Eleanor away to his fifth cousin Franklin in a simple ceremony at the New York home of Eleanor's aunt, Mrs. Henry Parrish, Jr. The couple later honeymooned in the United Kingdom and in Europe.

In 1910 Democrat Franklin Roosevelt ran successfully for the New York State Senate—after first getting a promise from Theodore Roosevelt not to campaign against him—in a district that had been carried by the Democrats only once since the Civil War. Franklin showed that he was a breed apart from other politicians when he toured solidly Republican Dutchess County in a two-cylinder red Maxwell that had neither windshield nor top. The new senator quickly earned a reputation for political toughness and ruthlessness. "I was an awfully mean cuss when I first went into politics," he recalled in later life. In 1913 President Woodrow Wilson appointed him assistant secretary of the Navy, a post that "Uncle Ted" had used as a stepping-stone to the presidency. Certainly from that time onward, FDR considered the Navy as somehow being "his." He even co-opted its hymn, "Eternal Father, Strong to Save," as his own.

As assistant secretary of the Navy, Roosevelt observed firsthand much of the idealism, internationalism, and moral superiority of President Wilson. In 1918, Eleanor discovered secret love letters from her social secretary, Lucy Mercer, to her husband.[9] She offered Franklin a divorce, but his mother, Sara, threatened to disinherit him should he abandon his family. Undoubtedly, Eleanor's discovery of these letters played a major role in Franklin's later aversion to committing things to paper. In 1920 Roosevelt ran as vice president on the unsuccessful James M. Cox Democratic ticket.

Personal tragedy struck on August 21, 1921. While visiting his summer home on Campobello Island, New Brunswick, Canada, he contracted poliomyelitis. He was thirty-nine years old. The attack resulted in (incomplete) motor paralysis from the waist down. The six-foot-two-inch Roosevelt was consigned to a narrow armless wheelchair, and he never walked again without heavy leg braces, crutches, canes, or the support of a son or an aide. Inconceivable today, through a gentlemen's agreement with the press, no photographs showing the president's disability were ever published. The Secret Service confiscated the film of any photographer who violated the "no picture" rule. Of the more than 35,000 photographs in the Franklin D. Roosevelt Library, only two have survived showing FDR in his wheelchair.

In 1928 Roosevelt won election as governor of New York by 25,000 votes, despite the fact that Herbert Hoover carried the state for the Republicans by a wide margin. Two years later FDR swept New York by a record 700,000 votes and reemerged as a national figure in Democratic presidential politics. In the elections of 1932 he easily defeated the colorless Hoover for the highest office in the land, receiving 22.8 million votes to his opponent's 15.8 million (and 472 electoral votes to Hoover's 59). *Time* magazine named him Person of the Year. On March 4, 1933 Franklin Delano Roosevelt was inaugurated as the nation's thirty-second president.

The public image of the new president had been carefully shaped. In hundreds of photographs and reels of press conferences, he came across as ebullient and radiant, the very personification of the American "can-do" spirit. He liked to pose for photographers with his large head thrown back, a broad smile on his pear-shaped face, the gleaming pincenez cocked on the bridge of his nose, his eyes a-twinkle, and the ever-present Camel in an ivory cigarette holder thrust upward at a jaunty angle. He could charm and mimic, berate and savage in the same sentence. Jack Bell, who worked the White House for the Associated Press, caught the essence of the Roosevelt style:

> He talked in headline phrases. He acted, he emoted; he was angry, he was smiling. He was persuasive, he was demanding; he was philosophical, he was elemental. He was sensible, he was unreasonable; he was benevolent, he was malicious. He was satirical, he was soothing; he was funny, he was gloomy. He was exciting. He was human. He was copy.[10]

Roosevelt had a masterful memory and an almost inexhaustible store of anecdotes. He could sidestep difficult questions as few others who occupied that powerful office. He was a master at planting a seed on any given issue—and then quickly stepping back from further exploration with his customary follow-up, "Of course, that's off the record, boys!" Through it all, in the words of his Secretary of the Interior, Harold L. Ickes, he kept his cards "close to the belly," revealing little in endless hours of palaver.

Franklin Roosevelt was the creator of the modern press scrum. Previous presidents had demanded that questions be written and submitted in advance. Now, to the delight of reporters, the press conferences became a spontaneous give-and-take. As David Brinkley recalled, Roosevelt would invite reporters into the White House press meeting room, where they "stood in a semicircle around the desk littered with cigarettes, holders, ashtrays, framed photographs, paperweights, and an array of miniature flags, pens, mementoes, and souvenirs."[11] The discussion would be free-flowing, with the president skillfully leading it in the direction he wanted. If reporters failed immediately to get the point he was driving at, Roosevelt would interject a helpful, "If I were writing your stories, I should say . . ." Photographers armed with black Speed Graphic cameras would aim their flashbulbs at Roosevelt's broad face, and the next day FDR would look out at millions of readers from coast to coast in front-page features. In 1934 *Time* magazine again proclaimed him Person of the Year.

Of course, not all press lords were enamored of "the sly squire of Hyde Park." Leading the pack of Roosevelt haters, apart from the denizens of the Hearst press, were Colonel Robert R. McCormick of the Chicago *Tribune*, Eleanor "Cissy" Patterson of the Washington *Times-Herald*, and her brother, Captain Joseph Patterson of the New York *Daily News*. While Roosevelt despised their newspapers, he nevertheless read them religiously—usually in the morning in bed, wrapped in an old stained and seared gray robe, furiously drinking coffee and smoking. Over time, he learned to circumvent their venom by way of radio "chats," his "pipeline" to the American people. And he waited to get his revenge. When Joseph Patterson, who had railed against the putative "dictator" for years, came to the White House to offer the nation his services four days after Pearl Harbor, FDR graciously allowed that he did, in fact, have one, and only one, wartime assignment for the owner of the *Daily News*—to reread all the vicious editorials against the Roosevelt Administration that his paper had published over the past six months. Patterson broke down and left the White House in tears.[12]

Roosevelt excelled at the spoken word. His was the first great American radio voice. Most Americans had never seen a president. Now, millions sitting in their living rooms or kitchens tuned in their radio to listen to that strong, vibrant voice broadcasting from the Diplomatic Reception Room in the basement of the White House what a reporter in May 1933 first described as a "fireside chat." Especially in the dark days of 1941, the president was most effective in using this medium to reach out to the public. A former editor in chief of the Harvard student paper *The Crimson*, Roosevelt refined multiple drafts of speeches prepared by a talented pool of writers before delivering them with exquisite timing, cadence, and clarity. Professor Lloyd James, linguistic advisor to the BBC in London, once suggested that FDR's diction serve as a standard for the English-speaking world.[13]

But his was not the language of the gentry, be it of the Hudson Valley in New York or of the Cliveden set in London. Rather, it was that of one in tune with the thoughts and feelings of the average American. His speeches were sprinkled with homely analogies, such as that of the garden hose, which he used to discuss the merits of Lend-Lease before its passage in March 1941. He let it be known that his favorite foods were ones "he could dig into," such as scrambled eggs, fish chowder, grilled cheese sandwiches, and hot dogs. At a time (1941) when the country was belting out hit tunes such as "Deep in the Heart of Texas" and "Chattanooga Choo-Choo," FDR confessed that his favorite was still "Home on the Range." He could recite the average price of nine out of ten common commodities, both at the time and a decade earlier. He openly admitted his obsession with philately and left behind an impressive 1.2 million stamps, most of which he derided as being little more than "scrap." An adoring public delighted in the attention that the president lavished on his friend at the White House, "Murray, the Outlaw of Fala Hill." Better known simply as Fala, the Scottish terrier had been given to him in November 1940 by his cousin, Margaret "Daisy" Suckley, and would first meet Churchill at the Argentia Conference in August 1941. The largely abstemious American public readily forgave the occasional photograph of FDR with martini shaker and glasses or with Orange-Blossom cocktails resting on a silver tray beside his chair. Millions of Americans had a picture of the president, often just a newspaper clipping, in their home.

The hungry, the poor, and the downtrodden of the world saw Roosevelt, like no other American president either before or after him, almost as a demigod. His fame spread as far as the remote villages of Calabria in southern Italy, where the exiled anti-Fascist doctor Carlo Levi was struck by one peasant cottage after another with cheap prints of two "guardian angels" usually hung on the wall over the bed: the "fierce, pitiless, mysterious" Madonna of Viggiano, an "ancient earth goddess"; and "the benevolent and smiling" Franklin D. Roosevelt, an "all-powerful Zeus."[14] He had become the Great Communicator four decades before that label was attached to the celluloid idol Ronald Reagan.

In terms of mentoring, Franklin Roosevelt took as much from his "Uncle Ted" as he did from his intellectual godfather, Woodrow Wilson.[15] Of course, FDR was left with a residue of Wilsonian views from his time as assistant secretary of the Navy. Like Wilson, he harbored strong fears about Prussian militarism in Europe and the "yellow peril" in the Far East. Like Wilson, he placed his hopes for the future in a democratic and Christian China, in free markets and free trade, and in the universal validity of the democratic ideal. And, like Wilson, he detested the negative influence of European colonialism. Later, as president, he was not above unabashedly borrowing Wilsonian concepts. Roosevelt's proclamation in January 1941 of the "Four Freedoms"— freedom of speech, freedom of worship, freedom from want, and freedom from fear—was a clear parallel to Wilson's "Fourteen Points" of 1918. His declaration (with Churchill) of the Atlantic Charter in August 1941 was pure Wilsonian rhetoric. His creation of the United Nations on New Year's Day 1942 clearly echoed Wilson's earlier League of Nations. He viewed the presidency as a place of moral leadership, but like the first Roosevelt, he also saw it as a bully pulpit.

Never an ideologue, Franklin Roosevelt had a sense of what has come to be called "the American way of life." Despite his patrician background, he felt an obligation to make the world a better place for those less fortunate. His optimism was grounded in conscience and in social concern. He had an uncanny ability to understand what ordinary Americans wanted. He believed that by exporting American values, he was increasing world peace and stability. He had a firm faith in the Anglo-Saxon race and in its Christian god. He believed in the ballot box and in the rule of law—if not always in the courts, as witnessed by his quixotic scheme in 1937 to "pack" the Supreme Court with as many as six additional judges to guarantee passage of New Deal legislation. He had no trouble identifying evil and exposing it to public scrutiny. He knew how to circumvent encrusted bureaucracies and how to control friction among his acolytes. Abe Fortas, a New Deal lawyer from Tennessee, presciently observed of his boss: "He was a real Toscanini. He knew how to conduct an orchestra and when to favor the first fiddles and when to favor the trombones. He knew how to employ and manipulate people." In a rare display of wit, Vice President Henry A. Wallace observed that FDR "could keep all the balls in the air without losing his own."[16]

Publicly, Roosevelt moved with caution and balance; privately, with broad purpose and (mostly) consistency. Administratively, what in the words of one of his greatest admirers looked like "confusion and exasperation on the operating level" was really a "competitive theory of administration" designed to keep control of a rapidly expanding bureau- cracy.[17] What to one historian was "infinite plasticity" in choosing means, was to Secretary of War Stimson "very much like chasing a vagrant beam of sunlight around a vacant room." Two-thirds of his trou- bles, Stimson noted in November 1941, stemmed from Roosevelt's "topsy-turvy, upside down system of poor administration."[18]

In the words of historian William E. Leuchtenburg, Franklin Roosevelt was America's "first modern president." Through four elec- tions, he held together a tenuous coalition of low-income ethnic voters in the great urban centers and white voters in the Deep South. He manipulated the press. He bullied and cajoled the Congress into passing his legislation. He kept the levers of power to himself. He appre- ciated the peculiar device of the presidential veto. In fact, by the end of his second administration Roosevelt had used almost one-third as many vetoes as all his predecessors since 1792. Friend and foe alike joked that FDR used his veto powers—on measures ranging from homing pigeons to tax bills—just to remind the Hill that it was being watched. He understood executive power and was not averse to using it. He appreciated the peculiar nature of the American polity. He authored the American century. And by the time he was done, he had established the Executive Office of the President, or what is now widely referred to as the "imperial presidency."

In the end, he became, and is likely to remain, America's longest-serving president (twelve years), breaking the taboo against a third term and even serving part of a fourth term. Largely because of him, in February 1951 the Congress in what has been called a "posthumous rebuke" ratified the Twenty-Second Amendment to the Constitution limiting a president to two terms.

Franklin Roosevelt's first two terms in office were perhaps the most tempestuous and hotly debated in American history. Between 1933 and 1938, he pushed through the Congress a dazzling plethora of social legislation designed to bring about what he termed "a permanent correction of grave weaknesses in our economic system." The so-called New Deal affected everything from agriculture to banking, housing to veterans' affairs, labor laws to trade laws, and public works to individual retirement. In the process, Americans were drowned with an alphabet soup of acronyms—CCC, FDIC, FHA, HOLC, ICC, NRA, PWA, SEC, TVA, and WPA, to name but a few—that defined what historian George Brown Tindall has called the "broker state."[19] Roosevelt sought to create a government that acted as an "honest broker," one that mediated among major interest groups and fostered competition.

Perhaps most important, Roosevelt worked to create a "New Deal" that in the words of historian David M. Kennedy can be summarized in a single word: security. "Job security, life-cycle security, financial security, market security"; these, Kennedy argues, were the "leitmotif" of all that Roosevelt's new style of "enlightened administration" attempted. There was to be security for "vulnerable individuals," security for "capitalists and consumers, for workers and employers, for corporations and farms and homeowners and bankers and builders as well."[20] Much of the legislation survived for the remainder of the twentieth century; some of it was cast aside after 1938, and some of it only at the start of the twenty-first century. All of it enhanced the power of the national government—power that the rising storm in Europe would make invaluable in the near future.

Like many an American president, Franklin D. Roosevelt believed that he understood foreign relations better than the starched shirts at the new Department of State building at dreary Foggy Bottom. Like many an American president, he sought to circumvent official diplomatic channels by way of a host of special representatives—to London, Berlin, Rome, Moscow, and eventually to Vichy and Madrid. And like many an American president, Roosevelt felt that he understood and could communicate with foreign leaders better than the Department of State. In fact, however, FDR's foreign policy record in the 1930s was less than stellar; some critics have labeled him a closet appeaser. He was not that, but his efforts to find the perfect balance between isolationists and interventionists often confused more than it revealed. When British prime minister Neville Chamberlain announced in September 1938 that he would go to Munich to meet Herr Hitler, the "head of the firm," to reach an agreement on carving up Czechoslovakia—surely the high point of appeasement—Roosevelt personally crafted a telegram to London with but two words: "Good man." Such comment made mockery of the president's bluster to Canada's governor-general, Lord Tweedsmuir,* that in case of war in Europe, the United States "would be in the next day"; to First Lord of the British Admiralty Duff Cooper, that America would come to the rescue "within three weeks"; and to King George VI, that the United States would be at war the minute the first German bombs fell on London.[21] (*Lord Tweedsmuir was the author of such popular novels as *Prester John, Thirty-Nine Steps*, published under the name John Buchan.)

Of all the countries in Europe, FDR claimed that he knew Germany better than his career diplomats. In part, this was because of his familiarity with that nation. Starting in 1891, his parents had taken him to Bad Nauheim no fewer than eight times. While his ailing father took the cure at the famous spa in the Taunus Mountains, Franklin enrolled for six weeks at a grammar school. In 1901, at age nineteen, he had a chance meeting with Kaiser Wilhelm II while sailing the

Norwegian fjords. Invited onboard the imperial yacht *Hohenzollern* for tea, Franklin stole a pencil bearing the kaiser's teeth marks. He would return to Germany later during his honeymoon.

Familiarity, at least in this case, bred contempt. Young Franklin learned to despise Germans from his Dutch Teutophobe parents. Like his mother Sara, he referred to Germans sitting at the dinner table as "swine." He mimicked their accent and denigrated their land. When he visited Europe as assistant secretary of the Navy in 1919, he found half-starved and half-naked German prisoners of war to be dull and dimwitted, and he verbally accosted them for their alleged atrocities. He believed that "Prussian militarism" constituted the heart and soul of the Bismarckian Reich—aggressive and dangerous, unstable and unreliable.

Once in office, Roosevelt's personal views changed little. He reminded the State Department at every opportunity that he had "studied" in Germany and that he spoke its language. Soon, German-American relations, in the words of Secretary of State Cordell Hull, consisted of "criminations and recriminations."[22]

For several months in 1933, Roosevelt deliberately delayed appointing an ambassador to Berlin. On numerous occasions that same year, he brushed aside feelers from Rome about a Four Power Pact designed to ease some of the harshest clauses of the Treaty of Versailles (1919). When Ambassador William Dodd finally arrived in Germany, one of his first acts was to lead a boycott of the Nazi Party Congress at Nürnberg. Relations quickly settled into an escalating spiral of diplomatic snubs. In May 1933, during a Washington visit by Germany's chief financial officer, Roosevelt and Hull kept Reichsbank president Hjalmar Schacht standing, while pretending to look for papers—and then cheerily told Schacht that Hitler was the right man for Germany! Roosevelt frequently blamed Berlin for the failure of disarmament, and he repeatedly demanded an economic blockade or a moral arms embargo against Germany. He informed Ambassador Joseph C. Grew, a kindred spirit from his days at Groton and Harvard, that he was, quite simply, prejudiced against the Germans.[23] Once he declared that America's frontier was on the Rhine—and then immediately denounced the quotation as a "deliberate lie." At news conferences, he regaled reporters with concocted stories about how Adolf Hitler's secret service was being followed by Joseph Goebbels' secret service, which was being followed by the army's secret service, which was being followed by the Gestapo.

Beginning with the withdrawal of Germany's most favored nation status in 1935, Roosevelt, Hull, and Morgenthau met every German foreign policy offensive—remilitarization of the Rhineland, annexation of Austria, dismemberment of Czechoslovakia—with punitive duties and restrictions. In October 1938 the president threatened to "quarantine" aggressors. In April 1939 he demanded that Hitler and Benito Mussolini refrain from aggression against thirty-one European and Near Asian countries. Hitler only heaped scorn and ridicule on these pronouncements. *Time* magazine made the Führer Person of the Year in 1938.

This icy veneer over German-American relations served Roosevelt well, however, for he had no German policy. To be fair, conflicting reports came at him from all quarters, not the least of which was the Department of State. Norman Davis, who had represented the United States at the Geneva Disarmament Conference, advised the president to try "political appeasement" with Hitler. Breckinridge Long, about to be appointed assistant secretary, recommended *Mein Kampf* to him as an "eloquent" tonic against "communism and chaos." Hull, a veteran of the Spanish-American War, assured FDR that it was best to think of Hitler and the Germans as in the days of the eighteenth-century poets Goethe and Schiller. Ambassador Joseph Kennedy from London let it be known that he supported both Germany's racial policy and its economic goals in East Europe. The bright but flaky Adolf A. Berle informed "the Boss," who had planted him as his personal security advisor at the State Department (sometimes referred to simply as "State") to spy on Hull, that it would be best to endorse a greater Germany alongside a reconstituted Austro-Hungarian Empire. To whom should he listen?

Official criticism was not welcomed. When Ambassador Dodd bravely continued to submit reports critical of Hitler and Nazism, he was first deemed "somewhat insane" by Hull, then recalled to Washington by Roosevelt, and finally ordered back to Berlin—only to find out on his arrival in the German capital that the president had fired him! When Truman Smith sent in detailed reports of the German air force's massive buildup after 1935, these elicited no immediate reaction. When General Albert Wedemeyer came back to the United States in 1938 bursting with news of the German military buildup, few listened. After all, he had a German name and so was easily impressed.

Partly because of conflicting advice and partly because of his personal predilection, Roosevelt dispatched a number of special representatives to Europe to report to him directly. The cavalcade included William Bullitt, Samuel Fuller, Sumner Welles, Hugh Wilson, William R. Davis, and James D. Mooney. On each occasion, Roosevelt's personal diplomacy via trusted envoys achieved exactly the opposite of what the president wished. Hitler and his lieutenants were, if anything, flattered by the president's attention. They feigned moderation while hardening their resolve in the face of Roosevelt's perceived weakness. When Sumner Welles made an extended trip to Germany on FDR's behalf in the spring of 1940, Propaganda Minister Goebbels was delighted. The Welles visit aroused "world attention," Goebbels wrote in his diary. Hitler had been "honest and open" with Welles. The British, he mused, "can fry in their own fat."[24]

Within six weeks, the German tone changed dramatically. On May 10, 1940, the *Wehrmacht* unleashed its massive invasion in the west, quickly crushing Belgian, Dutch, and French forces in its path. Thirteen days later, John Cudahy, a leading isolationist and U.S. ambassador at Brussels from January 1940 to January 1941, called on the Führer at his Alpine lair, the Obersalzberg, near Berchtesgaden. With victory in the west seemingly assured, Hitler took off the kid gloves he had worn during the Welles mission. He warned Cudahy (and through him American isolationists) that he would consider American escorts for transatlantic shipping to constitute "an act of war." He dismissed suggestions that Germany planned to invade the Western Hemisphere as "childish" and "foolish," as being "akin to claims that America planned to conquer the moon." Pouring ridicule on Roosevelt's statement that America's frontier extended to the Rhine, the Führer swore that "he had heard no German proclaim that the Reich's border ran along the Mississippi."[25] Upon arriving in America, Cudahy immediately published his interview with Hitler in the *New York Times* and later in *Life* magazine. That summer Hitler ordered the Americans to close down their ten major consular offices in Germany. The brief honeymoon in German-American relations was over.

The Soviet Union was another country that Roosevelt thought he understood. By the mid-1930s, he had concluded that the USSR was no longer a revolutionary state. Lenin was gone. Trotsky was in exile. Many of the Old Bolsheviks were dead. By way of Stalin's gentle touch, communism had been transformed into "a modified form of state social-ism." Stalin was a simple man of the people, waiting only for the right moment to open the Soviet Union's vast markets to American goods. While the "Rooseveltians" in Washington acknowledged that Stalin per-secuted religious groups, they nevertheless argued that the path of progress to peace, democracy, and social justice was often a messy one. And was the progressive "Great Leader and Teacher" of the Soviet people not preferable to the anachronistic imperialists who ruled in London and in Paris? Given this rose-colored view of the Soviet Union, it was hardly surprising that American analysts had no detailed infor-mation on the Soviet industrial system or its military installations.

Most tragically, Roosevelt and his clique of advisors developed what historian Dennis J. Dunn has called a "pseudoprofound theory of convergence," whereby the Soviet Union and the United States were on convergent paths. While Roosevelt was moving his country away from laissez-faire capitalism to welfare state socialism, Stalin was abandon-ing totalitarianism for social democracy.[26] Both Washington and Moscow were plotting out a policy of "collective security" against the Fascist dictators. Pluralism was inevitable; the ends justified the means.

Roosevelt's sunny view of Stalin and the Soviet regime survived the show trials of the late 1930s and even the murder of hundreds of thousands of Stalin's political opponents. Throughout this period, Ambassador Joseph Davies and military attaché Colonel Philip R. Faymonville fed the president a continuous flow of claptrap. The show trials, they reported, were fair and just, because they weeded out "trai-tors" and "fifth columnists." Surgery against conspiracy. For Davies, Red Army officers put on trial were Trotskyites and Bonapartists. He happily cabled Hull, "the danger of the Corsican for the present has been wiped out." Did he dimly recall a history class on the French Revolution from his days at the University of Wisconsin? When the ambassador shared his view of the show trials with Churchill during a visit to London in May 1937, Churchill sarcastically thanked him for this "completely new concept of the situation."[27]

Roosevelt's perceptions of Stalin and the Soviet Union began to change only in 1939, when Roosevelt named Laurence A. Steinhardt, a wealthy lawyer in the firm of Guggenheimer, Untermeyer and Marshall, to replace Davies in Moscow. Steinhardt was well connected to the Jewish community in New York. He was analytical, bright, articulate, witty, and fluent in three languages. Especially appealing to Roosevelt, Steinhardt, who had long seen the land of the tsars as the persecutors of the Jews, was an admirer of the Soviet Union. He was named ambassador on March 5, 1939.

No ideologue, the new ambassador brought to the position an Old Testament notion of justice, a highly developed sense of objective morality, and a great deal of pragmatism. He was no fan of social-sciences babble such as the "convergence" theory, and he instead demanded "reciprocity" in Soviet-American relations. Concessions by Washington, he argued, needed to be linked to concessions by Moscow. He was shocked by the Nazi-Soviet Non-Aggression Pact of August 1939 and by Stalin's subsequent role in the fourth partition of Poland. He informed Hull that the Soviet Union was acting as Hitler's major purveyor of war materials, as his "silent partner." He was outraged by Stalin's invasion of Finland in November, for the Finns were the only people that had repaid their war debt to the United States.

At first, Steinhardt seemed to bring about a slow but sure change in Roosevelt's perceptions of Stalin and the Soviet Union. In late 1939 the president seemed to have second thoughts about Russian behavior and even appeared to warm up to Steinhardt's notion of "reciprocity." He condemned the Soviet invasion of Finland and stunned Hull and Welles shortly thereafter by demanding suddenly that the United States "match every Soviet annoyance by a similar annoyance here against them."[28] He called for a "moral embargo" on American firms trading aeronautical goods with the USSR. But then his ambivalence reasserted itself. He began to ignore Steinhardt's increasingly bitter but realistic reports from the "Communist Utopia" and took in silence mounting Soviet harassment of the U.S. diplomatic mission in Moscow. The secret police followed American diplomats into public restrooms. They reduced food supplies. They first rationed and then cut gas. They piled snow high in front of the embassy and installed microphones throughout the building. And they subjected departing diplomats to physical searches. Worse, Roosevelt scoffed at the (proven) charge that Stalin had agents such as Alger Hiss working for him at State. His adversaries had a field day suggesting a linkage between Roosevelt and Stalin. H. L. Mencken put it perhaps most cruelly: "The smile of the sonofabitch in the White House and the smile of Holy Joe in Moscow have a great deal in common."[29] The comparison was outrageous, of course, but resonated with those conservatives who had all along believed that Roosevelt himself was the greatest single danger to American freedom. It strengthened them in their opposition to any American intervention in the war. Thus did FDR's own naïveté toward Stalin hurt his very real efforts to help the British.

When it came to understanding Great Britain, Roosevelt was on more solid ground. He spoke its language, had visited its capital, had met some of its leaders, was familiar with its history, and was conversant in its literature. At Groton he had devoured the *Illustrated London News*. He admired Britannia's traditions and institutions. He had available at State a stable of career diplomats who had served at the Court of St. James's. Likewise, he could call on a host of military and naval attachés with detailed knowledge about Britain's armed forces. He was dealing with a democracy, with a popularly elected government, and with leaders familiar with the give-and-take of political compromise. And not with some "Caucasian bandit" (Stalin) or "Austrian painter" (Hitler).

But on a personal level, Roosevelt brought to the table his share of impedimenta. Much divided Roosevelt and Churchill. While a student at Harvard, young Franklin had headed a movement for Boer relief during the Boer War of 1899–1902. In his early visits to Britain, he, and especially his wife, Eleanor, had been offended by the class-ridden gentry's arrogance and selfishness. "Too much Eton and Oxford," he crowed. At home, FDR was irritated by the snobbishness of Britain's diplomats—and especially of their wives, who resented having been posted "out there." Too many, in his view, had conveniently forgotten who had won the American Revolutionary War. He once told his Republican presidential opponent, Wendell L. Willkie, that the English were foxy and had to be dealt with as such. When at the height of the intense debate over Lend-Lease in March 1941 the British ambassador to Washington, Lord Lothian, in an unguarded moment blurted out, "Well, boys, Britain's broke; it's your money we want,"[30] that indiscretion had summed up for many Americans what Britain was all about.

On a formal level, there was the matter of EMPIRE, writ large. Imperialism was viewed by many Americans with distaste, perhaps as a consequence of the country's origin as a British colony. From President Wilson, Roosevelt had learned to despise empire in all its forms. It smacked of exploitation and racism. It divided him from the Churchills of the Anglophile world. To him, the very notion of "empire" was archaic in a progressive world. It constricted the free movement of both capital and goods. He knew well the militant history of that empire, which under Queen Victoria (1837–1901) had been at war somewhere in the world during every year of her reign. The Empire was, at least in part, responsible for the outbreak of the Great War, because the race for empire had set the European powers against one another and ushered in a mad arms race. Thus, FDR was as suspicious of Churchill and his fellow imperialists as he was of Neville Chamberlain and the "Birmingham Crowd" of arms makers. Moreover, the Paris peace conference of 1919 had degenerated into a sordid squabble over the colonies plucked from Germany. London's refusal to grant Ireland its freedom made mockery of the principle of self-determination imbedded into Wilson's Fourteen Points. India and Indochina became symbols of European avarice and greed for Roosevelt. He visited Egypt and Iran, Gambia and Morocco. He never set foot in London during the war, despite repeated invitations from Churchill.

Because Roosevelt never committed his deepest thoughts to paper, we can only surmise the general lines of his policy toward Britain. He was a keen student of geography, which he had not learned, in Anthony Eden's biting words, simply from his stamp collection. He knew his Alfred Thayer Mahan and appreciated that the Atlantic was America's lifeline to Europe and vice versa. He understood that the British fleet and, to a lesser extent, the French fleet were the guarantors of those vital sea lanes. Neither fleet must ever fall into an enemy's hand. He was a champion of democracies. He despised Germans in general and National Socialism in particular. He was revolted by Hitler's anti-Semitic policies.

Yet he also had his finger firmly on the pulse of the nation and knew that the country was deeply isolationist. Three hundred students at his alma mater, Harvard, signed a petition informing the president that they would never "follow in the footsteps of the students of 1917." Arthur M. Schlesinger, Jr., then a junior fellow at Harvard, in his auto-biography recalled that none of the national quarrels of his lifetime— over communism in the late 1940s, over McCarthyism in the 1950s, over Vietnam in the 1960s—so "tore apart families and friendships as the great debate of 1940–41." At Yale University, 1,486 students and faculty vowed never to go to war, "even if England is on the verge of defeat." The signatories included Kingman Brewster, a future president of Yale, and Gerald R. Ford, a future president of the United States.[31]

At the national level, the America First movement, with the help of such public figures as Charles Lindbergh, Colonel Robert McCormick, Lillian Gish, Father Coughlin, Henry Ford, and Alice Roosevelt Longworth, by late spring 1941 had organized into 700 chapters of about one million members. It was a polyglot collection of "pacifists, haters of Roosevelt, haters of Great Britain, anti-Communists, anti-Semites, admirers of Ger-many, American imperialists, devotees of big business, and [of] those who hated Europe." Just a few months before Pearl Harbor, Lindbergh publicly intimated that only three groups wanted the Republic to enter the war: "the British, the Jews, and the Roosevelt Administration."[32]

But Roosevelt also had an army of supporters who believed that America's first line of defense lay with Britain.[33] The Committee to Defend America by Aiding the Allies was a veritable Who's Who in America. It included Hollywood luminaries Tallulah Bankhead and Helen Hayes; playwrights and novelists Louis Adamic, Eugene O'Neill, and Robert Sherwood; financiers Herbert Lehman and J. P. Morgan; historians Henry Steele Commager, Carl J. Friedrich, and Edward Meade Earle; and boxer Gene Tunney. As well, the Committee had its share of political figures, such as Secretary of War Henry L. Stimson, Congressman J. W. Fulbright, and Dean Acheson of the Department of State. The Committee had established 600 chapters across the country by late 1940.

An Elmo Roper poll in 1939 found that 62 percent of Americans favored neutrality; a mere 2 percent were willing to go to war. Irish-Americans and German-Americans obviously had no great love for Churchill's empire. But many other Americans felt that the "war to end all wars" of 1917–18 had been an abject failure. Germany had been defeated at the cost of some 126,000 American lives, yet here it was again in 1939 about to set out on another war of conquest. Neither Britain nor France had made a major effort to repay their vast war debts. Neither had shown themselves willing to spill blood to defang Hitler while he was building his war machine. Why should the New World rally yet again to rescue the Old? "What did we get out of the first world war," many Americans asked, "but death, debt and George M. Cohan?"[34] In the words of historian David Reynolds, the country was "anglophile culturally" and "anglophobe politically."

Ambiguity and ambivalence were precisely Roosevelt's design, especially in the twenty-seven months between the German invasion of Poland and Pearl Harbor. The underlying reality that he had to cope with was that in a world at war, the United States was still virtually powerless. The American Army and Air Corps strength of around 1.5 million men in mid-1941 (up from 225,000 shortly after George C. Marshall became chief of staff) was inadequate even to the defense of the Western Hemisphere. In late September of that year the War Department admitted that only one infantry division, two bomber squadrons, and three pursuit groups were ready for combat. Moreover, the Army planned to release its older inductees and to retire all National Guard units from federal service. A mere 10 percent increase in ground forces was contemplated for the future. At best, the United States would at some distant point perhaps be able to commit sixteen divisions for overseas deployment.

Historians have recently applied descriptors such as "ambiguous," "ambivalent," and "indecisive" to Roosevelt. They have accused the president of playing "diplomatic chess," of "straddling" when he needed to lead, of always choosing "the path of least resistance," of constantly failing to "either fish or cut bait," of substituting "words for action, condemnation for policy," of acting "secretly as an agent of appeasement," and of retracting or breaking scores of promises, mostly to Britain. Perhaps the most biting of these indictments was that of historian Frederick W. Marks III. Roosevelt's foreign policy from 1933 to 1941 was like a house built on a bed of sand, Marks wrote: "The rain fell, the floods came, the winds blew and beat against that house, and it fell."[35]

Perhaps. Such attacks on the Roosevelt legacy are not new. They have been the staple of diplomatic historians since 1945. Robert Dallek was one of the first senior American scholars to address them in 1979.[36] To be sure, Roosevelt made his share of errors in conducting the Republic's foreign policy for twelve years, Dallek allowed, but on the whole the balance sheet was positive. The president had understood far better than many of his predecessors or successors that the American political fabric is delicately complex. He had appreciated that "effective action abroad" was impossible without "reliable consensus at home." He had waited for "dramatic events overseas" to "win national backing" from a divided country for his essentially pro-Allied measures. He had refused to "force an unpalatable choice upon the nation by announcing for war" prematurely.

Moreover, Roosevelt had remained in charge of the national agenda. He had refused to abandon national policy to the dogs of war. By a "mixture of realism and idealism, of practical short-term goals tied to visions of long-term gains," Roosevelt had skillfully "navigated the rapids," in the words of one of his advisors, Adolf A. Berle. Above all, however circuitous the means and however long the journey, FDR had managed to maintain his moral compass. One sentence in his Annual Address of the State of the Union to the joint session of the Congress in January 1942 elevates him above many other politicians: "There never has been —there never can be—successful compromise between good and evil."

3

THE SQUIRE OF CHARTWELL

WINSTON LEONARD SPENCER CHURCHILL WAS SIXTY-FIVE WHEN he took office as prime minister of the United Kingdom on May 10, 1940. He was at an age when most men have gone to their retirement. Indeed, it was almost ten years since his political life seemed to have drawn to a close. As far back as 1931 the political diarist Harold Nicolson had described him as "an elder statesman," with his spirits in decline, complaining of having lost "his old fighting power." Another of Churchill's colleagues had recorded in 1936 that he was "no longer so quick as he had been in grasping points."[1]

From the day that Britain and France declared war on Germany, his had been the only voice in the British Cabinet that had consistently called for decisive action. His fertile mind had churned out schemes for disrupting German war plans, cutting off the flow of German supplies, seizing the initiative. But Churchill had not been heeded in a cabinet that was still largely composed of the very men—Neville Chamberlain, Foreign Secretary Lord Halifax, Sir Samuel Hoare, Leslie Hore-Belisha, Sir John Simon, Lord Hankey, and others—who had so recently championed appeasement. Now, on the heels of the German conquest of Norway, while the *Wehrmacht* began to sweep into France, Denmark, the Netherlands and Belgium, Churchill inherited the mantle of leadership from Prime Minister Chamberlain. He quickly formed a coalition War Cabinet consisting of himself and Labour Party leader Clement Attlee, along with Labour Party members A.V. Alexander Arthur Greenwood and

Ernest Bevin, Liberal Party leader Archibald Sinclair, Neville Chamberlain, Lord Halifax, and Anthony Eden. Churchill took the all-important position of Minister of Defence, placing himself in direct charge of running the operational side of the war. If anyone thought that Churchill had neither the will nor the imagination to lead Britain in this most perilous time, they were woefully off the mark. On May 13, with German troops beginning to penetrate deeply into French defenses, Churchill gave a defiant definition of his policy:

> I would say to the House, as I said to those who have joined this Government: "I have nothing to offer but blood, toil, tears and sweat." We have before us an ordeal of the most grievous kind. We have before us many, many long months of struggle and of suffering. You ask, what is our policy? I can say: It is to wage war, by sea, land and air, with all our might and with all the strength that God can give us; to wage war against a monstrous tyranny, never surpassed in the dark, lamentable catalogue of human crime. That is our policy. You ask, what is our aim? I can answer in one word: It is victory, victory at all costs, victory in spite of all terror, victory, however long and hard the road may be; for without victory, there is no survival.[2]

Churchill was born at Blenheim Palace, his family's ancestral seat in Oxfordshire, on November 30, 1874. His family enjoyed the trappings of upper-class English society, but his father, Lord Randolph Churchill, had no real wealth. The family fortune belonged to Churchill's cousin, Charles Richard John Spencer ("Sunny") Churchill, the ninth Duke of Marlborough. Sunny was the inheritor of Blenheim and whatever other bits of the Marlborough fortune not already squandered by his father, the eighth Duke.

Churchill's parents were distant. His father, a strict, self-absorbed, cold man with a gift for oratory and strong Tory democratic convictions, had been a brilliant young rising political star in Winston's youth. He had achieved the high position of Chancellor of the Exchequer (senior minister of finance) in the Conservative government of Lord Salisbury in 1886 at the age of only thirty-seven. But then, in a stupendous act of political suicide, he resigned only a half year later. His career never recovered. In April 1874, it became known that he had been stricken with syphilis, possibly even before his marriage to Churchill's mother, the American-born beauty Jenny Jerome. The scourge eventually killed him in January 1895 with Winston just shy of his twenty-first birthday. In the meantime, forbidden to have sexual relations with her husband, Lady Randolph Churchill became one of the great courtesans of late Victorian England.

Lord Randolph was too caught up in the wreckage of his own political career and his deteriorating marriage to pay any real attention to young Winston. He was too much the disciplinarian to display either warmth or enthusiasm for his son when he did. Churchill's mother clearly loved the boy, but with her life focused on ministering to Lord Randolph and pursuing her own amours, she paid little attention to Winston either. Thus, Winston's early boyhood, spent at boarding school, saw a constant flow of letters from him to his parents beseeching them to visit him, to pay attention to him, to approve of him. None of these letters did any good.

Churchill barely scraped through Harrow, his public school. He did not qualify for admission to a British university. He only just managed to squeeze into the Royal Military Academy at Sandhurst after three tries at the entrance examinations, and with much tutoring. Sandhurst trained British army officers. It was almost entirely a practical school for the military, very weak on academics, and certainly not the equivalent of a university or a law school in either the arts or the sciences. Even when admitted, Churchill could not qualify for the infantry, which required a better entrance score. Much to his father's chagrin, he was put into the cavalry instead.

For all intents and purposes, Churchill educated himself. Even at Harrow he was drawn to English history; unnoticed among his mediocre Sandhurst entrance scores were very high grades in that one subject. But it was his first overseas military posting in 1896 to India with his unit, the 4th Hussars, which marked the real beginning of his learning. Unlike the typical British cavalry officer of the day, whose deepest interests ran to polo, women, cigars, and sartorial splendor, Churchill was determined to improve his understanding of the world around him—because he was keenly aware of his own ignorance. One day before he left for India, someone used the word "ethics" in a conversation with him. He thought about its meaning, its roots, its usages. Later, in India, he reflected: "But what were Ethics? . . . They had never been mentioned to me at Harrow or Sandhurst . . . here in Bangalore there was no one to tell me about Ethics for love or money. Of tactics I had a grip; on politics I had a view: but a concise compendious outline of Ethics was a novelty not to be locally obtained."[3] Nor were the meanings of other important concepts. He concluded that he would have to find out.

Churchill ordered cartons of books from England; his mother sent him others. In the long hot afternoons, he read Edward Gibbon's monumental *History of The Decline and Fall of the Roman Empire*, Henry Hallam's *Constitutional History of England*, Winwood Reade's *The Martyrdom of Man*, and the histories of Thomas Babington Macauley and other so-called "Whig" historians.[4] These early readings, with their heavy emphasis on history, empire, social Darwinism—set against the exotic majesty of the British Raj as only a young British cavalry officer could experience it—shaped much of his later thinking.

He began to see history as a grand human march to betterment and fulfillment. Not without its fits and starts and setbacks, progress and civilization were intertwined concepts. Rome had fallen and with its demise the march of progress had been set back a thousand years. But empire—ruled, organized, administered benignly, with only as much force as necessary to bridge the few crises that occasionally cut across its course—was the great engine of advancement. His understanding of the classics he read, combined with his father's paternalistic beliefs that the upper classes of British society were ultimately responsible for the welfare of the poor and had a sacred social duty to alleviate it, molded his political views.

Churchill's self-education left him with a sumptuous banquet of English words, phrases, concepts, and constructs before him in his growing Bangalore library; and with his flair for dramatic phrasing that was already in evidence in his schoolboy's letters to his parents, he developed an extraordinary power over the written language. As biographer William Manchester has written:

> [H]e . . . fashioned a soaring, resonant style, sparkling with eighteenth-century phrases, derivative of Gibbon, Johnson, Macauley, and Thomas Peacock, throbbing with the classical echoes of Demosthenes

and Cicero, but uniquely his own. . . . His feeling for the English tongue was sensual, almost erotic; when he coined a phrase he would suck it, rolling it around his palate to extract its full flavor.[5]

It is hard to see such an imaginative flexibility emerging in Churchill's writing had he experienced a classical British university education, let alone toiled in the stacks of some dusty law library.

At the time, as his friend Violet Bonham Carter later observed, "his relationship with all experience was first hand." She was the daughter of Herbert Henry Asquith, who became leader of the Liberal Party and prime minister in 1908. Her father and the other university-educated men of his class had built "their intellectual granaries [holding] the harvests of the past." Their knowledge of ethics, philosophy, economics, history, and geography were secondhand, gleaned from their professors and other students. But everything Churchill learned, he discovered himself. "His approach to life was full of ardour and surprise. Even the eternal verities appeared to him to be an exciting personal discovery . . . he was intellectually quite uninhibited and unselfconscious. Nothing to him was trite."[6]

But Churchill's exuberance could also be a mixed blessing. Once fixed, his ideas were often chiseled in stone. Then it did not matter what the evidence of his senses, or the entreatments of those around him, ought to have told him. "Mr. Churchill has scarcely, during a long and stormy career, altered them at all," philosopher and historian Isaiah Berlin wrote of him in the early 1960s.

> If anyone wishes to discover his views on the large and lasting issue of our time, he need only set himself to discover what Mr. Churchill has said or written on the subject at any period of his long and exceptionally articulate public life, in particular during the years before the First World War; the number of instances in which his views have in later years undergone any appreciable degree of change will be found astonishingly small.[7]

In those instances where Churchill was wrong, or misguided, or too much the child of his times—his dogged opposition to Indian self-rule is probably the best example—this singleness of purpose could result in personal disaster. In the outstanding instance when he was far more prescient than those around him—the menace of Adolf Hitler and Nazism—his stubbornness proved a blessing to humanity.

Churchill made his first mark even before he went to India. In October 1895 he secured permission from the army to go to Cuba to observe the war raging there between the Spanish army and Cuban nationalists seeking independence. At the same time he arranged to send dispatches of the fighting to the London *Daily Graphic*—his first newspaper assignment. In Cuba he came under fire from time to time; and in Cuba he developed his lifelong love of cigars. When he was published, his unique arrangement as both a military attaché and a war correspondent raised some eyebrows in military circles. But he left for India with the 4th Hussars before anything further came of it.

Though stationed at Bangalore in southern India, Churchill managed to get himself temporarily assigned to the northwest frontier, scene of constant fighting between British troops and Muslim rebels. Again, he took part in skirmishing, reporting the action to the London *Daily Telegraph*. His dispatches were published as *The Story of the Malakand Field Force* in 1898. His second book, *The River War* (1899), related his experiences with the British army in the Sudan, especially at the Battle of Omdurman, where he participated in one of the last cavalry charges in British history. This book too was based on his newspaper dispatches. It sold well and further introduced Churchill as a journalist to the educated public of Britain.

It is somewhat doubtful that Churchill ever saw the army—or even journalism—as more than a stepping-stone into politics. He chose to be a public man and to take up the profession of politics not just to advance his career, but also to redeem the waste of his father's potential. As he told Violet Bonham Carter after Lord Randolph's death, "All my dreams of comradeship with him, of entering Parliament at his side and in support, were ended. There remained for me only to pursue his aims and vindicate his memory."[8] To this end he cultivated his fame and glory and equipped himself further for a political career by practicing the art of rhetoric—public speaking. There he was challenged by the lack of preparation he might have had at a university or in appearing before the bar, and also by a slight speech impediment; he had some difficulty pronouncing the letters *r* and *s*. But Churchillian drive, aided by his already prodigious command of the English vocabulary, soon overcame both. He learned to painstakingly craft each speech, memorize it, and rehearse it in front of a mirror for hours. His object was to achieve a "striking presence." He recorded his thoughts about the importance of rhetoric in an unpublished essay. "Of all the talents bestowed upon men . . . none is so precious as the gift of oratory."[9] In 1899 he resigned his commission in the army and ran for Parliament as a Conservative candidate in a decidedly working-class riding. He was defeated.

It was a blessing in disguise. When the Boer War broke out in South Africa shortly after, Churchill was off once again to record the fighting, this time for the *Morning Post*. He was captured by the Boers after they ambushed an armored train he was on, but managed to escape. With the newspapers reporting his disappearance from a Boer prison camp and his subsequent arrival in neutral Portuguese territory and return to London, he became a national hero. When he ran for Parliament a second time in 1900, he was elected. Though nominally a Tory like his father, Churchill chafed under party discipline and was especially upset as the Conservatives drifted away from free trade and resisted any move toward Home Rule for Ireland. In 1904 he crossed the floor of the House of Commons to sit as a Liberal.

Churchill was appointed undersecretary at the Colonial Office in 1905 when the Liberal Party swept to power under Sir Henry Campbell-Bannerman. Thus began his meteoric rise to power. When Asquith followed Campbell-Bannerman three years later, he elevated Churchill to the Cabinet as President of the Board of Trade and, to Churchill's great delight, First Lord of the Admiralty in 1911. Vigorous, youthful, confident, meddling, iconoclastic, he prepared the Royal Navy for war. When Britain declared war on Germany on August 4, 1914, the fleet was ready. When the war bogged down into a battle of attrition on the Western Front, Churchill championed a quick naval attack through the Dardanelles to knock Turkey out of the war and turn Germany's flank. In the end, the campaign was a disaster—more the fault of others in its actual execution than Churchill's—but he was the man in charge and thus ultimately held responsible. When Asquith convinced the Conservatives to join a coalition government in the spring of 1915, Churchill's position at the Admiralty was one of the prices asked by the Tories. He was dismissed. When he failed to secure a position of any importance in the new War Cabinet, he begged a commission in the army and went to the Western Front in the fall of 1915 with the rank of major. The following January he was given command of a battalion.

Churchill was forty-two when he went to this fourth, and bloodiest, war. Successful command in any war is a young man's game, but Churchill seemed to take little notice of the dreadful surroundings, the fatigue, and the ever-present dangers of the Western Front. He was a resourceful, caring, and courageous commander. He came very close to being killed in an artillery bombardment, but seemed never to give his close shave a second thought. He did not revel in the experience, but undertook his duty to his men and his country with little reflection that but a year earlier he had overseen the world's mightiest navy and now was the commanding officer of perhaps 800 soldiers at the very edge of the battle. He did not resign his seat in the House, however, and by May 1917, eager to return to the center of power, he was back in the Cabinet at the request of David Lloyd George with the post of minister of munitions.

As Churchill had fought in war, so now he waged politics. In whatever cause he pursued, he did so fully and with abandon and little apparent thought as to the consequences. Violet Bonham Carter observed:

> [H]e was so wholly possessed by his own opinions that he often failed to take those of others into account, even as a practical factor in a situation. He never had his ear to the ground. Nor would he have felt much interest in its message even if he had heard it. It was his own message which concerned him and which he was determined to transmit.[10]

In the transmission, he frequently forgot, or took no heed of, the reality that politics is the art of the possible. Once his position was settled on a given issue, he had tunnel vision. He disregarded flanking fire. He steamed toward his objective like a battleship with guns blazing, whether his cause was well founded or ill considered. This rashness and doggedness led Chamberlain to fear that Churchill easily became a slave to his own rhetoric.

> I have often watched him in Cabinet begin with a casual comment . . . then as an image or simile comes into his mind proceed with great

animation . . . his speech becomes more and more rapid and impetuous till in a few minutes he will not hear of the possibility of opposition to an idea which only occurred to him a few minutes before.[11]

Churchill remained a whirlwind until age wore him down in the
early 1950s. He was a soldier, a newspaper correspondent, a politician,
a public speaker, a writer, a columnist, and a painter. He learned how to
fly and almost killed himself in the process. He was responsible for much
of the reconstruction of his beloved country home Chartwell—an estate
of 300 acres he purchased in September 1922—especially its gardens,
pools, and duck ponds. He spent most of his life working, even during
his so-called vacations. He was never still. Over the course of his life, he
authored or edited more than fifty books and wrote thousands of dispatches, columns, essays, and speeches. From the early 1920s, writing
was his chief means of livelihood.

His earliest books were all compilations of newspaper dispatches,
thrown together in great haste for money and fame. They are today
historical curiosities.[12] But his later works were invariably large, multi-
volume tomes. *The World Crisis*, his personal history of the First World
War written in the early 1920s, was five volumes. His biography of the
First Duke of Marlborough was four volumes. His two-volume biography
of his father ran to more than 800 pages. *A History of the English
Speaking Peoples*, completed in part before the Second World War but
not published until the 1950s, was four volumes. His best known work,
for which he won the Nobel Prize for Literature, was his six-volume
series *The Second World War*, which appeared between 1948 and 1953
—a runaway international bestseller.

Churchill's histories defined his ideas about history itself, Britain's
role in history, and the political destiny of the world as he saw it. As Isaiah
Berlin wrote, "Mr. Churchill's dominant category, the single, central,
organising principle of his moral and intellectual universe, is an historical imagination so strong, so comprehensive, as to encase the whole of
the present and the whole of the future in a framework of a rich and
multi-coloured past."[13] His histories are also the link between his personal story—his life, his antecedents, his accomplishments, his mark on

history, his destiny—and the unfolding story of civilization as he would have defined it. The observation has been made that both the starting and the ending of his historical works was his own experience[14]—as a son, as a descendent of the House of Marlborough, as First Lord of the Admiralty, minister of munitions, cabinet confidant of Lloyd George in the First World War, and as the man who led Britain in the Second. At the same time, he made no pretence to write history as a "professional" historian might have. In his personal histories of the two world wars, he saw himself a chronicler, setting down the record as he knew it, to be used by others who would attempt to write the history of those times.[15]

There is no better example of Churchill's history than *The Second World War*. With the exception of the first half of the first volume, *The Gathering Storm*, all the books are fundamentally autobiographical. Churchill weaves the story of his role in events together with large chunks of his speeches, of correspondence to and from him, of memos and reports he wrote, and of narratives of others. This technique—strongly discouraged in history students—is known as "scissors and paste" history. In Churchill's case, the process is meant not only to support his version of events, but to lay out the raw material of the history he used to underpin the narrative. Knowing as he did that many of the documents he used would not see the light of day for years, possibly decades, it was a perfectly reasonable way of putting the story of the war from his perspective on the record. It may also have been Churchill's way of claiming a place—without formal training either in the gathering of historical evidence or the writing of historical narrative—among those who craft history as a livelihood.

Churchill saw knowledge of the past as the key to understanding the present and finding insight into the future: "The longer you look back, the farther you can look forward," he once wrote. "This is not a philosophical or political argument—any oculist can tell you it is true."[16] He often looked back with nostalgia to the trappings and pageantry of another era. His frequent donning of his large collection of uniforms, hats and coats, mostly of a military or ceremonial nature, may also have been part of his way of linking with his own past. At the same time, however, he could be very much a man of the present, and even the future. He pushed the Royal Navy into converting from coal to oil. He championed the tank. He was fascinated by aircraft and their potential, and instinctively understood the threat posed by Germany's rapid construction of a modern air force.

Churchill's liking for things of the past was not nearly as important to the core of his values and ideas as his belief that history could reveal immutable truths about progress and civilization. As the British historian J. H. Plumb has written, "History was the heart of his faith; it permeated everything which he touched, and it was the mainstream of his politics and the secret of his immense mastery."[17] Robert Rhodes James may have put it best:

> No examination of Churchill's political career in the 1930s can ignore the significance of the tone and style of his historical writings. His sense of history was more emotional than intellectual but it is in this period of his life that the dominance of his faith in England's historical destiny, and his romanticized view of the past became particularly manifest. Much of his disgust for [Labour Prime Minister Ramsay] MacDonald, [and Conservative Prime Ministers Stanley] Baldwin and Neville Chamberlain was based upon his disgust at what he deemed to be their betrayal of England's grandeur and destiny.[18]

William Manchester has pointed out that "more than half of the fifty-six books he published were about war and warriors,"[19] touching heavily on Britain and its Empire.

It is natural that Churchill would have come to revere Britain and its institutions. He was the son of a parliamentarian. He was a military man. Before he was even twenty-five he had been to India—the crown jewel of the Empire—and to the Sudan. As undersecretary for colonial affairs from 1905 to 1908, he traveled widely across the Empire upon which the sun never set. He also embraced the Whig view of history, very Britain centered, which depicted the British as the one people who had created a stable, advanced, democratic, prosperous nation,[20] destined to lead others to the same happy state. The Britain that nurtured him had established a worldwide empire with a handful of soldiers, a very powerful navy, but mostly an efficient imperial civil service. It had led the world into the industrial revolution and embraced free trade. It had an age-old system of criminal and civil law (without a written constitution) that protected individual rights and balanced those rights against the welfare of the community. The great democratic reforms of the nineteenth century that had brought about universal male suffrage and reformed Parliament had come about peacefully. The emancipation of the slaves throughout the British Empire at the start of the nineteenth century had been done by an act of Parliament, not a bloody civil war. Churchill knew all this, took deep pride in it, even revered it as the example the world must follow if progress was to be made amidst peace and order.

However, Churchill was not blind to the very real inadequacies that still persisted in the United Kingdom, especially social injustice and the great disparity between classes. Like his father before him, he tended to believe that government had a responsibility to help the poor and the working classes. The new Liberal government elected in 1905 "was determined to lay this ugly specter of poverty, to redress the wrongs of the Industrial Revolution and to spread a net over the abyss," Violet Bonham Carter wrote of her father's administration. "It is to Winston Churchill's signal credit that he embraced these aims and worked and fought with all his heart and might to realize them."[21] Until his selection as First Lord of the Admiralty, he and Lloyd George were usually in the front rank of Asquith's ministers fighting against what they considered bloated navy budgets that diverted huge sums from the new social welfare schemes that the Liberal government had introduced. The socialist Beatrice Webb even thought of him at first as a "little Englander"—an opponent of Empire.[22] She was completely wrong.

Churchill had no real religious faith in the traditional meaning of the word.[23] His worldview was shaped not by the revelations of a supreme being but by his belief in the prevailing and everlasting civilizing mission of the British Empire. At the heart of his Empire were the British people; really, *his* British people, as he defined them: patriotic, loyal, courageous, tenacious, and morally decent. British men were manly and steadfast. They did their duty. If they grumbled at all in the course of said duty, it was only about small things, usually with a perverse sense of humor. They always faced their main challenges with resolve, especially when well led.[24]

He romanticized British women.[25] They were virtuous helpmates to their men, determined and loyal mothers of soldiers and sailors who sent their progeny to the dangerous borders of the Empire to guard their honor and their civilization. Even though Churchill grew to maturity in the a British upper class that openly flaunted its promiscuity and infidelities—he could not possibly have turned a blind eye to his own mother's many affairs—he was essentially a sexual innocent.[26] There is no evidence of his dallying with young women before he married, or any of infidelity afterward. Sexuality seemed to him a non sequitur and he was shocked when, on occasion in his adult life, he was faced with the blatant fact of it in someone he knew.

To Churchill, the British people were the heart and soul of two great institutions: the British Empire and the "English-speaking peoples," by which he meant the Americans. He believed that the relationship between the greatness of the British people and that of the British Empire was symbiotic. Britain stood as a shining peak on a mountaintop. The mountain rested upon the Empire—all of it, from the poorest colonial possessions of Africa and Asia to the burgeoning self-governing Dominions of Canada, Australia, and New Zealand. The mountain sustained British glory while it served British interests, both inextricably linked. Destroy the mountain and the mountaintop would crumble with it.

For most of his adult life, Churchill opposed any move to diminish the ties that bound that Empire. He was a staunch opponent of any sort of self-rule, let alone independence, for India (which then included Pakistan). He opposed the Statute of Westminster of 1931 that constitutionally granted independence to Canada and the other self-governing Dominions. He strongly supported the system of imperial preferences (lower tariffs among member nations of the British Commonwealth) instituted at the Ottawa Conference of 1932. In fact, he rarely used the words "British Commonwealth" to define the new post-1931 relationship of the Dominions to Britain—voluntary and ceremonial, cultural rather than constitutional, underpinned by loyalty to a common Crown. To him, there was one British Empire with its historical, cultural, and—still in the case of the colonies—constitutional heart in the British Isles. It led the civilized world and it guarded humanity against "the unpenetrated gloom of barbarism"[27] of the uncivilized that, in time, it would also lead into the light.

Empire was a chasm that separated Churchill from Roosevelt. Although it is technically untrue that the United States never acquired a formal colonial empire—the Philippines were an American colony for more than four decades—Americans could always claim that their empire was a temporary expression of their immediate national interests. When colonies were acquired, they were possessions, or commonwealths, or trust territories, not to be held permanently, but to be nurtured to self-government as in the case of Puerto Rico, or independence, as with the Philippines, or even permanent and full absorption, as with Hawaii and Alaska. Colonies and empire were aberrations in the American pursuit of self-interest, and many Americans looked upon colonies as, quite simply, un-American. Roosevelt was one of these people.

As a young man, Churchill seemed to harbor most of the prejudices toward the Americans that permeated the rest of upper-class English society. On the one hand, the latter could not fail but to be aware of the immense industrial power of the United States, its growing military power, its burgeoning population, its ever-increasing coterie of millionaires. Many of the second or third sons of the aristocracy—those with title but no inheritance—sought out the daughters of American millionaires to bring back to the United Kingdom as wives with fat checkbooks and important commercial connections. On the other hand, British upper-class prejudices against backwoods Yankee traders persisted. Even as millions of poor British subjects poured into the United States as immigrants, adding to the great potential of American society, many of Churchill's counterparts—and sometimes Churchill himself—saw America as "crude and vulgar, an arriviste among the cultivated nations of the world." Although publicly friendly—he depended too much on American readers and audiences for a large chunk of his writing and speaking income—he often could not "disguise the . . . genuine differences of opinion, often expressed acrimoniously, that emerged between himself and his would-be American brothers."[28]

Nonetheless, Churchill's vision of a great civilizing process led by the British Empire included those brothers, now broken away, who after all had come from the same political, constitutional, historical, and cultural roots. Perhaps he simply understood the Americans better than most of his contemporaries. His mother was American and that part of his family traced its roots as far back as the American Revolution. In the first half century of his life, he traveled extensively in the United States on speaking tours and made many wealthy, powerful, and important friends. He also read extensively in American history, particularly the history of the Civil War, and counted Abraham Lincoln as one of history's great leaders. There is more than a trace of Lincolnesque determination in a number of Churchill's early wartime speeches, and, like Lincoln, he held a strong belief in the moral rightness of his cause.

Churchill was the epitome of fidelity, and with the notable exception of Violet Bonham Carter in the first half of his adult life, he had practically no female friends. Certainly, they formed no part of his inner circle, ever.[29] His marriage to Clementine Hozier on September 12, 1908, was a true love match; Winston nurtured a strong and affectionate bond with Clementine that lasted his lifetime. She was his wife, but she was also the supporting, forgiving mother that Winston had never had.

It was not an easy marriage for Clementine.[30] She and Winston had five children: Diana (born July 1909), Randolph (born May 1911), Sarah (born October 1914), Marigold (born and died in finfancy in 1921), and Mary (born September 1922). Churchill's unstinting work, his constant occupation with causes, his unceasing demands on their always limited funds, tested her endlessly. He spent too much. He was sometimes too intemperate in his public utterances. She disliked (or distrusted) many of his political associates. And in the 1930s, when he was out of power, immersed in his writing, fighting his lonely and often futile battles against self-rule for India, against appeasement, against the abdication of King Edward VIII, she began to take long trips without him. He pined for her presence, but he learned to tolerate the absences.

Churchill ate, drank, and entertained as he spoke and wrote, with gusto and exuberance. He invariably made himself the center of attention at dinner parties, his own or others'. He loved costumes, hats, and travel to southern France or other warm climes during the cold wet English winters. He loved brandy, champagne, whisky and soda, and Cuban cigars. He dressed well and almost always formally. His relaxation was always private—painting alone, working outdoors at Chartwell, bathing in warm seas, or lying on hot sands.

It can fairly be said that much of Churchill's productivity prior to his becoming prime minister was the sheer need to earn money to support his extravagant lifestyle. For all intents and purposes, he was penniless; he earned his living and he worked hard to do it. Twice he lost a small fortune on the stock market, first in the great crash of 1929 and then again in the mini-collapse of 1937. Chartwell alone was an endless source of heavy expense and at one point in the 1930s he seriously entertained the notion of selling it. It was saved only when Churchill was given a helping hand with a generous loan from an admirer. In addition to the costs of acquiring, rebuilding, maintaining, and staffing Chartwell, the Churchills leased an apartment in London. Winston insisted on a full larder and a well-stocked liquor cabinet at both residences. He entertained frequently. He depended on a large staff to tend to his personal needs and to help him research his books and write his speeches.

When Churchill at last achieved the crowning glory of his political life and became prime minister on May 10, 1940, his need for money rapidly diminished. It was not that the job paid so well; but as leader of the nation in wartime, his lifestyle changed drastically. Chartwell effectively was closed for the duration. The entertainment was not so lavish or frequent—though Churchill never attempted to live on normal British wartime rations. But his energy remained unbounded. He tried to direct the massive, worldwide British war effort himself. He is famous for his daily afternoon naps and baths, but he worked from the moment he woke to the moment, usually far past midnight, when he retired. The prodigious Churchill energies that had previously been devoted to writing, speaking, painting, and Chartwell were now all harnessed to the task of running the war. This was certainly not rooted in the need for money.

Churchill's depression—his "black dog"—has long been written of. William Manchester speculated that the affliction may have arisen from an aggressive temperament turned inward: "Having chosen to be macho, Churchill became the pugnacious, assertive fighter ready to cock a snook at anyone who got in his way"; and when "the deep reservoir of vehemence he carried within him backed up . . . he was plunged into fathomless gloom."[31] Perhaps. But as Manchester also observes, no one is really sure what produces depression, though suspicion falls heavily on heredity. Churchill's father and five of the seven dukes of Marlborough suffered from it. Many persons of great accomplishment from national leaders to writers, artists to businesspeople, have suffered from it. There seems to be a link between depression and creativity, as if a precocious preoccupation with mortality drives a person to achieve as much as possible before the flame of life expires. Violet Bonham Carter recorded her first-ever encounter with Churchill in 1906:

> He turned on me with a lowering gaze and asked me abruptly how old I was. I replied that I was nineteen. "And I," he said almost despairingly, "am thirty-two already. . . ." Then savagely: "Curse ruthless time! Curse our mortality! How cruelly short is the allotted span for all we must cram into it!"[32]

However depression is caused, it is generally cyclical. Its comings and goings challenge the afflicted with the constant choice between surrender to the blackness or confronting it. In those who have it, the blackness often reappears during periods of forced or sustained idleness, when things consistently do not go well, when endless effort seems to be fruitless, when there are no markers to measure life's progress.

The great British essayist, philosopher, historian, and biographer Thomas Carlyle could not have been unknown to Churchill, since he was one of the most famous historical writers of his age. He too suffered from depression. His therapy was work. In *Past and Present*, published in 1843, he wrote that there "is a perennial nobleness, and even sacredness in Work. . . . there is always hope for a man that actually and earnestly works: in Idleness alone is there perpetual despair." In Carlyle's view, there was no sense in trying to understand why one was depressed. The best course was simply to accept it and cope with it through work: "Know what thou canst work at; and work at it, like a Hercules! That will be thy better plan."[33]

Whether Churchill came to his personal therapy through reading Carlyle, or arrived at his own fundamentally same way of coping with his "black dog," does not matter. What is pertinent is the obvious link between his depression and his very active life.

Churchill remained a prominent member of Lloyd George's government beyond the Armistice of 1918, first in the War Office and then as colonial secretary. At times, however, his main preoccupation seemed to be the defeat of the new Communist regime that entrenched itself in Russia in October 1917. Churchill hated communism. He did everything in his power as a member of the British Cabinet to encourage Western military intervention in the Russian civil war that followed the revolution in a vain effort to expunge the "red menace." He was obsessed by the effort and only acquiesced in the withdrawal of British support for the anti-Bolsheviks after Britain was abandoned by Canada and other intervening countries in 1919.

In 1922 Lloyd George's Liberals were defeated and Churchill lost his seat. The Liberal Party was clearly in decline, battered by the rising Labour Party. Churchill sought refuge once again in the Conservative Party. He was elected as a Tory in a by-election in the fall of 1924. In November of that year Prime Minister Stanley Baldwin somewhat unexpectedly named him Chancellor of the Exchequer. He held the post for five years, until Baldwin's government was defeated in May 1929. Churchill kept his seat. In fact, he remained in the House of Commons until 1964. But the loss of his cabinet post began his ten-year-long sojourn in the desert of British politics—the so-called "wilderness years."

Churchill first laid out the framework for the story of the "wilderness years" in *The Gathering Storm*. In Chapter 5, which he entitled the "The Locust Years," he described the four years of the coalition government formed by MacDonald (Labour) and Baldwin (Conservative) from 1931 to 1935. That coalition did almost nothing when Hitler came to power in January 1933 and began to rearm Germany. This is the pivotal chapter in Churchill's account of how the Second World War was rooted in the failure of Britain and France to stop German rearmament. It is the pivotal interpretation behind the popular view that Churchill's lonely stand against the appeasement of Germany was the only real cause of the virtual destruction of his political career during the 1930s.

In fact, Churchill's political isolation stemmed not only from his strong opposition to appeasement, but also from his long and persistent battle with Baldwin through most of the decade against any sort of liberalization of British rule in India and from his moral support for King Edward VIII during the abdication crisis of 1936. The former position is relatively easy to explain. It came from Churchill's strong belief in the need to keep the Empire whole in order to sustain British greatness. It was fed by his archaic and romantic reminiscences of the Raj as he found it in the late 1890s. He had no sympathy whatever for Mahatma Ghandi and the Indian nationalists, though he had no solution either to the problem of how a truly liberal Britain could long prevail over 600 million people who resisted its rule. He absolutely had no sympathy for the unbridled use of force against the nationalists either; he had been one of the very few public figures in Britain to openly condemn Brigadier General Reginald Dyer, who had perpetrated the machine-gun massacre of 379 men, women, and children, and the wounding of at least 1,500 more, in the Punjabi city of Amritsar on April 13, 1919.[34] The Empire Churchill believed in did not gun down innocents in the streets.

But what of about Edward VIII? Churchill's support for the king's efforts to retain the throne while marrying the twice-divorced American Mrs. Wallis Simpson defies explanation. It is also evidence of the Churchillian tendency to sometimes nail his colors to a flag and persist in his course on the basis of an ill-considered view or emotion, rather than facing unalterable realities. His useless public pleading for Edward even endangered the Arms and the Covenant movement, which he helped to found, that favored rearming Britain and enforcing the Covenant of the League of Nations against Hitler.

Churchill's campaign to stop Hitler through rearmament, especially in the air, and through enforcement of the Treaty of Versailles, was both prescient and unassailable. But it is best seen in its proper historical context. For example, Churchill was not worried about Benito Mussolini's fascism and believed, virtually until the German attack on France on May 10, 1940, that the Italian dictator might be a leavening influence in Europe and a counterweight to Hitler. He saw Mussolini as essentially a domestic tyrant who posed no threat to the Empire or even to Italy's European neighbors. Despire his bluster, the Italian dictator had put the Communists in their place—largely in prison—and accepted the rules of international diplomacy.

Churchill saw Francisco Franco's Nationalists in the Spanish Civil War very mulch as he saw Mussolini and his Facists. Franco, after all, claimed to be fighting to overthrow a Republican government that had become dominated by Communists. The problem was that although Churchill obviously—and rightly—saw Hitler in a much different light than Mussolini or Franco, not many of his contemporaries saw much difference at all. As Robert Rhodes James has observed, Churchill "failed to see that in the eyes of many people fascism was indivisible, that the same specter that haunted Germany now stalked through Italy and brought death and devastation to Spain." Not until the summer of 1938—two years into the Spanish Civil War—did Churchill oppose Franco. The switch came primarily because he concluded, after a visit to Spain by his son-in- law Duncan Sandys, that Franco ultimately posed a greater menace to British interests than the Republican government did.[35]

The central theme of the story of the "wilderness years" has stood the test of time: Churchill was among the first to understand the menace Hitler posed to the British Empire, to international order, and to western civilization. It has become fashionable in some recent historical writing to denigrate Churchill's great foresight, even to claim that he understood Hitler because they shared similar leadership characteristics.[36] The claim is absurd. It ignores the whole corpus of Churchill's writings, his speeches, and his long history of great political battles for the integrity of Parliament and the British system of constitutional liberty.

Yet it is surely an oversimplification to explain Churchill's passionate opposition to Hitler simply by exclaiming that he "loathed Nazism because he hated persecution and prejudice."[37] In the main that was certainly true, but Hitler represented far more than that in Churchill's eyes. Almost from his first notice of the Nazi leader, Churchill recognized Hitler as a man who might well succeed in harnessing the enormous military potential of Germany to the purpose of revenging the kaiser's defeat. Even worse, Churchill understood that Hitler would do this using his spellbinding demagoguery to promote racial hate as an instrument of state policy, that he would literally suspend the norms of Judeo-Christian civilization throughout Europe and beyond if he succeeded.

Churchill seems to have awakened to Hitler in the summer of 1932 when his son Randolph covered the German elections for the *Sunday Graphic*. Randolph was but twenty-one at the time, but he wrote of the Nazis: "Nothing can long delay their arrival in power. . . . The success of the Nazi Party sooner or later means war. . . . They burn for revenge. They are determined once more to have an army. I am sure that once they have achieved it, they will not hesitate to use it."[38] As Churchill watched Hitler achieve power in January 1933 and begin immediately to ignore the Treaty of Versailles, scorn the League of Nations, and then to rearm Germany, he saw the danger. Hitler's regime was ruthless in crushing its political opponents and unstinting in its efforts to disenfranchise Germany's Jews. With the concentrated power of the state's police, security apparatus, and army at his fingertips, Hitler would, if not halted, eventually hold sway over central Europe, whether he actually conquered it all or not. When that happened, Churchill knew, Britain and France would find themselves isolated and directly threatened by Hitler's growing air force. Thus, a powerful Nazi Germany at the very geographical heart of Europe, within easy striking range of London or Paris, promised not only to dominate Europe, but also to pose a mortal danger to both nations.

That core belief—that the fate of Britain was tied to the whole of Europe—formed one layer of Churchill's reaction to Hitler. Another layer was Churchill's early recognition that Hitler was his own man, had his own agenda, and could not be manipulated by others. Churchill hated communism, but he knew from the start that trying to placate Hitler in order to use him as a bulwark against the Soviet Union would not work and would only allow him more time to build his military. Finally, he saw that Hitler had no respect whatever for international agreements. He wielded force and he respected nothing else.

Nowhere did Churchill sum up the basic fear that fueled his long struggle against the appeasement of Hitler better than in his speech to the House of Commons of June 18, 1940, upon the surrender of France:

> Hitler knows that he will have to break us in this Island or lose the war. If we can stand up to him, all Europe may be free and the life of the world may move forward into broad, sunlit uplands. But if we fail, then the whole world, including the United States, including all that we have known and cared for, will sink into the abyss of a new Dark Age made more sinister, and perhaps more protracted, by the lights of perverted science.[39]

Churchill's return to the Admiralty and the Cabinet on September 3, 1940, was widely cheered among the people at large. They knew little of how impetuous he had been in that post during the First World War, or of how he had virtually assumed control of the navy. His Dardanelles sin was now long forgotten, well overshadowed by his steadfast opposition to Hitler throughout the decade. The Royal Navy was not so sure that his accession to the office was a blessing. Rear Admiral Sir John Godfrey, Director of Naval Intelligence, later wrote, "I . . . wondered if Mr. Churchill's long years in opposition to all governments left him with a feeling that, during his early days at the Admiralty, we all shared the delinquencies of those politicians that he had so consistently [condemned] in public."[40]

Churchill insisted that his former office in the Admiralty Building be restored as close as possible to its original configuration in 1915. He demanded that his old 20 x 30-foot map of the world, on which he had plotted all British ships and fleet movements, be put up again; he found the map precisely where he had left it rolled up in the spring of 1915. He also brought back his old way of running the Admiralty. He was far from content being the Royal Navy's civilian boss, representing it to the Cabinet, protecting it at the highest political levels, and conveying the government's wishes to the Board of Admiralty that commanded it. Almost immediately, he assumed command. And, as in 1914, the Admiralty's powerful radios allowed him to keep close watch on his ships and their captains at sea and all too often to interfere in their command.

Working at his desk into the small hours of the morning, Churchill seemed to miss no detail, large or small, in the command, administration, or buildup of the fleet. He fired out memos to the naval staff late every night—each beginning with the phrase "Pray tell me," or "Pray inform me"—which greeted them on coming to work each morning. Godfrey remembered those "Churchill prayers" memos: "they put one on the defensive and added greatly to the strain of those early months."[41]

Nor had Churchill's basic approach to war changed. Wars are not won by waiting for the enemy. He had no control over the land or air forces, but he did control the navy and was determined to use it to strike at Germany in whatever way he could. Some of his schemes were badly thought out; sending British ships into the Baltic, into the teeth of German air power, for example, would have resulted in mass slaughter. But at least, as Abraham Lincoln had once said of Ulysses S. Grant, he wanted to fight.

Churchill and Roosevelt renewed their acquaintance in the 1930s, when Churchill sent Roosevelt all four volumes of his Marlborough biography. On September 11, 1939, Roosevelt decided to reacquaint himself by opening a personal correspondence with Churchill with the letter excerpted below:

> It is because you and I occupied similar positions in the World War that I want you to know how glad I am that you are back again in the Admiralty. Your problems are, I realize, complicated by new factors but the essential is not very different. What I want you and the Prime Minister to know is that I shall at all times welcome it if you will keep me in touch personally with anything you want me to know about.[42]

Churchill recorded his receipt of that letter in *The Gathering Storm*: "I responded with alacrity, using the signature of 'Naval Person,' and thus began that long and memorable correspondence—covering perhaps a thousand communications on each side, and lasting till his death more than five years later."[43] Until their first meeting at Argentia, Newfoundland, fifteen months later, the Churchill-Roosevelt correspondence became the chief means by which both men communicated their needs, views, and difficulties to each other. It was far more important than the letters, notes, and telegrams that went from embassy to embassy.

Churchill certainly knew better than to take this first note as a sign that the United States might enter the war. Until the fall of France, neither he nor anyone else in the Cabinet, nor in Washington, thought that it might be necessary, or even possible. Thus, Churchill's correspondence with FDR over the next eight months was mainly informative and moderate in tone. When he wrote his first letter to the president as prime minister on May 15, 1940, however, that situation had changed drastically, and so had Churchill's message.

> We expect to be attacked here ourselves, both from the air and by parachute and airborne troops in the near future and are getting ready for them. If necessary, we shall continue the war alone and we are not afraid of that. But I trust you realise, Mr. President, that the voice and force of the United States may count for nothing if they are withheld too long. You may have a completely subjugated, Nazified Europe

established with astounding swiftness, and the weight may be more than we can bear.[44]

The gathering storm that Winston Churchill had first detected on the far political horizon of Europe in early 1933 had now broken. Could he count on FDR to find shelter, and succor, in the maelstrom?

4

DAY OF INFAMY

THE ESCALATING PACE OF WAR PREPARATIONS AND MUSHROOMING bureaucracies had transformed the sleepy capital into a bustling metropolis—and offended many Southern sensibilities. But Sunday was a day of leisure and Sunday, December 7, 1941, was no exception. Housewives had done their weekend shopping and discovered just how richly stocked the city was and how reasonable groceries still were: spareribs went for 22 cents per pound, ground beef for 15 cents, fresh ham for 29 cents, bacon and butter for 39 cents, and cigarettes for a mere $1.29 per carton.

As well, there was entertainment galore. The Don Cossacks Chorus was at Constitutional Hall, home of the Daughters of the American Revolution. The new National Gallery had just opened its doors. The stage was abuzz with talk of the 1941 Pulitzer Prize-winning play, Robert Sherwood's *There Shall Be No Right*, a saga about the Soviet invasion of Finland in 1939. Sherwood, as everyone knew, was one of the president's speechwriters. Film theaters were showing that year's glorious hits, John Ford's *How Green Was My Valley* and Orson Welles' *Citizen Kane*. For those so inclined, the hurly-burly Gayety Theatre had announced its star attraction: Rosita Royce, the "Dove Girl."

Baseball was over, with the Yankees taking the Dodgers in five games. But at creaky old Griffith Stadium, Sammy Baugh was ready to lead the National Football League's Washington Redskins into the final game of the season against the Philadelphia Eagles. A crowd of 27,000 screaming fans was expected.[1] As the morning progressed, a brisk

December wind stiffened and the sun finally broke through the gray clouds. The weather turned warm and peaceful.

At the White House, Eleanor Roosevelt was set to hold court. She had invited thirty guests to the State Dining Room for a "small lunch." Her husband had also been invited, but he had declined. The dampness of Washington had caused his sinus congestion to flare up again, and he also had a cold and a headache.

In fact, Franklin Delano Roosevelt, in the first year of an unprecedented third term, had heavier matters on his mind than his wife's lunch. The Japanese, against whom he had taken a tough and unyielding line concerning further expansion in the East, seemed unimpressed by his warnings and embargos on raw materials. On the evening of December 6, the special codebreakers known as the "Magic" team had intercepted and decrypted an angry Japanese message rejecting Secretary of State Cordell Hull's latest proposals for a peaceful settlement of Pacific affairs. Roosevelt considered Japan and the Pacific to be an American concern, one aggravated by anachronistic empires run from London, Paris, Lisbon, and, before the fall of the Netherlands, The Hague. He had received the "Magic" intercept with the terse comment, "This means war."[2]

Thus plagued by poor health and political worries, the president remained in his upstairs bedroom on December 7. It was a square chamber, dominated by a heavy dark wardrobe, an old bureau, an old-fashioned rocking chair, and a small, narrow white iron modified hospital bed. Beside the bed was a white table littered with aspirin bottles, nosedrops, bits of paper, pencil stubs, books, ashtrays, cigarettes, and telephones. Secretary of Labor Frances Perkins was impressed by the Victorian mantelpiece, carved with grapes, which held a collection of miniature pigs in all shapes and colors; propped up behind them, were snapshots of children, friends, and expeditions.[3] The walls of the bedroom were plastered with prints of the clipper ships *Sweepstakes*, *Dreadnaught*, and *Nightingale*; a color print of *Commodore Preble's Squadron at Tripoli, August 5th, 1904*; a watercolor of the *Amberjack II*; a portrait of Isaac Roosevelt (1726–94); and a framed certificate of membership in the New York Marine Society, to which a good number of his Delano relatives had belonged.[4] This room was under the command of Arthur Prettyman, Roosevelt's chief butler. The presidential flag stood outside the door.

That December 7, FDR sat in the bedroom wrapped in a turtleneck sweater awaiting further developments in Japanese-American relations. He ate his lunch from a trolley with luncheon trays.[5] All the while, he discussed unfolding world events with presidential advisor Harry Hopkins, the White House's "permanent" guest since, in 1941, FDR had invited him to occupy the Lincoln Bedroom. After lunch, Roosevelt turned to his stamp collection while Hopkins, casually dressed in slacks and a sweater, lounged lazily on a couch. It was, after all, Sunday afternoon.

At Fort Myer's Quarters Number 1, Chief of Staff George C. Marshall made his way to the red-bricked stables and mounted his bay horse for a leisurely trot along the fort's crest by the Potomac River. It was a beautiful, warm day. Looking across the water to the capital, the general could see the tip of the Washington Monument as well as the golden Goddess of Freedom atop the Capitol dome. Upon returning to Fort Myer, he was called to the telephone. Someone at the War Department asked that he come in. No urgency. Just come in. Marshall casually showered and dressed. He reached his office at 11:10 A.M.

The Japanese Embassy on Massachusetts Avenue likewise was quiet that Sunday morning. There had been quite a party the night before, with food larders emptied and Scotch whisky flowing freely. The first risers called up a grocer with an order of $200 worth of food, including 500 pounds of rice, 75 loaves of bread, 36 dozen eggs, and assorted juices and jellies. The translators were still drunk and struggled to translate into English a coded telegram from Tokyo for Secretary of State Hull—the very message that FDR had already read.[6] An angry Ambassador Kichisaburo Nomura and special envoy Saburu Kurusu paced up and down in the Embassy's parlor, waiting to take Tokyo's latest missive to the State Department.

Over at Sixteenth Street, Maxim Litvinov and his English wife, the Fabian Society darling Ivy Low, had just taken up residence that day at the Soviet Embassy, the former Italian-French cupid-and-swag palace of Mrs. George M. Pullman. The new Soviet envoy, only recently resurrected from political exile by Joseph Stalin, had arrived in a rumpled and grubby gray denim suit, one that reminded the denizens of Sixteenth Street of those issued to roadwork gangs.

Franklin Roosevelt's "desuetude" was ended abruptly at around 1:40 P.M. by a telephone call from Secretary of the Navy Frank Knox.[7] He took the call in the Oval Room, Hopkins by his side. The Navy had picked up a radio report from U.S. Navy commander in chief Honolulu, Knox informed "the Boss," that an "air raid" was on, and that it was "no drill." Hopkins was thunderstruck. There "must be some mistake"; surely, Tokyo "would not attack in Honolulu." Roosevelt at first likewise seemed baffled by the news, and merely muttered "No!" upon hearing Knox's report. Then the immensity of the moment hit him: the United States would now be in the war. What had been philosophical musing at Argentia in August was about to become hard reality. Decisions could no longer be avoided. True to form, Roosevelt recovered quickly. He confided to Hopkins that the report rang true and that he had feared such an act for quite some time now. There was no escaping its greater implication. "If the report is true," he told Hopkins, "it has taken the decision out of our hands." As more devastating news filtered in from Honolulu, Secretary Knox's reaction was blunt: "Those little yellow bastards!"[8]

At 2:05 P.M. the president called the secretary of state, who was expecting Nomura and Kurusu, both delayed by their inebriated decoders. The seventy-year-old Hull was in an especially mean mood. Everyone in Washington, he informed an aide, seemed to be meddling in foreign policy matters. "They all come at me with knives and hatchets."[9] The president instructed his secretary to treat the envoys "coolly" and then to "bow them out." Sitting stiff and erect in his tall chair, Hull cut a stern Victorian figure in his black suit, white shirt, black necktie, and white hair. After letting the Japanese cool their heels for fifteen minutes, Hull left them standing on their feet while he dressed them down about their "infamous falsehoods and distortions" during past conversations. He denied later reports that he had subjected them to some choice "Tennessee mountain language," calling them "bastards" and "piss-ants."[10] At 2:28 P.M. Admiral Harold R. Stark, chief of naval operations, confirmed to Roosevelt by telephone that the fleet was under attack and that there had been loss of life. Two minutes later, the president dictated a news release about Pearl Harbor to Press Secretary Stephen T. Early. Then he called a conference for 3 P.M. of those leaders who were in Washington.

"The President wants you right away. There's a car on the way to pick you up. The Japs just bombed Pearl Harbor!" It was Louise "Hackie" Hackmeister from the White House switchboard, summoning Grace

Tully to her boss' side. As she approached the White House, FDR's personal secretary noticed that the physical landscape had already changed. The grounds were "swarming with extra police and an added detail of Secret Service men." Reporters were running to the Executive Wing. State, War, and Navy officials were scurrying into the White House. When she reached the second floor around 3 P.M., Tully discovered that Secretary Knox and Secretary of War Henry L. Stimson were already "with the Boss"; Secretary Hull and General Marshall were expected any moment. What became in effect the first council of war took place in the Oval Room, with FDR's advisors seated on leather sofas and brocade chairs. They at once put forces in the Philippines on high alert, and at home ordered guards for all munitions factories and bridges. Lend-Lease shipments then loading at American ports were stopped; the United States would now need that equipment for its own forces. Roosevelt, outwardly calm but with "rage in his very calmness," personally took call after call on the first ring. "With each new message he shook his head grimly and tightened the expression of his mouth,"[ii] Tully recalled. Eleanor had seen him like this before. "His reaction to any event was always to be calm. If it was something that was bad, he just became like an iceberg."[12] Finally, the expected call came from London.

Winston Churchill was at his official country estate, Chequers, that Sunday night (London was five hours ahead of Washington and ten hours ahead of Honolulu). Ironically, U.S. ambassador Gilbert Winant and Roosevelt's special envoy, Averell Harriman, were with the prime minister. He turned on the BBC news just after 9:00 P.M., London time. "There were a number of items about the fighting on the Russian front and on the British front in Libya, at the end of which some few sentences were spoken regarding an attack by the Japanese on American shipping at Hawaii, and also Japanese attacks on British vessels in the Dutch East Indies." The news took a moment to sink in. Harriman spoke up: there had been something about the Japanese attacking the Americans. Everyone sat up. Then Churchill's butler came into the room. "It's quite true, we heard it ourselves outside. The Japanese have attacked the Americans."[13] Winant would later recall: "We looked at one another incredulously. Then Churchill jumped to his feet and started for the door with the announcement, 'We shall declare war on Japan.'. . . 'Good God,' I said, 'you can't declare war on a radio announcement'." Churchill stopped. 'What shall I do?'" Winant offered to telephone the White House to find out from the president just what was happening. Churchill added, "And I shall talk with him too." When Winant got Roosevelt on the line, he was able to confirm the news of the attack. Then he added that he had a friend with him who wanted to talk to him. "You will know who it is, as soon as you hear his voice."[14] Churchill took the receiver. "Mr. President, what's this about Japan?" FDR confirmed the news, then declared: "We are all in the same boat now."[15] These were the words that Churchill had longed to hear for years. "I went to bed," he later recalled, "and slept the sleep of the saved and thankful."[16]

At 5 P.M. on December 7 Roosevelt summoned his secretary to the Oval Room. "Sit down, Grace. I'm going before Congress tomorrow. I'd like to dictate my message. It will be short."[17] Furiously puffing away on cigarettes, FDR dictated the 500 historic words that he would address to the Congress the next day. Hull and Hopkins went over the draft with him. The president rejected Hull's call for a wordier document detailing American-Japanese relations. And he rejected suggestions that he include Germany and Italy in his message to Congress, for "Magic" had intercepted a cable from Berlin to Tokyo November 29 in which Germany pledged to join the war immediately should Japan become engaged in a war against the United States. Satisfied with his labors, Roosevelt went down to the infirmary to have his sinus congestion treated. He then retreated to the second floor and had a light dinner with Hopkins, Tully, and his son James, a captain in the Marines. Eleanor made the one dinner she knew how to cook well—scrambled eggs in a silver chafing dish. The kitchen added cold cuts, a salad, spoon bread, and an apricot Bavarian (!) cream pie.

At 8:30 P.M. on the dot, the Cabinet assembled in the White House study. Frances Perkins, the only woman in the Cabinet, was so struck by what she called her "strangest cabinet meeting," that she immediately scribbled a detailed description of that historic gathering on a White House memo pad.[18] There was none of the usual Roosevelt banter and levity. He was silent and withdrawn. His voice was low. He was grim. His complexion had "a queer, gray, drawn look." His face was "puckered," with an unusual "pursed-in" expression. With the Cabinet seated in a semicircle around him, the president told the group that this was the most serious cabinet meeting since Abraham Lincoln had met with his on the outbreak of the Civil War in 1861. He reviewed the day's events, and informed them that he would go before the Congress the next day to read his message. Perkins recalled that FDR had physical difficulty declaring that "his" Navy had been caught asleep. It was now apparent that four battleships had been severely damaged or sunk. Twice he asked Knox, "Find out, for God's sake, why those ships were tied up in rows." He was less than thrilled with the secretary's bureaucratic reply, "That's the way we berth them."

At 9:30 P.M. Roosevelt invited Vice President Henry A. Wallace as well as a select group of senators and congressmen to share the news. It was agreed that he would address both houses of Congress at 12:30 P.M. the next day. The delegations left the study around 11 P.M. At midnight, waiters brought in beer and sandwiches. FDR's last two guests were Edward R. Murrow, a CBS reporter, and "Wild Bill" Donovan, the president's coordinator of information. Sitting in a room lit only by a small puddle of light from a desk lamp, the former assistant secretary of the navy could only lament, "They caught our ships like lame ducks! Lame ducks, Bill!"[19]

Monday, December 8, revealed what Grace Tully called a "new normality" at the White House. Sentry boxes, manned by special units of military police, had been constructed both inside and outside the black iron fence. The regular White House police presence had been beefed up with extras from the Metropolitan Police Force. Colonel Edmund W. Starling, head of the White House Secret Service, had called agents in from the field. But that night, when Secretary of the Treasury Henry J. Morgenthau, Jr., discovered only three men patrolling the long block at the back entrance of the White House, he gave Starling "the most terrific dressing down you ever heard of." Next day, with the president's consent, he replaced Starling with his second in command, Michael F. Reilley.[20]

When Chief Usher J. B. West arrived for work at 6 A.M., "I thought all the policemen of Washington had gathered on the White House grounds." Soldiers were rushing in from Fort Myer to guard the Executive Building. The flag, which flew over the White House only when the president was in residence, was now ordered flown every day as a security measure. Members of Congress, members of the Cabinet, and top military aides flitted in and out of the mansion. At first, West feared that the White House had been bombed.[21] Thousands of Washington's "cave dwellers" already were gathering in Lafayette Square in the early morning hours, just to be close to their president in this hour of despair. Automobiles slowly crept down Pennsylvania Avenue and their occupants craned out of windows to catch a glimpse of someone, anyone, at the White House.

At precisely 12:05 P.M. on December 8, 1941, Howell Crim noted in the usher's log, President Roosevelt, wearing his navy blue cape, was helped into the black presidential limousine at the White House. A G-man man clung to each running board. To either side were open Secret Service automobiles manned by agents holding riot guns; on each running board were three other agents, armed with .38-caliber revolvers. Slowly, the cavalcade made its way past the barren trees of Constitution Avenue toward the Capitol. What had started as a lovely, warm day had become bitterly cold. Along the route, only a few onlookers braved the weather. Inside the Capitol, the Justices of the Supreme Court, the Cabinet, Vice President Wallace, and Speaker Sam Rayburn joined the joint session of Congress. And there was a very special invited guest, Mrs. Woodrow Wilson. FDR arrived at 12:12 P.M. A thunderous roar welcomed him. All rose to their feet, save one, a Republican Representative from Montana.

Roosevelt took just six minutes to deliver his momentous speech. It was simple, direct, vintage Roosevelt. "Yesterday, December 7, 1941—a date which will live in infamy—the United States of America was suddenly and deliberately attacked by naval and air forces of the Empire of Japan." The president then listed the targets of Japanese aggression: Malaya, Hong Kong, Guam, the Philippines, Wake Island, and Midway Island. Before asking the Congress to declare a "state of war" to exist between the United States and Japan, he spoke the one sentence that Hopkins had inserted into the speech: "With confidence in our armed forces—with the unbounding determination of our people—we will gain the inevitable triumph—so help us God."[22]

The Senate passed the measure 82-0 forty-two minutes later; the House 388 to 1 thirty-two minutes after the Senate. The only dissenting vote was that of Republican Representative Jeannette Rankin of

Montana, who had also voted against war in 1917, her only other term in Congress. She then sought refuge in a telephone booth and broke down crying. Her career in Congress was finished. Just after 4 P.M., Roosevelt, back in the White House, with his own pen noted "Approved" on the war resolution. Using twelve other pens, to be distributed to the joint congressional delegation that had brought the document over, the president wrote "Dec. 7, 1941, 4:10 P.M., E.S.T. Franklin D. Roosevelt."[23] From this point on, he took seriously his role as commander in chief. At 10 P.M. the next day, FDR addressed the American people. He promised them "a long war," "a hard war," against what he called "crafty and powerful bandits."[24] Sixty million people, the largest listener group in American history according to the Hooper ratings, had heard both speeches. The BBC in London also carried it live.

At the Japanese Embassy on December 8, a crowd had gathered to watch smoke rise from the rear garden. The staff of fifty brought out cardboard boxes, each with a fuse protruding from the end. They lit the fuses, one by one. When the destruction was complete, the Japanese were rounded up and held in a small building with sleeping accommodations meant for ten. They ordered mattresses and pillows and soap from the Woodward and Lothrop store, and then turned to other purveyors for five cases of Old Paar and five cases of Johnny Walker Black Label Scotch whisky, as well as beer, oysters, French bread, and aspirin. Each deliveryman demanded cash. Eventually, the staff was interred at the Homestead Hotel at Hot Springs, Virginia.

Winston Churchill at once grasped the enormity of the possible implications for Britain of the attack on Pearl Harbor. Now that the United States had been dragged into the war by Japan, would Roosevelt even think of trying to involve the Republic in a war with Germany and Italy? Churchill was certain that Adolf Hitler would declare war against the United States very soon, but would the Americans stick with the "Europe-first" strategy they had agreed to in the "ABC-1 Staff" accord in March 1941? It was one thing for Washington to have made theoretical war plans in a vacuum—when it was not at war—but another when American servicemen had been killed without warning, raising America's ire against Japan to fever pitch.

What would happen to Lend-Lease supplies destined for the United Kingdom? Surely, most American war production would now be diverted into building up the nation's stocks as quickly as possible. What role would Britain play in shaping overall war strategy, in deciding what was to be done with food production, munitions, ships, and aircraft now that it was one of three major protagonists, and the smallest at that? What could he do to make sure that British plans, needs, strategic interests, and the preservation of the British Empire were placed as high on the new Allied war agenda as those of the United States and the Soviet Union? This last issue was especially important in light of the president's well-known antipathy to imperialism. It could easily threaten Britain's absolute need, as Churchill saw it, to keep the Empire united, and under British lead, so as to enable him to marshal Empire assets in a bid for equality with the United States and the Soviet Union.

Almost immediately, Churchill made up his mind to go to Washington to meet Roosevelt.[25] The day after Pearl Harbor he wrote King George VI:

> I have formed the conviction that it is my duty to visit Washington without delay, provided such a course is agreeable to President Roosevelt as I have little doubt it will be. The whole plan of the Anglo-American defence and attack has to be concerted in the light of reality. We have also to be careful that our share of munitions and other aid which we are receiving from the United States does not suffer more than is, I fear, inevitable.[26]

The decision to rush off to the United States was wholly in character and in keeping with Churchill's long-held conviction that nothing substituted for face-to-face meetings and firsthand, on the spot, reconnaissance. Before he could leave, however, he had to overcome the opposition to the trip of his foreign secretary, Anthony Eden, and the reticence of Roosevelt and his top advisors to have Churchill on their hands so soon after Pearl Harbor.

Robert Anthony Eden both admired and disrusted Churchill. At forty-four he was a relatively young man for one so high in the ranks of British political leaders. A decorated veteran of the British army in the

First World War, he had won a seat in Parliament in 1922 at just twenty-five years of age, only months after graduating from Oxford with First Class Honours in Persian and Arabic. Eden joined the Cabinet of the Baldwin National government in 1935 and became one of the youngest foreign secretaries in British history.

Eden's resignation from Prime Minister Neville Chamberlain's Cabinet in early 1940 has given him a place in popular memory as a Churchill supporter during Winston's long fight against appeasement. In fact, he was nothing of the kind. His resignation was due primarily to his refusal to countenance Chamberlain's arbitrary decision-making in the field of foreign affairs. Eden did not harbor the deep suspicions of Hitler that Churchill did and was inclined to oppose resolute diplomatic action against either Hitler or Benito Mussolini. He thought the Treaty of Versailles had placed somewhat of an unfair burden on Germany and was never prepared to defend that treaty to the letter. He thought Churchill alarmist, unpredictable and untrustworthy, and he was constantly annoyed by what he believed to be Winston's rash decisions. There is no evidence that he felt any warmth for Churchill and much that he resented living in Churchill's shadow, as he did throughout the war and into the early 1950s, until he finally became prime minister in 1955.

Eden's hesitation about Churchill's proposed visit to Washington grew from the fact that he was about to embark on a long-planned journey to Moscow on the very eve of Pearl Harbor. On the afternoon of December 7 he left London's Euston Station to begin the long train journey to Scapa Flow, where he and his party were to board a cruiser for the sea voyage to the USSR. He took Sir Alexander Cadogan, permanent undersecretary of the Foreign Office, and Ivan Maisky, Soviet ambassador to the United Kingdom, with him. Eden was easily the best man in the British War Cabinet to go to Moscow, to sound out Stalin on Soviet war aims and military needs. In 1935 he had been the first British minister to pay an official visit to the Soviet Union since the Bolshevik revolution, and he had in no way been taken in by Stalin, whom he considered to be a man of implacable ruthlessness.

On the train north from London, Eden learned about the Japanese attack. The next morning he was run-down, ill from gastric flu, and running a temperature. He was eager to board his ship, but a message came from Churchill telling him to call. "A. [Anthony Eden] rang up P.M.," Cadogan wrote in his diary, "who said he was off to America! A. horrified, but didn't succeed in dissuading him." Eden did not see how he and Churchill could be out of the country at the same time, especially in light of Washington's imminent declaration of war against Japan. He quickly called Clement Attlee, who was deputy prime minister and who would assume the position of acting prime minister in Churchill's absence, as well as U.S. Ambassador Winant; both agreed that the trip should be discouraged. Attlee vowed to oppose it at that afternoon's Cabinet meeting. Both Oliver Harvey, Eden's private secretary, and Cadogan were convinced that the Americans would not want Churchill there and that he would have nothing to do when he arrived.

When Cadogan called Churchill late on the afternoon of December 8, he learned that the prime minister had carried the Cabinet easily and planned his departure for Thursday, December 12. "I said A. was distressed at idea of their both being away together. He said 'That's all right: that'll work very well; I shall have Anthony where I want him.'"[27] The next day, December 9, Britain declared war on Japan.

Few Americans had noticed that in his declaration of war, the president had spoken in the plural when referring to the "gangsters" and "bandits" that had brought on the war. But Germany had no hand in Pearl Harbor and was not obligated under the Tripartite Pact of September 1940 to join Japan in the war. It took a horrendous blunder in Berlin to release Roosevelt from this apparent contradiction.

On December 8, 1941, Hitler was at his military headquarters near Rastenburg, East Prussia. He was anxious about reports from the East stating that the Soviets had mounted a major counteroffensive to save Moscow. He received the news of Pearl Harbor courtesy of BBC Radio. While his Luftwaffe officers rushed to find the American naval base on an atlas, the Führer "slapped his thighs, jumped to his feet as if electrified, and shouted 'Finally.'"[28] He immediately called Propaganda Minister Joseph Goebbels to share his delight. And then he headed off to Berlin.

Hitler was in high spirits. On December 10 Goebbels reported him to be "filled with joy." The war was now truly a world war. Roosevelt,

the Führer averred, had acted like a boxer, saving his best combinations
for the fifth or sixth round—only to discover, like Max Schmeling in his
June 1938 rematch in New York with Joe Louis, that he could receive a
knockout punch in the first round.[29] The Japanese sinking of the British
capital ships *Prince of Wales* (of Argentia fame) and *Repulse* off Kuandan,
Malaya, that same day had brought more cheer. Goebbels called it
simply "the greatest sensation of the war at sea to date."[30] The only sour
note was that Pearl Harbor had forced Reinhard Heydrich of the SS to
reschedule to January 20, 1942, a conference slated for December 9 in
the Berlin suburb of Wannsee to deal with the "final solution" of the
"Jewish question."

At 3 P.M. on December 11 Hitler, repeatedly interrupted by deliri-
ous shouts from his Reichstag sycophants, delivered a ninety-minute
diatribe against Roosevelt and his "plutocratic clique." He compared
Roosevelt, a scion of the "so-called upper ten thousand," to the "para-
lytic professor" Woodrow Wilson. He decreed both presidents to have
been "mentally ill" at the time of their decisions for war. He drew the
dissimilarities between Roosevelt's life of luxury with his own life of
struggle. He denounced Roosevelt as a "tool of the Jews" and "an old
Freemason." He ridiculed the Atlantic Charter as being equivalent to
a bald barber recommending a surefire hair restorer. He ended by verbally issuing the American chargé his passports—in fact, the Gestapo
had already taken American embassy personnel to Bad Nauheim, where
Roosevelt had spent so many childhood days—and by declaring "a
state of war with the United States to exist." The world's largest male
glee club celebrated the tumultuous session by singing the national
anthem, "Deutschland über alles," and the Nazi party anthem, the
"Horst Wessel Lied." The secret SS reports on the mood of the nation
concluded that most Germans saw the declaration of war as "the only
possible answer" to Roosevelt's "continued interference in European
affairs." Unfortunately for Germany, few, if any, had any idea of how to
conduct a war against the United States.[31]

While Hitler spoke in Berlin, Chargé Hans Thomsen burned official papers in Washington. Then he left his residence, "a hideous,
pigeon-stained pile of dark brownish-red brick" on Massachusetts

Avenue, six blocks from the White House, to deliver the German declaration of war to the State Department. He was in high spirits. As
Thomsen stepped into his black Buick, he happily cried out to the gathered Washingtonians, "Anybody want to buy a nice car?" He eventually
received $1,000 from Olivia Davis, owner of a nightclub one block from
the German Embassy.[32] Secretary Hull kept Thomsen waiting for an
hour to deliver his message. Six special buses hauled some 200 staff
members from the Embassy to Union Station, where they were taken
by train to the Greenbrier Inn at White Sulphur Springs, West Virginia.

Throughout these terrible days, Roosevelt remained calm and in
control. When his close friend Sam Rosenman visited the president on
the night of December 9, he found FDR leisurely at work over his
stamps. "There was no excitement here now, no hectic atmosphere of
false rumors; there was no fear—not even disquietude." Rosenman
poured himself a ginger ale and Roosevelt a beer. FDR coolly continued
to work on his stamps, the familiar cigarette firmly emplaced in the long
holder. There was only one indication of the darkness of the hour: "His
face was resolute, even grim."[33] Roosevelt spent his evenings with small
dinner groups, personally carving the pheasants and wild ducks brought
down from Hyde Park. Eleanor had the staff brighten the dining room
with carnations and spirea.

A few days after Pearl Harbor, FDR, taking advantage of the tidal
wave of patriotic sentiment, invited business and union leaders to the
White House. He asked them to take a no-strike, no-lockout pledge for
the duration of the war that lay ahead. The discussions with his aides
quickly broke down in angry debate when the industrialists refused to
accept union shops. At that moment, Roosevelt wheeled into the room,
congratulated them on what they had agreed on, ignored what they
could not agree on, wished them all a merry Christmas, and sent them
home. It was the classic Roosevelt touch. Roger Lapham, chairman of
the American-Hawaiian Steamship Company, summed up the angry
sentiments of many as he walked out of the White House doors: "I've
been raped in Macy's window at high noon."[34]

On December 11, 1941, Roosevelt in a written message asked the
Hill to pass a resolution declaring the Republic to be at war with
Germany. At 3:05 P.M. the Congress did so unanimously—by a recorded
vote in the Senate and by a voice vote in the House, the latter perhaps

to get around a second "no" vote from Representative Rankin. FDR then turned his attention to another pressing matter: since December 8, Churchill had badgered him with repeated requests to come to Washington to coordinate Allied policy and strategy.

Within twenty-four hours after the Japanese attack on Pearl Harbor, Churchill had secured the acquiescence of the Cabinet and the king to an immediate trip to meet Roosevelt. Now, he had to get the president's approval. On December 9 he wired Roosevelt.

> Now that we are, as you say, "in the same boat," would it not be wise for us to have another conference? We could review the whole war plan in the light of reality and new facts, a well as the problems of production and distribution. I feel that all these matters, some of which are causing me concern, can best be settled on the highest executive level. It would also be a great pleasure for me to meet you again, and the sooner the better.

He proposed to leave "in a day or two," to come by warship, and to bring Admiral Sir Dudley Pound, Chief of the Air Staff Sir Charles Portal, Lord Beaverbrook, and the recently relieved chief of the Imperial General Staff, Sir John Dill, with him.[35]

Churchill's telegram caused disquiet in Washington, which was already in an uproar. Senior civilian and military officials were rushing about trying to find out what had really happened at Pearl Harbor. The Japanese had already opened attacks on the Philippines and assaulted Wake Island. Would they come back to Hawaii? Was the West Coast under threat? What military resources were left in the Far East to bolster the Dutch in the East Indies, the Australians, the New Zealanders, and the British themselves?

FDR's first inclination was to put Churchill off. "Early stages of mobilization complete here and situation in Pacific more clarified," he said in an unsent telegram. In a second note, again written but not sent, he told Churchill, "My first impression is that a full discussion would be more useful a few weeks hence than immediately." In the view of Roosevelt biographer Kenneth S. Davis, FDR's desire for delay "agreed with, if not determined by, the opinions of [General George] Marshall and [Admiral Harold] Stark, both of whom (Stark perhaps more than Marshall) were suspicious of 'perfidious Albion.'"[36] The feeling among these men was no doubt strong that the time for Churchill and his war chiefs to come to the United States was after Washington had settled its basic war strategy and decided its production and shipping priorities, and not to have Churchill meddling in the making of those decisions. The weekly summary from the British Embassy in Washington to the Foreign Office in London noted for the week of December 17 that there was "an extraordinary reluctance" on the part of the American military leaders "to start joint staff conversations in Washington," even though there was "a new tendency on the part of the Americans to seek our advice and the fruits of our experiences. . . ."[37] Churchill, of course, had no purpose other than to meddle as effectively as he could in American war planning.

In Washington, Halifax worked hard to convince Roosevelt to see Churchill without delay. On the morning of December 9 he went to the White House to see the president. Roosevelt seemed "genuinely pleased" at the prospect of another meeting, but was worried about the prime minister's safety. There was another factor on Roosevelt's mind, however, as Halifax told Churchill:

> [H]e was not sure if your coming here might not be rather too strong medicine in the immediate future for some of his public opinion that he still feels he has to educate up to the complete conviction of the oneness of the struggle against both Germany and Japan. I wouldn't overstate it, but I think it was definitely in his mind. . . . They are terribly shaken here, as you can well suppose, and fully realize that they have been caught napping.[38]

Halifax pushed Roosevelt as hard as he dared. So did Churchill. At one point, when he was drafting another note to send to the White House insisting on a meeting, someone told him that his tone should be a little less assertive. "Oh," Churchill replied dismissively, "that is the way we talked to her while we were wooing her; now that she is in the harem we talk to her quite differently."[39] The prime minister then sent the president another note insisting that whatever personal danger he might be in, it was nothing compared to the danger the Allied war effort would incur if the two leaders did not meet without delay. Roosevelt finally relented.

> Delighted to have you here at the White House. . . . I know that you will bear in mind that the production and allocation problems can and will be worked out with complete understanding and accord. . . . Details of production and allocation can be handled at long range. Naval situation and other maters of strategy require discussion.[40]

Thus began the conference that was to be called ARCADIA. The code name was chosen by Churchill, likely in an ironic reference to the mythical land of Arkady, where the sun always shone on pastoral landscapes and shepherds played pipes as they tended to flocks of contented sheep—a sharp contrast to the freezing and brutal war then raging at the gates of Moscow, or on the cold and rolling North Atlantic where Hitler's "gray sharks" were relentlessly killing men and destroying cargoes bound for the United Kingdom. Even the idyllic South Pacific and Southwest Asia were now awash in the blood of American, British, Australian, and Dutch soldiers, sailors, and airmen.

On the morning of Wednesday, December 10, Churchill was in bed as usual at No. 10 Downing Street, opening dispatch boxes and dictating notes in reply, when his phone rang. It was Admiral Pound with the shocking news that the only two major British warships in Asia, the old battle cruiser *Repulse* and the new battleship *Prince of Wales*, had been sunk with heavy loss of life by Japanese aircraft off the east coast of Malaya. Churchill would later write, "In all the war I never received a more direct shock."[41] He had steamed to Argentia to meet Roosevelt aboard the *Prince of Wales* in August; her captain, Sir Thomas Phillips, had been one of the key men at the Admiralty in the hunt and destruction of the *Bismarck* the previous May; he and Churchill had renewed their acquaintance on the voyage over. Now Phillips was dead, lost in the sinking. In the relative calm of the American capital—an Arkady in the global storm—Roosevelt and Churchill would meet.

Was Churchill right to push so hard for a meeting as quickly as possible? The "Christmas in Washington" that took place in December 1941 was his initiative. He was not by any means solely responsible for its eventual success, but had he not used his considerable persuasive powers over his own Cabinet and even at long distance over FDR, the meeting would not have happened when it did. Churchill's instinct to push for an immediate conference was surely correct. These were the key weeks in the formation of the Grand Alliance, which, in the first half of the war at least, was an alliance largely based on the London-Washington connection. This is not to belittle the major contribution that the Soviet armed forces were already making to the war of attrition against Nazi Germany in December 1941. But the reality is that the Soviet Union was fundamentally alone in its fight, isolated from the making of grand strategy and heavily dependent on American and British aid.

With America's entry into the war, then, the opportunity presented itself in the last weeks of 1941 and the first weeks of 1942 to forge a truly united Anglo-American war effort. That would not only entail coordinating the grand strategy of the United States and Britain (with its Empire and Commonwealth partners) on land, at sea, in the air, across the globe, but integrating virtually the entire war productive capacity of the two nations and their lesser allies. The aim was to create a joint war effort unique in history, one that truly brought the English-speaking peoples together as one integrated ally despite national differences. Of course, the reality of those national differences always threatened to intrude and sometimes did, especially as the war dragged on. But that does not obviate the impact that the united war effort had in magnifying the war-fighting capabilities of both partners and eliminating, to an impressive degree, overlapping and competitive endeavors. Had Churchill not seized the moment—before American war plans had solidified—it is more than likely that such a degree of integration would never have been achieved.

5

NORTH ATLANTIC CROSSING

AT 10:30 P.M. ON DECEMBER 12, 1941. WINSTON CHURCHILL'S special train left London's Euston station for the north. Most of the people selected to go to Washington aboard the battleship *Duke of York*, sister ship to the *Prince of Wales*, had accompanied Churchill the last time he had crossed the Atlantic—with the notable exception of Chief of the Air Staff Charles Portal and Lord Beaverbrook, who had flown to Newfoundland from the United Kingdom. Beaverbrook had "his private saloon on the train, and had a dinner party there before the train started," Colonel Ian Jacob, one of the party from the Ministry of Defence, later recalled. "We got the luggage all stowed away before the Prime Minister arrived. It was generally given out that the party was to be headed by Lord Beaverbrook and that the Prime Minister was going to see him off."[1]

William Maxwell Aitken was known as Lord Beaverbrook to the public, "the Beaver" in private, and "Max" to his friends. Small, with a large head, wide mouth, and an ever-present Canadian drawl, he affected wide-brimmed hats with his rumpled suits, but both his looks and his demeanor were carefully cultivated to draw attention away from his sharply honed intellect and his tremendous power over British public opinion. It was said that he was the only man in English public life who could truly match wits with Churchill. He was a major influence on key political questions confronting Britain in the decade before the outbreak of war, and in that decade he was more often opposed to Churchill than in agreement with them.

Born in 1879 in a small town in Ontario, Canada, Max Aitken considered a career in law before finding his true talent as an entrepreneur. Before he was forty, he had already set up a number of major Canadian corporations, especially Royal Securities. He moved to the United Kingdom in 1910 and immediately established connections with Andrew Bonar Law and the Tories, winning a seat in Parliament in a by-election by a small majority later that year. His friendship with Bonar Law, his great wealth, and his extensive financial connections quickly marked him as a man to be listened to in British politics. In late 1916 Aitken—now Lord Beaverbrook)—purchased the first newspaper of what would shortly be a journalistic empire. Thereafter, he kept tight editorial control over his papers, which became virtual extensions of his personality and political views.

Beaverbrook was elevated to the peerage in 1917 as his reward for helping to maneuver British Prime Minister Herber Asquith's Liberal government out of office and replacing him with Lloyd George's Liberal-conservaive coalition. He was a political fixer, a mischief-maker par excellence, and an adroit behind-the-scenes manipulator of men and institutions. He was also a naturally born entrepreneur. "If Max ever gets to heaven, he won't last long," H. G. Wells once declared. "He will be chucked out for trying to pull off a merger between Heaven and Hell after having secured a controlling interest in key subsidiary companies in both places."[2] One of Churchill's biographers has described him this way:

> Beaverbrook's was a complex personality, in which good and bad were so intermixed than an objective judgment is exceptionally difficult to make. He could be mean and vindictive; he could be generous and magnanimous. He could harbor and nourish bitter grievances; he could forgive and forget injustices and disappointments. He could be cruel; he could be overwhelmed with remorse over a minor social peccadillo. . . . He loved argument, yet welcomed sycophants.[3]

Beaverbrook and Churchill had been at odds for most of the 1930s. He distrusted Churchill's judgment and what he saw as his capacity for self-deception. He disagreed with Churchill on the dangers of war, on the perils of Stalin's regime, and, most important, on Adolf Hitler's evil intent. He, like Churchill, was a passionate believer in a

British Empire whose constitutional and historical ties were buttressed by the Ottawa Free Trade agreements; he excoriated Churchill for being insufficiently supportive of those agreements. In the late 1930s he did whatever he could to try to deny Churchill access to the English papers in a conscious effort to dampen down any war feeling that Churchill might have been whipping up. On the only public matter the two men agreed upon—the need to try to preserve Edward VIII on the throne—Beaverbrook later admitted he sided with the king for the fun of it while Churchill had done so on principle.

Yet Churchill had long recognized Beaverbrook as a man of great energy and organizing genius and appointed him to the Cabinet as minister of aircraft production shortly before the Battle of Britain began. It had been a brilliant choice. Brooking no opposition, no objection, no recalcitrance from Britain's tradition-encrusted aircraft industry, nor from the Royal Air Force, Beaverbrook worked a miracle in fighter production. Where factories such as Supermarine and Hawker had once turned out a dozen or so fighters a month, they began to produce hundreds a month over the high summer of 1940. Beaverbrook was as responsible for the British victory in the Battle of Britain as "the few"—the weary RAF fighter pilots. His job done, Beaverbrook resigned from his post in May 1940, but Churchill succeeded in convincing him to stay, first as a minister of state (without portfolio), then as minister of supply—in effect, as czar of all British war production.

In some ways, Beaverbrook was facing the toughest challenge of all those who set out from the United Kingdom on this crucial journey to Washington. The heads of state and the generals and admirals might talk grand strategy all they wanted, but without the adequate tools of war, allocated by national need and not by which nation produced what product, the war could not be fought. There were four major issues that Beaverbrook would have to settle with the Americans: How much could be produced? Who should produce it? How was it to be allocated? And the key question: who was to control the process, the civilian authorities or the military?

No one ever doubted that Beaverbrook was his own man, never to be dominated by, or beholden to, Churchill. The same could not be said of Sir Alfred Dudley Pound, First Sea Lord and thus the chief of naval staff of the Royal Navy. Born in 1877, Pound had gone to sea when he was just fourteen. By the outbreak of the First World War, he had achieved command rank, serving as a flag captain at the Battle of Jutland in 1916. Sir Roger Keyes, best known as the Royal Navy's chief of staff, Eastern Mediterranean, during the Dardanelles offensive in 1915, later wrote of him:

> I was immensely struck by his high professional ability, his grip of affairs, and his unbounded energy. A leader who demands a high standard of service & invariably gets it. . . . Possessed of excellent judgment, he is a wise counselor. I consider that he shd. be, and I believe that he will be, 1 S.L. [First Sea Lord] before his career comes to an end.[4]

Keyes was correct in his forecast, but in the peacetime navy of the interwar years, advancement for senior officers was slow and Pound was no exception. He did not reach the rank of rear admiral until 1926, when he was forty-nine. It took him nine more years to become a full admiral. In 1936 Pound was placed in command of the all-important Mediterranean Fleet, but the early onset of a number of physical ailments slowed him down considerably. He seems also to have lost the intellectual edge that Keyes had once detected. One senior administrator wrote of him in 1936, "He is too pig-headed; too unwilling to recognize that there may be another side." Admiral Sir John Tovey, commander in chief of the Home Fleet at the time of the *Bismarck* chase, thought Pound "neither a great tactician or strategist [though] unfortunately he believed he was."

Pound was probably too old to assume the position of First Sea Lord in June 1939, just before war broke out, but death and illness had removed all potential rivals. In effect, he was the last man standing. When the ever-dominating Churchill took over the Admiralty in September, Pound still had sufficient strength and self-confidence to, on occasion, resist his exuberant meddling in the actual command of Royal Navy ships and task forces at sea. Sir Alan Brooke, who replaced Dill as chief of the Imperial General Staff in December 1941, thought Pound "insufferably slow and complained that he dozed at long meetings."[5] He did. He suffered painful arthritis in one hip and slowly advancing brain cancer, which eventually killed him in 1943. He rarely passed a good night's sleep. One colleague, who saw him shortly after the start of the war, noticed "with horror" that he had become "a worn-out old man."[6] Pound was also a man who could no longer stand up to Churchill by the time the sea voyage to Washington began. His principal duty at the conference would be to try to coordinate the Battle of the Atlantic with the Americans, especially with the notoriously anti-British Admiral Ernest J. King.

Churchill's chief of the Air Staff, Charles Frederick Algernon "Peter" Portal, was almost the complete opposite of Pound in his relationship with the prime minister. Slim, well proportioned and of average height, Portal had a prominent nose and a long face. He always wore his RAF cap square on his head, with no rakishness at all. Well mannered and soft-spoken, he was quiet, unemotional, and unassuming. John Colville, one of Churchill's private secretaries, described the air marshal as a man "who only spoke when he had something significant to say, listened intently and neither made promises unless he knew he could fulfill them nor allowed himself to be the victim of undue optimism or pessimism."[7]

Portal's quiet countenance came from supreme confidence in his abilities, a sureness earned over a long career of flying. Born in 1893, he volunteered for service in the British army as soon as war broke out in 1914 and spent the first year of the war as a motorcycle dispatch rider. At the end of 1915 he volunteered for the Royal Flying Corps. He graduated from pilot training in the spring of 1916 and flew countless missions over the front during the battles along the Somme in the summer and fall of that year. By the summer of 1917, he had been awarded the Military Cross and the Distinguished Service Order and was in command of No. 16 reconnaissance and artillery observation squadron. It was then that his life changed irrevocably. His squadron was assigned to carry out night bombing missions behind enemy lines, a task for which they were neither equipped nor trained. Portal trained himself in the then highly dangerous skill of taking off, flying and landing a fully loaded bomber in the dark.

His great talent as a pilot and his success as a leader of men brought him to the attention of Sir Hugh Trenchard, first marshal of the

Royal Air Force, shortly after its creation as a separate branch of the British armed forces. Portal became one of Trenchard's disciples—a "bomber baron"—a strong believer in air power and strategic bombing and a fierce defender of the independence of the RAF from the older services. He spent almost his air force career between the wars commanding bomber squadrons in the United Kingdom and the Middle East, competing for bombing trophies and advocating air war as the only means of avoiding the grueling trench warfare of the Western Front in future conflicts. In late October 1940 he reached the pinnacle of his career when he was promoted chief of the Air Staff.

Portal's major challenge in Washington would be to bridge the doctrinal gap between the RAF and the U.S. Army Air Forces and to try to rally the Americans to add their weight to the night bombing campaign that he intended to ramp up in 1942. The United States had its bomber barons—H. A. "Hap" Arnold, commanding general, Army Air Forces, was one of them. But whereas RAF bombing doctrine had long advocated mass night attacks against enemy cities, aimed as much at enemy morale as at enemy production, the Americans had trained for and designed aircraft for long-range "precision" daylight raids primarily against what they termed "nodes of production." They thought heavily armed bombers in tight formation could get through enemy defenses in daylight without fighter escort. They would eventually suffer appalling losses in these daylight bombing efforts, but in December 1941, after studying the results of the British night bomber campaign, they were convinced they had nothing to learn from the Royal Air Force.

Field Marshal Sir John Greer Dill was the only one of the four senior military officials accompanying Churchill who did not command anything. Born in 1881, Dill had graduated from Sandhurst before he was gazetted with the 1st Battalion of the Leinster Regiment during the Boer War. In the First World War he was wounded in action but eventually achieved the rank of brigadier general, serving in both command and staff positions. After the war he was posted to a number of overseas assignments in India, Palestine, and Trans-Jordan, rising steadily to the rank of lieutenant general by the outbreak of war. On May 27, 1940,

Dill succeeded Field Marshal Sir William Edmund Ironside as chief of the Imperial General Staff (CIGS).

Dill was by all accounts a handsome man with a "thin, distinguished soldier's face," a scholar's mien, a thorough knowledge of all aspects of modern soldiering, and a strict dedication to the norms, practices, and codes of the British professional soldier. His military colleagues had great respect for his ability and his demeanor. Dill took command of the British army as France was collapsing and the evacuation of Dunkirk was well under way. It was his great misfortune to lead those forces through the disastrous eighteen months that followed. Under him, Britain prepared to meet the German invader; under him, the British army lost campaign after campaign. He and Churchill tussled constantly; the prime minister always demanding that the Germans be made to bleed here or struck a blow there, while Dill kept uppermost the need to husband the ground forces for the defense of Britain and to use the core that had survived Dunkirk to train the mass army that would eventually need to fight its way back to the Continent. To make matters worse, his wife of thirty-three years lay dying in the first six months of his tenure as CIGS. He visited her in the hospital as often as he could while he put in inhumanly long days at the War Office, sat in interminable meetings, and visited military installations throughout the country. His health deteriorated, he tired easily, and his ability to stand up to Churchill's constant prodding drained.

Dill, in the view of Major General Hastings "Pug" Ismay, was incapable of "the one thing that was necessary, and indeed that Winston preferred—someone to stand up to him."[8] His successor as CIGS, Sir Alan Brooke, could and did stand up to Churchill—for the rest of the war. He would later write: "Dill's character was too fine and highly tempered to be able to put up with the 'gangster' transactions of politicians. It all jarred on him and put him on edge."[9] It was inevitable that Dill would eventually go the way of all British senior commanders who did not satisfy Churchill in their zeal to kill Germans or who did not have the temperament to handle him when he was being unreasonable and pugnacious. In time, he "wilted before the blast of Churchill's sleepless energy."[10] By the fall of 1941, in the words of one private secretary, Churchill had "got his knife right into Dill and frequently disparages him." On November 16, he met with Alan Brooke, commander in chief

Home Forces, and announced that he was going to dismiss Dill. He asked Brooke to replace him as CIGS. Brooke was momentarily taken aback, but in the end had no choice. Dill was sacked, pensioned off to the Far East with a field marshal's baton and the nominal title of governor of Bombay.

Pearl Harbor saved John Dill from his impending exile to India. Churchill could not take all of his chiefs of staff with him and Brooke was newest on the job. He thus chose Dill to go instead and proposed that he stay in Washington in some capacity as his personal military representative. Brooke supported the decision, which turned out to be one of the best that Churchill made.

On the morning of December 13 Churchill's party arrived at Prince's Pier, Gourock, Scotland, and transferred to the *Duke of York*. There were thirty-eight in all, from the chiefs of staff to private secretaries and six official photographers and newsreel cameramen. Gilbert Winant, the U.S. ambassador to the United Kingdom, and Averell Harriman came along to expedite the inevitable discussions over the future of Lend-Lease. Churchill's personal physician, Sir Charles Wilson (the future Lord Moran), came along, as did Colonel Ian Hollis. It was a cool gray morning with low cloud and a stiff southwest wind. Around noon, the battleship departed with an escort of three destroyers. By nightfall, the little flotilla cleared the south coast of Ireland and set course for the New World—straight into a full southwesterly gale.

Few historical documents are as prosaic as a ship's log; the *Duke of York's* for this journey is no exception. At 6:00 P.M. on Sunday, December 14, the log records the ship heading southwest, to Bermuda, with a Force 9 wind, a shaft speed of 83.8 revolutions per minute, the barometer at 990.7 millibars and falling, and a speed of 10.5 knots.[11] What this meant to the men on board was that the battleship of some 37,000 tons, with a top speed of 28 knots, was pitching and rolling violently with winds of 50 to 60 miles an hour whipping the gray Atlantic into a heaving surface of forty-foot waves. The strong gale force winds drove the tops of the waves into dense streaks of foam and flung it across the seascape. The wind shrieked and moaned through guy wires, around radar and radio antennas, through the scuppers, and around the barrels and blast shields of the guns. Inside the ship, all was in motion. A simple walk down a passageway was a challenging adventure through an obstacle course. Even at 10 knots, the little destroyers rolled violently, threatening to founder.

Churchill was accommodated in the admiral's sea cabin, high in the superstructure, in case the battleship took a torpedo hit. But, as one of the ship's officers later recorded:

> [H]e did not spend much time there, he used to wander through the mess decks, whatever the weather, smoking a cigar which was very necessary as the decks smelt high to say the least of it after being battened down for days because of the continuing atrocious weather.

Every night, no matter how badly the ship rolled, Churchill watched movies. "He would sit watching, complete with cigar and relays of brandy. Seated by him were some of the big shots looking very green."[12] Westerns and war movies dominated the list: *The Fighting 69th* with James Cagney and Pat O'Brien, *Santa Fe Trail* with Errol Flynn, Olivia de Havilland, and Ronald Reagan, *North West Mounted Police* with Gary Cooper and Paulette Goddard; and *Boom Town* with Clark Gable, Spencer Tracy, and Claudette Colbert, to name a few.

When he was not wandering the mess decks, Churchill did his best to keep up with war events via the radio. The news that filtered through the radio room was almost universally bad as the *Duke of York* plowed westward. On December 13, British, Canadian, and Indian troops withdrew from their positions on the mainland at Hong Kong and manned the defenses of Hong Kong Island. It had taken the Japanese less than six days to roll up the Gin Drinkers' Line across the Kowloon peninsula and to capture Kai Tak airport.

That same day, as the British pulled out of Victoria Airport at the extreme southern tip of the Kra Peninsula in Malaya, the Japanese moved in right on their heels. Japanese attacks on Borneo gave promise of imminent landings there. In North Africa, however, Erwin Rommel was in headlong retreat, while at sea submarines and aircraft attacked convoy HG-76 from Gibraltar to the United Kingdom. The German naval attackers had the bad luck to run into the Royal Navy's ace U-boat killer, Commander Johnny Walker. They lost five subs; the British lost the escort carrier *Audacity*, one destroyer, and two merchant ships. Winston wrote Clementine, "it should touch the spirits of the survivors [of the U-boats] when they get home to see how many of their companion vessels have been sent to the bottom."[13] On the Eastern Front the news was even better, as a major Soviet counterattack pushed the German Army farther away from Moscow; but on December 19, came news that Hitler had taken over full control of his army. In the heavy seas, the *Duke of York* had to slow to 5 knots to try to accommodate her struggling destroyers—before leaving them behind.

Three days out of Scotland, Churchill began to lay out the strategy he would propose to Roosevelt and the American military chiefs upon his arrival in Washington. Churchill's official biographer has summed up the thrust of his strategy this way: "the creation of a European front, and a massive American commitment to it, within a year and a half."[14] The prime minister was also determined to cajole the Americans into straightening out their interminable war production problems so as to reach their full potential as quickly as possible. He laid out his plans in five memoranda—the most important three were entitled "The Atlantic Front," dictated on December 16; "The Pacific Front," on December 17; and "The Campaign of 1943," on December 18 . They were followed by full staff meetings on the eighteenth and nineteenth at which the documents were discussed in detail.[15]

Churchill's most immediate concern was that the Americans stick with the "Europe-first" plan. As he radioed South African prime minister Jan Smuts from *Duke of York* on December 21, "I hope to procure from [Roosevelt] assistance in a forward policy in French North Africa and in West Africa. This is in accordance with American ideas, but they may well be too much preoccupied with the war in Japan."[16] Assuming (or hoping) that he would find the "Europe-first" policy intact, Churchill wanted to get the Americans blooded as quickly as possible in a three-phase strategy that would end the war by 1943. He called the three phases "closing the ring," "liberating the populations," and mounting the "final assault on the German citadel."[17]

In the first phase, he aimed to wear down Japanese naval power by attrition, turn the tide in the Battle of the Atlantic, bomb Germany to erode the morale of its citizens and the productive capacity of its industry, and get the Americans into action on the ground. He wanted

Washington to station troops in Northern Ireland, thus freeing up British soldiers, and he wanted the American troops to take the lead in landings in North Africa, which he proposed for late 1942. He hoped to convince the Vichy French to join the Allies before that endeavor—and to be able to reconcile Charles de Gaulle's Free French Forces to the prospect—but if not, he advocated taking them on directly. And he wanted American bomber squadrons transferred to Britain as soon as possible to add their weight to the RAF bomber offensive, which he admitted was not proceeding well.

In his second phase, Churchill aimed to confront and destroy the Japanese navy after new British and American capital ships had put to sea. The bombing of Germany would intensify and the Allies would pour aid into Europe to encourage the resistance of the captive peoples. He held out some hope—but not too much—that the heavy bombing of German cities might bring about a downfall of Hitler's regime.

All this was certainly feasible and, to a degree, did form the blueprint for Anglo-American strategy in the first eighteen months of the war. Yet, Churchill's third phase was far from the mark and ran directly counter to American strategy. In that phase, Churchill did propose an invasion of Europe—but single, powerful, concentrated blow preparatory to a concerted drive on Berlin. Rather, it was to consist of "three or four" landings on the European periphery needing no more than 600,000 troops led by armored forces. Churchill believed that if successful, these landings would cement the growing resistance forces that would "supply the corpus of the liberating offensive." He also wanted to delay those landings "as long as possible" so as to take advantage of the popular uprisings he hoped for.[18]

He was simply wrong. The eventual number of Allied divisions in Western Europe in 1945—British, American, Canadian, and French— approached ninety, with two million combat troops and another eight million in support. Even that proved insufficient for a quick victory. And his notion about the role that liberation forces would play in the defeat of Hitler was hopelessly optimistic. On the Western Front they produced a bare handful of fighters and, with a few notable exceptions, were in most cases a mere nuisance to the Germans.

Churchill ordered the memoranda and draft agenda for his meetings with Roosevelt as well as for the staff meetings between military leaders to be radioed ahead to Lord Halifax in Washington as soon as the battleship was close enough to the American coast that it was safe to break radio silence. Thus, he and the president could begin their talks with a common set of British documents.

6

A GUEST AT THE WHITE HOUSE

THE YULETIDE SEASON OF 1941 WAS NOT A HAPPY TIME FOR Franklin and Eleanor Roosevelt. Their sons were all in the service—James in the Marines, Elliott in the Army Air Forces, and both Franklin, Jr., and John in the Navy. Robert Todd Lincoln had been the only other son of a president in office who had marched off to war. Their daughter, Anna, was in Seattle; their son-in-law, John Boettiger, was stationed in England. For the first time in nine years, there would be only two small stockings hung in the White House—one in the president's bedroom filled with rubber bones and toys for Fala, his black Scottish terrier; and the other in Harry Hopkins' bedroom, where he resided with his ten-year-old daughter Diana.

Eleanor, only recently returned from a trip to the West Coast, was in poor spirits. Her dear friend and regular White House guest, Joseph P. Lash, head of the socialist American Student Union, had been drafted. She had tried unsuccessfully to get him a commission, but in the end only managed to have him posted to the Air Corps at Bolling Field, just across the Potomac River from Washington National Airport. To the unbridled anger of the White House staff and of senior military leaders, Lash—a private—at Eleanor's insistence was driven to and from the mansion by an army major.

The president and his chiefs of staff had more pressing matters on their mind. News of the pending arrival of Prime Minister Winston Churchill had energized them. Ever so slowly, they began to shake off the immediate shock of Pearl Harbor and think in grand strategic terms. Secretary of State Cordell Hull, knowing that the president would desire another proclamation like the one issued at Argentia, as early as December 14, 1941, had one of his advisors, Maxwell M. Hamilton, compose a first draft of a possible "joint declaration." That declaration would become one of the basic documents of Allied grand strategy. It pledged each government to deploy its "full resources" against the Axis until victory was achieved; to coordinate the military effort against "the common enemies"; and "to continue war against, and not to make a separate peace with, the common enemies or any of them."[1] At the same time, Hull set his staff to work to outline possible machinery for the actual joint conduct of the war.

On December 18 FDR received the first of Churchill's planning documents along with an agenda for the upcoming talks radioed in from the *Duke of York*. It included: "fundamental basis of joint strategy"; "terms of immediate Military measures"; "allocation of joint forces"; "long-term programme . . . including forces to be raised and equipped required for victory"; and "joint machinery for implementation."[2] Roosevelt at once called a meeting of his top military advisors for 3 P.M. that day. It included Admirals Ernest J. King and Harold R. Stark, General George C. Marshall, Secretary of War Henry L. Stimson, Secretary of the Navy Frank Knox, presidential advisor Harry Hopkins, and the new commander of the fleet, Admiral Chester Nimitz. The president shared with them Churchill's agenda, instructed them to discuss the British document, and ordered them to prepare an American equivalent. FDR was not about to be bulldozed again by a British mission with a British agenda as at Argentia in August 1941. The breathtaking scope of an emerging "grand alliance" was beginning to take shape in Washington. Secretary Stimson noted: "[T]his was a matter that I must get into with all my mind and strength." And given what he called "the President's unmethodical habits," he took it upon himself to keep FDR "straight as far as possible" in the days ahead.[3]

Secretary of War Henry L. Stimson was one Cabinet member with whom Roosevelt seldom played games. Born on September 21, 1867, in New York City, his family lines on both sides ran back to the

Massachusetts Bay Colony in the early seventeenth century. He was educated at Yale University and Harvard Law School; in 1893 he married Mabel White, whom he had met at Yale. Stimson entered politics after a career in the law firm of Root and Clark when his close friend President Theodore Roosevelt appointed him U.S. Attorney for the Southern District of New York in 1906. After his only run for elective office—an unsuccessful bid to become governor of New York in 1910—Stimson would eventually serve in six presidential terms. William H. Taft made him secretary of war in 1911, Herbert Hoover secretary of state in 1929, and Franklin Roosevelt secretary of war in 1940. The latter appointment resulted in Stimson being read out of the Republican Party. At age forty-nine, he had volunteered for service in the Great War and seen active duty in France as an artillery officer; now, at age seventy-two, "a very tired, decayed old man" in the words of a colleague, he became secretary of war.

A Victorian patrician through and through, Stimson resided at Woodley Oaks, his estate in Northwest Washington, where he rode horse almost daily. His views of fellow human beings were defined by class and by racial bias; he usually found "character" only in fellow Yale and Harvard men. He and his wife refused to have visitors who had been divorced. He once moved to block a donation to Columbia University because the school was under "tremendous Jewish influence." His physical well being was tenuous at the best of times: he suffered from insomnia, poor digestion, lumbago, rheumatism, and chronic bouts of weakness. He was often short-tempered. He refused to move into the new War Department building on Virginia Avenue at Foggy Bottom (it became and remains home of the Department of State) because the facade looked like the entrance to a "provincial opera house."[4] He is best remembered for the bon mot "Gentlemen do not read each other's mail" with which he explained his closure of the State Department's cryptography office ("the Black Chamber") in 1930. Two years later he formulated what became known as the Stimson Doctrine, which proclaimed that the United States would not recognize any "situation" or "agreement" brought about by threats or acts of war.

Stimson was a loyal Rooseveltian, supporting the president's destroyers-for-bases deal with Britain in September 1940 as well as Lend-Lease in March 1941. First and foremost, the "Great Victorian" was pro-British. He firmly believed that America's national security demanded all aid short of war to beleaguered Britain, and he rejected suggestions of accommodation with the Germans or the Japanese. In May 1940 he joined the nonpartisan Committee to Defend America by Aiding the Allies. He was annoyed by what he perceived to be Roosevelt's ambiguous policy with regard to the dictators in the 1930s and availed himself of every opportunity to impress his views on Cabinet colleagues. He judged the president to be incapable of following "a consecutive chain of thought" and of mounting any consistent policy. Instead, FDR seemed to have a predilection for "government on the jump," for allowing "stories and incidents" to dominate Cabinet discussions. Stimson, a man of rigor and discipline, found what he called the president's "happy-go-lucky snap-of-the-moment" and "topsy-turvy, upside-down" method of administration poorly suited to the crises of the 1930s. Perhaps most important, Stimson forged an exemplary harmony of interests ("the door was always open") with General Marshall, one that would stand the War Department well in the trying war years of 1941–45.

Acting on the president's orders of December 18, 1941, Stimson set his staff at the War Office to work on preparing the American agenda for the Churchill visit. The task was completed within forty-eight hours. Working hand-in-hand with Chief of Staff Marshall, General Henry H. Arnold of the Army Air Forces, Chief of War Plans Division General Leonard T. Gerow, and the latter's deputy, General Dwight D. Eisenhower, on December 20 Stimson submitted his "Suggested Analysis of the Basic Topics and their Attendant Problems" to the president. Therein, the War Department identified the North Atlantic as America's "principal theatre of operations," whose safety "must underlie all our other efforts in the war." It agreed with the British suggestion that American forces take over "the defense of Ireland," and thus relieve British forces in Northern Ireland. It suggested that the American garrisons in Iceland and Greenland be reinforced, especially in light of the expectation of "a violent renewal of submarine activity" in the North Atlantic after Adolf Hitler's declaration of war against the United States.

Stimson at once appreciated that the war would be global in scope. The "most difficult and important problem of the conference," he forecast, was the need to shape operations in four distinct theaters: the southwest Pacific, western Africa, Syria and Iran, and Egypt and Libya. He ranked the southwest Pacific as the most important of these. After all, it was from there that "a new combatant power," Imperial Japan, had challenged America's "position in the Pacific." And it was there that the most immediate Japanese threats arose: at Singapore, in the Dutch East Indies, in Australia and New Zealand, and in China. Stimson and his planners offered three immediate courses of action. First, the United States needed to secure its North Atlantic communications "with our fortress in the British Isles covering the British fleet." Second, it had to protect its communications with the Near East and the Far East by air and by water. And third, it had to build up as quickly as possible "air and sea communications in the Pacific with Australia."[5]

Stimson recalled there was potential cause for friction between the Americans and the British in the forthcoming talks. No one seemed to question that Germany was the greatest menace and that the agreements arrived at in March 1941 during the initial American-British staff talks were still intact. But that left open to interpretation the question of how much American effort would go to the war against Japan in the immediate future. Stimson seemed to want to make Japan at least a tactical or temporary American priority, and he was not alone, as events would tell. After all, it was the Japanese who had attacked the United States, and Japanese forces who were sweeping across the Pacific, killing Americans in large numbers. Surely, the Germans could await their turn to receive American punishment even if, in the long run, they would absorb the greatest part of it.

One day later, December 21, 1941, the Joint Board sent the president its evaluation of the "broad strategic objective" to be followed by what it still called in First World War terminology, the "Associated Powers." For the moment, there was little to do but to "hold where necessary while building up strength." In other words, the United States and Britain would maintain the strategic defensive and conduct only "local offensives in appropriate theatres." But a "successful air offensive" against Germany was to begin immediately. Ultimately, the Allies would have to conduct "an all-out offensive," first against Germany and its European allies and then against Japan.[6]

The War Department's memoranda occasioned a critical conference with Roosevelt on the afternoon of December 21, which included Hopkins, Secretaries Stimson and Knox, Generals Arnold and Marshall, and Admirals King and Stark. Roosevelt carefully went over the two memoranda point by point. He agreed with the suggested agenda for the upcoming conversations with the British, ranging from Ireland and the North Atlantic to Syria and Egypt. He also approved the recommendations for the creation of a "supreme allied war council," a military "joint planning committee," and a "joint supply committee."[7] This time, unlike at Argentia, the Americans would be ready for the arrival of Churchill with his army of officers and clerks and his sheaves of position papers.

Eleanor Roosevelt's mood turned sour on the morning of Monday, December 22, 1941. The president, who only two days earlier had spoken to her of spending the weekend at Hyde Park, had told her to expect "some guests" who would be staying at the White House for several days.[8] She was to include these guests in all family Christmas affairs and to see that one of the second-floor sitting rooms was made ready as an office and map room. She was to make sure that "we had good champagne and brandy in the house and plenty of whiskey." But she was not allowed to know "who was coming nor how many" there would be. It was all too much secrecy for Eleanor. She had already been greatly displeased by what she called the Secret Service's "idiotic restrictions"—from the "rather soiling process" of fingerprinting to the "fluoroscoping" of all packages arriving at the White House. Now, the G-men further annoyed her by announcing that no one at the White House was to leave their offices or to walk the halls that afternoon.

The president summoned his butler, Alonzo Fields, to his study to begin preparations for the visit. As Fields approached the door to FDR's second-floor bedroom, he heard Eleanor's agitated voice. "You should have told me. Why didn't you tell me? I can't find Mrs. Nesbitt anywhere. If only I had known."

Roosevelt, seeing Fields approach, tried to calm his wife. "Now,

Eleanor, all that little woman would do even if she were here is to tell Fields what we can tell him ourselves right now. Fields, at eight tonight, we have to have dinner ready for twenty. Mr. Churchill and his party are coming to stay with us for a few days."[9]

There, it was out: the "guest" would be the leader of the anti-Hitler crusade—and of the British Empire. The first lady vented her anger on having this surprise sprung on her before the entire nation in her newspaper column *My Day* on Christmas Eve. "It had not occurred to him," she petulantly wrote, "that this might require certain moving of furniture to adapt rooms to the purposes for which the Prime Minister wished to use them."[10]

Franklin was not in a much better mood. The news from the war fronts had been all bad. On December 17 he had received word that Japanese forces had landed at North Borneo. Twenty-four hours later he had been informed that Japanese troops had stormed Hong Kong Island. As a "former naval person," FDR was thunderstruck by the high British losses in the Mediterranean: *Galatea* off Alexandria, Egypt, on December 14; *Neptune* off Tripoli five days later; and the battleships *Queen Elizabeth* and *Valiant* in Alexandria harbor on December 20.

At home, hundreds of thousands of young men stormed recruiting centers not yet ready to receive them. Those taken in trained with dilapidated equipment. Most expected to ship out to the Far Pacific. The Navy was rounding up every available diver and yard worker to dispatch to Battleship Row on Oahu Island to see what could be done about the sunken fleet. Industrialists feared that the torrent of new government orders already coming in for trucks and tanks, aircraft and artillery, could bring with them bothersome government regulations and oversight. Rumors continued to spread like wildfire about German and Japanese saboteurs at work in the United States. There were even reports of enemy landings in the Aleutian Islands. Henrietta Nesbitt, the White House cook, later recalled some of those rumors: "Strange planes off Florida. Subs off New Jersey. Santa Barbara shelled by Japanese submarine."[11] The Congress was gathering steam for what Secretary of the Navy Knox feared would be "a nasty investigation" into the debacle at Pearl Harbor.[12] Might this turn into a full-blown review of the Administration's Japan policy?

FDR spent much of December 22 on routine matters. The day

was warm with gentle winds; the temperature hovered near the 50 degree mark. At 10:50 A.M. he received the new Soviet ambassador, pudgy and smiling Maxim Litvinov. The three-piece suit that Litvinov had hurriedly acquired amused the president. "You get that suit in Moscow?" he mischievously asked the ambassador.[13] Across the mahogany table in the small dining room, FDR then rather nastily reminded Litvinov that the ambassador had been brought up "in a God fearing family and educated to be a Rabbi." And he reminded him of what lay ahead. "Some day you will die and you will probably know beforehand that you are to die and you will remember your parents and all they meant to you and what then?" Poor Litvinov headed back to the Soviet Embassy with former U.S. Ambassador William Bullitt, mumbling that "he did not like the president—he was afraid of a man like that."[14]

Later that morning Roosevelt saw the ambassadors of China (Dr. Hu Shih) and the Netherlands (Dr. A. Loudon). He closeted himself with Harry Hopkins over lunch, then called Canadian prime minister William Lyon Mackenzie King in Ottawa and invited him to come to Washington to meet "a certain person who is on his way." Mackenzie King had only recently been informed about Churchill's visit and had immediately extended an invitation for him to take a side trip to Ottawa to address Canada's Parliament. The president implied to Mackenzie King that some basic decisions concerning the conduct of the war had already been made: "There will have to be a Supreme Council, and I am determined that it shall have its headquarters in Washington." Roosevelt acknowledged that "there will possibly be quite a time over this," but he was determined to have his way on the matter.[15] At 5:55 P.M., an hour after sunset, the president mysteriously left the White House by car. His destination was the Anacostia Flats Naval Air Station, across the Potomac River from National Airport; it was time to greet Churchill to the New World for the second time since the outbreak of war.

Late in the morning of December 22 *Duke of York* was still battling heavy seas on its approach to Chesapeake Bay. In the expectation that the battleship would reach calmer waters, Churchill had accepted an invitation to join the president and a number of guests for dinner at the White House that night. But progress was slow in the face of the high winds. Churchill grew anxious about reaching his destination in time. Sir Charles Wilson, his private physician, recorded in his diary, "He was like a child in his impatience to meet the President. He spoke as if every minute counted. It was absurd to waste time; he must fly."[16] As the great warship approached the Virginia coast, Churchill cancelled the original plan to steam up the bay, land in northern Virginia, and then motor on to Washington. He wired his ambassador, Lord Halifax, "Impossible to reach Mouth Potomac before 6:30 P.M. which would be too late . . . I should like to come by airplane to Washington airfield reaching you in time for dinner."[17]

The *Duke of York* disembarked Churchill and his entourage at Hampton Roads Gate. The White House scrambled a Lockheed Lodestar aircraft, which took on board Churchill, Wilson, Portal, Harriman, and Beaverbrook for the forty-five minute flight up the Potomac. What the passengers saw was staggering. Used to years of blackouts, the British party marveled at the sea of lights that spread out below them. Churchill's personal bodyguard, Commander C. R. "Tommy" Thompson, recorded: "It was night time. Those in the plane were transfixed with delight to look down from the windows and see the amazing spectacle of a whole city lighted up." Obviously, the capital's residents had not yet taken to heart recent blackout orders. "Washington represented something immensely precious," Thompson went on. "Freedom, hope, strength. We had not seen an illuminated city for five [sic] years. My heart filled."[18]

Those in the British party who did not fly to Washington traveled to the capital aboard a special train provided by the vice president of the Baltimore and Ohio Railroad. The journey began at the station at Phoebus, Virginia, at 7:45 P.M. As the train rolled through the cool Virginia night, the crew served "a first rate sandwich dinner consisting of cold chicken, two hard boiled eggs, salad, coffee and fruit." Colonel Ian Jacob, deputy to General Hastings Ismay (who had stayed in London), played bridge with some of the others to while away the time. Jacob recorded in his diary that the train arrived in Washington after midnight. A fleet of cars took them swiftly through the dark Washington streets to the Mayflower Hotel.

The "grand dame" of Washington hotels had been placed on a war footing. Windows and doors had been covered with lightproof blinds, and skylights blacked out. Two air-raid sirens and an emergency first-aid station had been installed on each of the hotel's ten floors. The barbershop had been stocked with hospital supplies, and the roof manned by lookouts against aerial attack. Box springs were ready to be turned into stretchers and tablecloths and napkins into bandages.[19] At the Mayflower, the British party found "plenty of whiskey and beer . . . ready on the ice," various vouchers and passes, and $50 in cash. "We were glad to tumble into bed after a most fatiguing day," Jacob later wrote.[20]

When the Churchill plane rolled to a stop at Anacostia Flats Naval Air Station just before 7:00 P.M., the passengers saw a tall man propped up against a large, black limousine. Churchill came out first and at once went over to Roosevelt. He clasped Roosevelt's "strong hand with comfort and pleasure," and introduced him to Wilson. The doctor and the president commiserated about the lives lost at Pearl Harbor. Then the limousine, confiscated by the Treasury Department from Al Capone, sped the two leaders and Beaverbrook off to the White House.

There, the arriving party was met by a small group of reporters and press photographers at the South Portico entrance. As always, no pictures were allowed while FDR was lifted out of the limousine and "walked" to the mansion's doorway. Then, an explosion of flash bulbs and camera clicks. Press Secretary Stephen T. Early, who had just that morning warned the press that any "leak" about the important visitor would "violate the Censorship Act,"[21] was almost trampled as reporters rushed to nearby telephones to call in their story.

Inside, Eleanor greeted Winston as he and the president came out of the elevator on the second floor. She showed "Tommy" Thompson to Room 13, the Yellow Bedroom, and John Martin, Churchill's private secretary, to Room 14, the Small Blue Bedroom. Next, she found quarters for the two Scotland Yard men (Room 31) and Churchill's valet (Room 33). She proudly showed the prime minister the Monroe Room on the second floor. It had been emptied of furniture and would serve as Churchill's "map room," modeled on the one in the Cabinet War Rooms beneath the New Public Offices in London. White House carpenters had mounted five map holders and electricians had installed two fluorescent lights for each. Then she took Churchill to the Lincoln Bedroom, just off the West Hall, which she had selected as the prime minister's while at the White House.

It would not do. The bed did not suit him. Without invitation, Churchill roamed over the second floor, trying the beds and pulling out drawers in each room. He finally selected Room 12, the Rose Bedroom, with its prints of scenes of Victorian England at the east end of the floor. Did he perhaps remember that Queen Elizabeth had used that room in 1939? Eleanor was not amused by his antics. Still, she dutifully invited Churchill for tea in the West Hall. Alonzo Field supervised the White House staff busily preparing dinner. It also had not been told who the White House's special guest was that evening.

The tea, Eleanor quickly discovered, had been changed to what she called "more stimulating refreshments." To get the jump on Churchill, who had taken the first round at Argentia, Roosevelt had Mrs. Nesbitt retrieve from storage at Garfinkel's the lion-skin rug that Emperor Haile Selassie had given him. "Leo the Lion" was thus on the president's floor to remind Churchill of the evils of empire.[22] At 8:15 P.M. FDR, sitting in the Red Room beside a small table filled with glasses and shakers and bottles, set about mixing drinks. Churchill, who liked his spirits uncontaminated by nonalcoholic ingredients, was aghast at the exotic drinks the president served up. There were special martinis, whose secret proportions FDR hid from view, topped with a dash of Pernod. There were bourbon Orange-Blossom Specials. And there were Haitian Libations that included dark rum, chilled orange juice and lemon juice, egg whites, and brown sugar.[23] FDR had another trolley brought in with his favorite delicacies—caviar, smoked turkey, smoked clams, and imported cheeses. The prime minister took it all in stride. He was delighted to report to the president that he had code-named their secret meeting ARCADIA. Roosevelt concurred.

Before sitting down to dinner, Churchill made the rounds, greeting each guest with a warm, "How-de-do—how-de-do."[24] The prime minister was dressed in what FDR's friend Huybertie "Bertie" Hamlin called a "reefer jacket." In fact, it was the very same uniform of the Elder Brothers of Trinity House that Churchill had worn at Argentia: a knee-length double-breasted coat "buttoned high" in seaman fashion, and a cape with a circled insignia on it. "He reminded me of a big English bulldog," Mrs. Hamlin noted, "who had been taught to give his paw." Dinner began at 8:45 P.M. The "colored waiters" were smartly decked out in tuxedos and black bow ties, the rest of the male staff in white coats, white shirts, and black bow ties. The maids were dressed in black taffeta uniforms with white collars and cuffs, and organdy embroidered aprons. Red roses adorned the center of the dining table. The president had invited Secretary of State and Mrs. Hull, Under Secretary and Mrs. Sumner Welles, Lord Beaverbrook, Lord Halifax, and various guests, including Hopkins and some of the president's other personal friends. For dinner, the White House kitchen served up broiled chicken and vegetables, finished off with a vanilla ice cream and strawberry cake.

Throughout the dinner, Churchill and Roosevelt engaged in light banter, each seeking to grab center stage from the other. At one point FDR laughingly pointed out to Churchill that as president of the United States, he could leave the country without having to get the permission of the Cabinet. "That," Roosevelt drove on, "meant that the secret of the Atlantic Charter meeting probably had leaked out from the British side." Churchill, "laughing and eyes twinkling," at once riposted, "It must have been the women who did it." Mrs. Hamlin was charmed by the prime minister, who now in his enthusiasm reminded her of "the jolly-sea-dog type." She admired his massive head, "as if cut from granite," and was amused by the "mass of wrinkles" that highlighted his shirtfront. "But his eyes twinkle with the most kindly expression."

Just before dinner ended, FDR raised a glass of champagne: "I have a toast to offer—It has been in my head and on my heart now for a long time—now it is on the tip of my tongue—'To the common cause.'"

Then, at 10 P.M. the president led Churchill, Beaverbrook, Halifax, Hopkins, Welles, and Hull away from the table to the Oval Room. It was FDR's inner sanctum, an amazing place. The plaster walls were a flat battleship gray, the woodwork a glossy white. Tall mahogany bookcases were crammed with books all stacked up on their sides. Ships' models were everywhere. The well-worn brown and green leather sofas and chairs stemmed from Theodore Roosevelt's yacht *Mayflower*. Green carpet covered the floor.

For Churchill, the first moment of truth had come. He was edgy, desperate to know how Pearl Harbor had affected the president's thinking. Would Roosevelt stick to the old "Europe-first" strategy? Or would he yield to the public clamor that he strike out against Imperial Japan? FDR obviously appreciated the prime minister's concerns and immediately assured him that there would be no change in strategy from "Europe first." Churchill was greatly relieved; his worst fears had been laid to rest.

FDR and Churchill discussed "general questions . . . covering the initial situation, the present status, and relations with the Vichy Government and with Portugal." They also prepared a draft of a declaration covering their "joint" intentions, which included the provision "that no power would make peace without an agreement with the associate powers."[25] But the main topic of conversation North Africa. The prime minister emphasized the potential danger to the Allied cause of leaving Algeria in the hands of the Vichy French. In part he was concerned about the two modern French battleships based there, *Jean Bart* and *Richelieu*, but his basic motive was far deeper. He had decided shortly after the Italian entry into the war in June 1940 to make North Africa a major British war priority. That was no doubt due to the possibilities North Africa held as one theater where the British might make the Axis bleed.

Left unsaid in his initial talks with Roosevelt, however, was his concern that the Mediterranean had become an Axis lake after June 1940, effectively cutting the lifeline between Britain and the Far East. The British held Gibraltar, Malta, the Nile Delta, and Suez, but if Hitler succeeded in cajoling Spain's Francisco Franco into allowing German troops to attack Gibraltar from the land side—as Churchill greatly feared—the very entrance to the Mediterranean would be sealed off. Prior to Japan's entry into the war, that might have seemed more a matter of British imperial interest—the route to India—but after Pearl Harbor, Britain's ability to hold Singapore and its other territories in southeast Asia had become an American concern as well. Besides, Roosevelt wanted to get American troops into action as quickly as possible if for no other reason than to get the point across to his countrymen that they were now in a real war. He agreed that American troops should join the North African campaign in Algeria as the United State's first offensive priority, whether the Vichy French agreed to allow the Allies in, or fought to keep it under their own control.[26] The next morning Churchill wired Deputy Prime Minister Clement Attlee, "Arrived here by air after a very rough sea journey. Long invaluable talk with the President last night. We begin high level conferences this afternoon (December 23)."[27]

The men returned from the Oval Room about midnight, having received news that Japan had launched a major offensive in the Philippines. Eleanor could barely keep awake—she had attended half a dozen pre-Christmas celebrations that day, ranging from the Salvation Army to the American Committee for British Catholic Relief. And so much more lay ahead.

Still, the deep differences of opinion about grand strategy already evident at Argentia had quickly resurfaced. Added to these now were equally grave worries within the British camp about the new relations with the Americans. Halifax, the British ambassador to Washington, left the meeting suddenly aware of the vast disparity of thought between himself and Churchill as well as Beaverbrook. He would write to a friend in early 1942:

> Part of my feeling here . . . is affected by my awareness of how remote my mind and thoughts are from Winston's and Max's. When they were here . . . I was profoundly conscious of how differently their minds worked to my own, and how impossible it would be for me to establish any real community of sympathy in thought with them. I don't know quite what it is. Partly intellectual, partly moral . . . I was terribly shocked by Winston's growth in the egotistic habit of thought. I can do this: I won't do that, etc., etc. . . .[28]

But Churchill was happy. Roosevelt had reaffirmed his cherished "Europe-first" strategy. He had accepted the prime minister's North Africa strategy. He had agreed that no ally would make a separate peace with Hitler. In fact, he appeared to have agreed to just about everything Churchill had proposed. But had he? FDR was in no position to make firm commitments to Churchill about military matters, even ones that lay at such a high level. He simply did not know what the American military was capable of at that point in the war and he had neither the means, nor the inclination, to order strong-willed men such as Marshall or King about, even if Chief of Naval Operations Stark was more than likely to do his bidding. In any case, he had long ago developed a talent for making his beseechers believe that he agreed with their every demand, when in fact he was just nodding and reserving his options to act, or not to act at all, at a later time. Churchill would see the first sign of this within twenty-four hours.

Just before midnight, Churchill called for his personal physician. A White House car picked Wilson up and he was brought to the second floor. Churchill assured him that his pulse was regular, but wanted to know whether he could take a sleeping pill. The prime minister was simply too excited to sleep. He had sold the president on the main tenets of the grand strategy he had mapped out on the stormy voyage across the Atlantic. It had been a triumphant first White House meeting with Roosevelt. "He must have a good night," Sir Charles wrote in his diary. The doctor prescribed two "reds," barbiturate sleeping pills, and left the prime minister "bottling up his excitement."[29]

No member of the White House staff had ever seen the likes of Winston Churchill. Nor would any of them ever forget him. Alonzo Fields was the first of the staff to encounter him. Churchill invited the butler into the Rose Bedroom the morning of December 23. The room was in a shambles, with crumpled bedclothes on the bed, newspapers strewn all over the floor, and the leader of the British Empire in bare feet and long underwear. "Now Fields," he began, "we had a lovely dinner last night but I have a few orders for you. We want to leave here as friends, right? So I need you to listen." No guest had ever spoken to Fields in this manner. "One, I don't like talking outside my quarters; two, I hate whistling in the corridors; and three, I must have a tumbler of sherry in my room before breakfast, a couple glasses of scotch and soda before lunch and French champagne and 90 year old brandy before I go to sleep at night." Fields did not miss a beat: "Yes, sir."[30] Churchill still was not done. He instructed Fields every breakfast to bring him something hot—"eggs, bacon or ham, and toast"—and something cold—"two kinds of cold meats with English mustard and two kinds of fruit plus a tumbler of sherry." The butler was most amused by what he called Churchill's "air-raid suit,"[31] actually a Royal Air Force jumpsuit.

Henrietta Nesbitt, who had run a bakery in Roosevelt's old political stomping grounds, Dutchess County, New York, was known for being the worst cook in White House history. Morning after morning, she served the president oatmeal for breakfast, simply because she decreed that it was good for him. At one point, FDR in exasperation had sent Mrs. Nesbitt an advertisement from the morning paper: "Corn Flakes! 13 ounce package, 19 cents! Post Toasties! 13 ounce package, 19 cents! Cream of Wheat! Two for 27 cents!" She blissfully ignored the president's "gentle reminder."[32] Day after day she offered up chicken salad with more celery than chicken, turkey and candied yams, broccoli (which she knew he hated), rolls without butter, and cake without frosting. No one could figure out why FDR kept her on—and even raised her pay from $1,500 to $1,620 per year.

But she was delighted to have her staff feed the food-deprived British guests, who seemed to enjoy whatever she brought them. Churchill's principal private secretary, John Martin, marveled at being served "*eggs*—the wonderful eggs. I hadn't eaten an egg in years, times were so hard at home. It seems we did nothing but order up eggs."[33] Second helpings were routine, of everything from soup to nuts. Nesbitt, a woman of German descent in her late sixties, bespectacled and strong-jawed, took pity especially on the prime minister, who she decided had a "poor-colored and hungry" look. She served him (and the president) special meals such as grilled kidneys, calves' liver, roast beef, and roasted game (quail, pheasant, and wild ducks). She made sure that there always was an ample supply of Scotch on hand. When the $2,000 of his salary of $75,000 that FDR turned over to Mrs. Nesbitt every month for the White House food and liquor budget ran out, she managed to get the State Department to pay for more libations. She kept the ushers on duty twenty-four hours a day to look after her special guest's every need. She even got Churchill English soap for his twice-daily hot baths. And like Fields, she was amused by what she called the prime minister's "zipper suits."[34] FDR joked that he would get a "siren suit" like Churchill's, if the Office of Production Management would only let him have the wool.

Lillian Rogers Parks, on the other hand, was not enamored of Churchill. He simply had taken over the White House "as if he belonged there." The maid disliked his loud "cussing." She was offended when Churchill committed the unpardonable sin of cold-shouldering Hopkins' young daughter, Diana. She howled upon learning that "the prime" always curled up in bed with a hot water bottle, and that his

Scotland Yard bodyguard would apparently inject mice with samples from his Coronas. "If the mouse did not drop dead, the new box of cigars was safe to smoke." She was troubled by the fact that the first lady feared Churchill's bad influence on her husband's alcohol consumption. When Eleanor once broached the subject with Franklin, he cut her cruelly with the comment that it was not *his* side of the family that had a drinking problem—a brutal reference to her father Elliott and brother Hall both alcoholics.

When Parks arrived at work early one morning she found Churchill "stalking" the halls of the second floor of the White House, bellowing, "Where is my man?" He wanted his valet and, upon seeing Parks, instructed her that he never rose before 11 A.M., that he in fact had not yet risen, and that she was to tell no one that he had risen. Worst of all to her, Churchill was cheap. Whereas other guests to the White House had often left generous tips, "All Churchill came up with was a bunch of cheap little photos of himself, which he didn't even bother to autograph. Adding insult to injury, the word 'souvenir' was printed on them."[35] Parks' one great moment was when the president had the cooks serve up pigs' knuckles in a special sauce and Churchill, "trying to be gracious," had shut his eyes and eaten them, becoming "sicker by the minute as he pretended enthusiasm." When FDR threatened to serve the same meal in a day or two, the prime minister "surrendered," whereupon Roosevelt called off the threat.[36]

The White House was a changed place with Churchill in residence. Simply put, he turned it into the staff headquarters of the British Empire. Officers, diplomats, and secretaries would rush in and out of the mansion carrying their red letter-dispatch cases stuffed with official papers. Typewriters clicked at all hours of the day and night. Phones rang around the clock. In the afternoon Churchill demanded his nap; bedtime all too often came at 3 A.M. The walls of the Monroe Room soon were covered with giant maps of all the war theaters, with colored pins daily tracking the movements of British troops and ships.

Of course, FDR was not about to be outdone by Churchill in managing the war. Thus, he instructed Lieutenant Robert Montgomery of Naval Intelligence, who had seen Churchill's map room in London, to build him a similar one right away.[37] The only quarters that could be found in the crowded mansion was a pale green ladies' coatroom in the basement. It was a low-ceilinged, rectangular room. Pipes protruded where once there had been marble lavatories. But a host of workmen quickly transformed the coatroom into a map room. Blackout shades were secured over its single window. New "scrambler" telephones were installed. Under tightest security, twelve officers—six Army and six Navy—under the command of Captain John L. McCrea, FDR's chief naval aide, staffed the new White House Map Room. Soon, the Signal Corps ran all military and diplomatic correspondence through it. Only seven men, mostly senior military leaders and Hopkins, were allowed inside. Neither Eleanor nor the White House Secret Service detail was given access. Mrs. Nesbitt was instructed to find a boy to clean the room. "Find us a dumb one," she was told, and so she selected one "I knew wouldn't be interested in military plans."[38] A White House policeman stood watch at the door twenty-four hours a day, and each night the wastepaper baskets were emptied by an officer on duty and their contents incinerated by an officer of the watch.

To outdo Churchill, "Bob" Montgomery even devised special pins for special people. The head of the Roosevelt pin was in the shape of a long cigarette holder; that of Stalin a briar pipe; and that of Churchill a big cigar. Other pins showed the whereabouts of battleships, aircraft carriers, and heavy cruisers. The destroyer on which FDR's son, Franklin, Jr., served was especially large headed so that the president could always check it first. The watch officers quickly noticed that even in the map room, the angle of FDR's cigarette holder gave away his mood. At this stage of the war, when most of the news from the Philippines, Guam, and Wake Island was bad, it descended "from its usual rakish angle to hang loosely in his mouth."[39] It was hanging loosely almost all the time these days.

7

GETTING DOWN
TO BUSINESS

FRANKLIN ROOSEVELT AND WINSTON CHURCHILL WOULD SPEND fourteen days under the White House roof. They would have dinner together (with Harry Hopkins) every day but one.[1] And they would hold at least eight major White House meetings with their staffs. True to form, the "sly squire of Hyde Park" had no American minutes or notes of conversations recorded—save for the final dinner meeting on January 14, 1942. Thus, a host of subjects was discussed with no record save Churchill's memoirs. These ranged from the future borders of the Soviet Union in Eastern Europe to the possibility of undertaking "sacrifice landings" on the Continent sometime in summer 1942; from the "political situation in India" to the military and political significance of China; and from the issue of British "imperial preferences" to sending relief supplies to Greece.[2]

In the course of those weeks the leaders also discussed two highly secret matters. The first was atomic energy research. Edwin McMillan and Glenn T. Seaborg that year had discovered plutonium, thereby opening up the prospect of a new and powerful weapon. The second was Britain's most closely guarded secret, "Ultra." While it is not known precisely how much Churchill shared or omitted in his talks with Roosevelt concerning the British codebreakers at Bletchley Park, it is known that he did inform the president that until Pearl Harbor, British cryptographers had been breaking State Department ciphers![3] Yet again, FDR's refusal to commit anything to paper prevents further exploration of what could potentially have been a conference-breaking admission by Churchill. Thus, much of what we know about "Christmas in Washington" from the American perspective comes from the notes and papers of Harry Hopkins.

Harry Lloyd Hopkins was unquestionably the most controversial and shadowy of figures around the president. Born in Sioux City, Iowa, on August 17, 1890, young Harry was raised in a deeply religious family drawn to the brilliant rhetoric of William Jennings Bryan and other populists. He attended Grinnell College, then steeped in the Christian reformism of the social gospel movement. Upon graduation in 1912, Hopkins moved to the Lower East Side of New York City, where he found work in a social settlement called Christadora House. There he married Ethel Gross, a Jewish immigrant and social worker; they had three sons.

When the United States entered the First World War, Hopkins joined the Gulf States Division of the American Red Cross, serving first in New Orleans and then in Atlanta. Hopkins returned to New York in 1922; two years later he landed a job as director of the New York Tuberculosis Association. In 1931 then governor Franklin D. Roosevelt appointed him to run the New York State Temporary Relief Administration, the nation's first relief organization during the Great Depression. Unable to manage his personal finances and in love with a coworker, Barbara Duncan, Hopkins divorced his wife in May 1931, leaving him free to marry Duncan.

When FDR became president, Hopkins followed him to Washington and helped establish much of the New Deal's alphabet soup of acronyms: AAA (Agricultural Adjustment Administration), CCC (Civilian Conservation Corps), CWA (Civil Works Administration), FERA (Federal Emergency Relief Administration), NRA (National Recovery Administration), and WPA (Works Progress Administration), among others. As Federal Emergency Relief Administrator, Hopkins cheerfully spent $9 billion in federal relief money, forever earning him to sobriquet of a "big government" free spender. In fact, Hopkins was shocked upon arriving in Washington to note that the federal government financed most of the nation's relief work. "I was the most surprised man in the world when I got to Washington," he told a group of social workers, "and found that the federal government was paying eighty percent of all unemployment relief in the United States." In December 1938 FDR appointed Hopkins secretary of commerce.

Then personal tragedy struck. First, his wife Barbara died of cancer in 1937, leaving Harry to raise their young daughter, Diana. Soon thereafter, Hopkins underwent surgery for stomach cancer, which left him thin and frail, constantly in and out of hospital. Friends feared for the life of the lanky, frenetic workaholic. He resigned his Cabinet post in August 1940, but is appetite for rich foods and alcohol slowed his recovery.

Hopkins returned to Roosevelt's side in 1941. The president dispatched him to Britain to catalogue its military needs and in March 1941 appointed him to head up the Lend-Lease program. A self-designated "glorified office boy," Hopkins traveled to Moscow in July 1941 to establish contacts with Joseph Stalin and to evaluate the Soviet Union's ability to withstand the German onslaught. He accompanied Churchill to Argentia in August of that year. As Lend-Lease administrator, Hopkins built an informal network of aides, later known as "the Hopkins Shop," that included future leaders such as Edward Stettinius, James Burns, and Averell Harriman. By December 1941, he was at the heart of the action, occupying the Lincoln Bedroom on the second floor of the White House, just down from Roosevelt's study and across the hall from Churchill. Utterly disorganized in his private affairs, Hopkins was a tough poser of important questions and a relentless advocate of rearmament programs, qualities that prompted Churchill to call him "Lord Root of the Matter."

Hopkins understood power. His dream of one day occupying the White House as president never materialized, so he did the next best thing—he moved into the White House as Roosevelt's special assistant. Proximity to power satisfied Hopkins' immense ego. He was responsible for his actions to no one but Roosevelt, and he controlled access to the president. His relations with Eleanor were strained from the start, for he did not share her Pollyannaish view that the war provided an opportunity to rapidly expand the social programs of the New Deal; rather, it had to be won first and at all cost. Gaunt, chain-smoking, acid-tongued, a lover of beautiful women and fast horses, Hopkins, in the words of historian Randall B. Woods, "was one of the most hated and feared men in wartime Washington."[4] Few dared cross swords with him, for Hopkins enjoyed ready access to the president.

While Roosevelt and Churchill dined together for the first time on the evening of December 22, the initial meeting between a British and an American chief of staff took place at the War Department. Both military staffs knew that the devil in these discussions would be in the details, and those details were chiefly going to be their purview. Their first-ever meeting at Argentia in August had not gone well. A wide chasm had quickly developed in their separate views of how the war was to be waged and won. George Marshall especially was aghast at Churchill's strategy to defeat Germany by way of strikes on the periphery of "Fortress Europe" and by encouraging the subject peoples to rise up against the tyrant. It was naïve, in Marshall's view, to believe that Germany could be defeated in any way other than a landing on the Continent and another brutal drive on Berlin, as in 1918.

Marshall decided that "Hap" Arnold, chief of staff, U.S. Army Air Forces, should lead off the talks with Portal, his British counterpart. He was keenly aware of the fact that the two airmen were only equals in an informal sense, and perhaps this might break the ice. Not only was Arnold's rank junior to Portal's, as heads of the two air forces but more important, he had been included in the staff discussions first at Argentia and now in Washington essentially on Marshall's sufferance. Moreover, the United States had no separate air force (it would not have one until 1947) and Arnold was, in fact, technically commander of a branch of the Army.[5] Portal, on the other hand, was the commander of the Royal Air Force, which had enjoyed independent status since 1918. The disparities in rank and status might encourage collegial discussion.

At first, Marshall's hunch seemed to pay off. Arnold was delighted when Portal basically accepted the U.S. War Department's agenda. But the vast differences in outlook and attitude between the Americans and the British quickly surfaced. Arnold was annoyed by the overall tone of the meeting. It is debatable whether or not Portal intended to convey an air of superiority, but that was exactly what Arnold picked up. He was especially offended by Portal's strong hint that what Britain needed most in the way of air support from the United States was American bombers—without American crews—to "help out [the British] bombing effort."[6] Was Portal suggesting that the United States enter the war as a "junior partner"? Arnold was also less than enthused about Portal's suggestion that the United States Navy order its aircraft carriers to "steal up rapidly to the vicinity of Japan" and carry out an American Pearl Harbor. This was "wishful thinking" at best; at worst, it would divert American heavy bombers from Britain to the Far East.[7] Unlike the Churchill-Roosevelt discussions at the White House that night, the first official staff contact ended with suspicion and, for Arnold, more than a touch of acrimony.

The meeting was a preview of what was to come. At the start of the ARCADIA conference, the American military leaders thought their British counterparts to be arrogant know-it-alls. They were convinced that the British were only interested in poaching as much U.S. military hardware and troops as they could get without American participation in the decisions as to how those assets were to be used. They did not trust them. They suspected the British of harboring narrow national motives and of being interested only in advancing selfish interests.[8]

The British chiefs were no more generous in their assessment of the Americans. They thought them unorganized, bureaucratic, ignorant of the realities of the war, and still reeling in shock from the Japanese attack. They quickly noticed, and had little sympathy for, the obvious interservice rivalries that popped up at virtually every meeting.[9] In fact, as Forrest C. Pogue, Marshall's biographer, has written, the Americans were still in nursery school as far as the war was concerned:

> Despite the efforts made over several decades to develop close-knit collaboration among the President, the cabinet, and the Chiefs of Staff, no integrated system of defense control existed in Washington. Sir John Dill was not far wrong when he reported to General [Alan] Brooke in 1942 that 'the country has not—repeat not—the slightest conception of what the war means, and their armed forces are more unready for war than it is possible to imagine.'[10]

And Dill, unlike some of the other British chiefs, was a good friend and admirer of the Americans.

The Arnold-Portal meeting confirmed Hopkins' innermost fears that the Americans, despite Secretary Stimson's earnest preparations, would not be ready for the British. Several days before Churchill's arrival, he had confided these fears to Ambassador Halifax. Undoubtedly, Churchill "would come much better prepared with practical and specific suggestions," as he had at Argentia. That could only evoke "negative replies" from American planners from Marshall on down. Hopkins appealed to Halifax to remind British staff officers that such initial "negative replies from [the] U.S. Staff . . . should not, repeat not, be taken too seriously."[11] Staff relations by December 22 were electric and fraught with the danger of failure.

American military leaders were not at all happy that Churchill was staying at the White House, literally down the hall from the president. They worried about what commitments Roosevelt might make to Churchill, perhaps over drinks, or in an expansive moment when both men were talking together about lofty war aims and high strategy. They knew that FDR was a neophyte in military affairs compared to Churchill, despite his having been assistant secretary of the Navy in the First World War. They also jealously guarded the special position they held as chiefs of their respective branches of the military responsible not only to the president as their constitutional commander in chief, but also to the Congress and to the American people beyond.

They had reason to be concerned. Churchill was the supreme British war leader: prime minister and minister of defence, he was boss to the British military chiefs. As John Colville, one of his wartime private secretaries, would later write, Churchill never held himself aloof from the British chiefs. He routinely critiqued their decisions and conveyed to them in general political terms where they ought to steer the British war effort. "He would dictate 'directives' for them to consider. . . . They were the instruments by which Churchill sought to direct the conduct and strategy of the war."[12] Sometimes he listened when they argued against some plan or other of his, and changed his mind. But the engagement with his military chiefs was always close, detailed, intricate, personal, and immediate. By December 1941, after twenty-eight months of war, Churchill and the British chiefs had developed "a sixth sense of understanding common to partners in a long and harmonious marriage."[13] The "marriage" was certainly not always harmonious, but it was far tighter than the relationship between FDR and his chiefs. This difference in both the personality of the two men and their constitutional roles as heads of their respective militaries would be a source for much misunderstanding and suspicion over the weeks of the ARCADIA talks.

When "Bertie" Hamlin arrived at the White House early in the morning on Tuesday, December 23, she was awestruck by how it had changed from the night before.[14] "There is a delicious smell of evergreens all over the house." The gardeners had hauled "tubs of Box trees" onto the portico. Two tall Christmas trees stood guard on each side of the front door. The windows on the lower floor all had wreaths hung in them. The front hall was resplendent with "gorgeous red Poinsettias" in carved stone flower tubs at each door. The Blue Room and East Rooms as well as the West Hall upstairs had Christmas trees, with lights and ornaments. A large "potted Acacia" had also been brought up to the second-floor hall. Small Southern pines and greens completed the transformation of the mansion.

That same morning, Grace Tully, FDR's personal secretary, spied "a chubby, florid, bald-headed gentleman dressed in one-piece, blue denim coveralls and with a big cigar in his mouth"[15] roaming the grounds. She opened the door to the colonnade connecting the White House to the Executive Building, and invited the prime minister to come in. Over a vegetarian lunch of kedgeree and grilled tomatoes, Churchill formally presented Roosevelt with the four memoranda he had written on the *Duke of York*. There was more talk about North Africa and a discussion with American diplomat H. Freeman Mathews, stationed in London but then in the United States, as to the likelihood of the Vichy French leader in Algeria, General Maxime Weygand, betraying Marshall Henri-Philippe Pétain and giving Algeria up without a fight. Matthews thought that highly unlikely.[16]

Later in the day, Churchill changed into more formal attire: a short black coat, striped trousers, and a polka-dot bow tie. At 4 P.M. he joined Roosevelt for his first official appearance in Washington, the president's seven hundred forty-ninth press conference. The "press closet," as it was known, was a small room just inside the entrance to the West Wing of the White House. It was cluttered with tiny desks and battered chairs. Whatever was wood, in the words of David Brinkley, was "blackened with cigarette burns, the walls, ceiling and curtains smoke-stained into a color close to that of an egg yolk." It reeked of "smoke, sweat, whiskey and dust."[17] FDR, the master of the press conference, mockingly warned Churchill that the "wolves" were about to enter the room in "sheep's clothing."

The official occasion of the press conference was for the president to announce the formation of the Office of Defense Transportation under Joseph Eastman to coordinate the nation's rail, road, and water traffic.[18] But it quickly turned into a showcase for the famous visitor.

When reporters in the back of the room could not see Churchill, who was a full head shorter than Roosevelt, the president asked him to stand up. Churchill did him one better, standing up on his chair, to "loud and spontaneous cheers and applause." When asked when he thought the new Allies "may lick these boys," Churchill responded: "If we manage it well, it will only take half as long as if we manage it badly. [*Laughter*]." When asked whether the United States' entry into the war could be construed as another of his "great climacterics," he delighted them with a cheeky, "I think I may almost say, 'I sure do'. (*Laughter*)." When asked whether the fate of beleaguered Singapore was "the key to the whole situation out there," he nimbly sidestepped that thorny issue with a general comment. "The key to the whole situation is the resolute manner in which the British and American democracies are going to throw themselves into the conflict." He delighted the press by suggesting that if the Allies pressed the war vigorously, they might, as in the last war, "wake up and find we ran short of Huns."[19] It was a stunning opener for the prime minister. Columnist Ernst Lindley of the *Washington Post* summed it up well: "Churchill Conquers the Press."[20]

The first full meeting of the two leaders and their chiefs of staff took place at 5:00 P.M. at the White House. After the testy meeting between the "bomber barons"—Arnold and Pound—the night before, it was important that this meeting go well. It did not. The room first selected was too small and it took time to shuffle into the more spacious Cabinet Room. General Marshall was embarrassed that his staff had fumbled such a trivial detail. As well, the American chiefs were still concerned about Churchill's proximity to Roosevelt at the White House. As a result, in the words of Marshall's biographer, Forrest C. Pogue, they went into their first full meeting with the British chiefs "ill at ease, edgy about the Prime Minister's influence over the President and uncertain of their ability to cope effectively with the British proposals."[21] They knew that, in effect, they were about to become players in a game where the British did all the pitching and they would either hit or field the ball as well as they could, or strike out. Their worst fear was that there would be no joint planning at all this afternoon, just more British ideas about a British war to be fought in pursuit of British interests.

Roosevelt opened the meeting with a brief summary of most of what he and Churchill had agreed to the night before. The president then ruminated about action to be taken in each of the major theaters of war: America troops were not going to the "far east at this time"; the British would hold Singapore and the Americans would "build up in Australia" while trying to save the Philippines; and existing British and U.S. transport ships were to be used as, and where, needed without regard to flag. He announced that talks about supply issues would start "in one or two days" and would involve Beaverbrook and William Knudsen, Chairman of the Office of Production Management.[22] Unlike the night before, FDR was strangely ambivalent about North Africa. Again, according to Marshall's biographer, Pogue, "It was the President's opinion that if Germany goes into North Africa we must get there first. On the other hand, we can't take any action that might cause Vichy to turn the fleet over to the Germans."[23] That observation directly contradicted the assurances Roosevelt had given Churchill the previous night.

Churchill followed. He had not come all this way to act the shrinking violet. As he had the night before, he bore in on North Africa. It must be taken. The British had more than 55,000 troops virtually ready to go in. Certainly, the Americans should go into Morocco if they were invited. In any case, he wanted the two staffs to study the issue. FDR agreed. "He considered it very important to morale, to give this country a feeling that they are in a war, to give the Germans the reverse effect, to have American troops somewhere in active fighting across the Atlantic."[24] The president offered no specific dates or troop numbers. Then Roosevelt threw Churchill a curve: major operations in Europe might have to wait until 1944. Churchill had planned for 1942. Was this another Roosevelt prevarication or did he really believe that the Allies would require two years to storm the Continent?

Colonel Ian Jacob, military assistant secretary to the War Cabinet, was impressed by Roosevelt's demeanor, but not by his grasp of strategy, or by the nation's state of readiness:

> The President is a most impressive man, and seems to be on the best of terms with all his advisors. By the side of the Prime Minister, he is a child in Military affairs, and evidently has little realization of what can and cannot be done. He doesn't seem to grasp how backward the U.S. is in its war preparations, and how ill-prepared his army is to get involved in large scale operations. To our eyes the American machinery of government seems hopelessly disorganized. . . . the President is Commander-in-Chief, but he has no proper machinery through which to exercise command.[25]

It was a disappointing meeting. Little had been accomplished. No specific proposals had been laid on the table. While Roosevelt had offered positive rhetoric on the need for action in general and in favor of a landing in North Africa in specific, he had dumped cold water on Churchill's plans to operate somewhere on the Continent in 1942.

The twenty-third of December ended with cocktails in the Red Room at 8 P.M., followed by dinner fifteen minutes later. Mrs. Nesbitt flattered her guest with roast beef and a fine cream pie. Doing his best to gloss over the day's disappointing exchanges of views, the prime minister kept expressing his delight at finding two poached eggs on his breakfast tray that morning—at home he was limited to one per week. Putting the best face on Anglo-American relations, he assured FDR that Scotch whisky and Dundee marmalade would continue to get through to America regardless of the U-boats. And should Roosevelt ever come to Britain, Churchill laughingly stated, he would appoint him Archbishop of Canterbury at the next vacancy.

That same evening, the military men went their own way for dinner. At the Carlton Hotel, Secretary of War Stimson and Secretary of the Navy Frank Knox hosted a formal dinner for the British and American chiefs of staff. It now fell to Stimson to get the difficult first day of meetings behind one and all. The "Great Victorian" rose to the occasion. Stimson toasted the king and stated that ARCADIA was "the fulfillment of our life's dreams of British cooperation." The new allies, in his opinion, would "win both the war and the peace." The secretary allowed that he was well pleased with the first contacts between the two groups. "There was a very hearty spirit of cooperation and good will evidenced on all sides," he concluded, "and not a single note, so far as I could see, intervened to mar the earnest spirit of harmony and endeavor which pervaded everybody."[26] It was typical after-dinner fare, full of good cheer and camaraderie, but it was hardly true.

The news of Churchill's dramatic journey to Washington went around the world. In Berlin, Roosevelt's and Churchill's remarks at their joint press conference on December 23 were closely followed. Propaganda Minister Joseph Goebbels dismissed the press conference as a "media circus" and forbade any mention of it in German newspapers. Neither Roosevelt nor Churchill, he gleefully confided to his secret diary, "could magically make the Pacific Fleet reappear" from the bottom of Pearl Harbor! It was all a "propaganda maneuver." One desperate leader was out to offer sustenance to the other. Adolf Hitler's analogy on December 11 of Roosevelt being like a bald barber recommending a hair-restorer to a customer, Goebbels concluded, applied equally to Churchill.[27]

Goebbels had Churchill's remarks at the press conference in Washington translated and presented to Hitler. The Führer informed an invited inner group of devotees over his usual vegetarian meal that he was delighted that he had taken such a hard line with Roosevelt in his war declaration of December 11, 1941. The American president, he informed his guests, "is truly mentally ill!" The press conference, Hitler stated, had turned into pure theater, "truly Jewish." How could two such "impostors" have deceived a nation such as America? "The Americans," he concluded, "are the dumbest people that one can imagine!"[28]

1. FDR and Eleanor at the President's third inauguration. No other US president had ever been elected to a third term, but Roosevelt earned his victory largely by promising Americans that he would keep the United States out of the war. Until his victory, he did little to aid Britain, but soon thereafter he conjured up the "Lend/Lease" scheme.

2. Between May 26 and June 3, 1940, the Royal Navy, aided by virtually every British boat owner on the southern coast of England, took some 328,000 British and French soldiers off the beach near the French port of Dunkirk. Under constant air attack from the Germans, the Allied soldiers lined up for days, waiting for evacuation. Hitler's failure to allow his ground forces to destroy these troops remains a mystery to this day. The bulk of the British army saved, but most of their equipment lost. "Wars are not won by evacuations" Churchill proclaimed afterward.

3. Though shocked at the magnitude of the damage to his beloved Navy, FDR was galvanized by the December 7, 1941 assault on Pearl Harbor Churchill was relieved. After talking to Roosevelt on the night of the attack he recalled that the "went to bed and slept the sleep of the saved."

4. *Five out of six meals that FDR and Churchill ate together at Argentia were aboard the cruiser USS Augusta. Here FDR is flanked by Churchill and Sir Alfred Dudley Pound, First Lord of the Admiralty (commander in chief of the Royal Navy). Harriman and Hopkins are in the second row on the left next to Admiral King. FDR's dog Falla sits at the president's feet.*

5. The President found both standing and walking with his heavy steel braces an extremely demanding physical chore. Yet every effort was made to keep the truth of his paralysis, caused by polio, from the American public. In photos like the one above, he is often seen standing beside his eldest son Franklin Jr. In fact, Franklin Jr. was always struggling to hold his father upright.

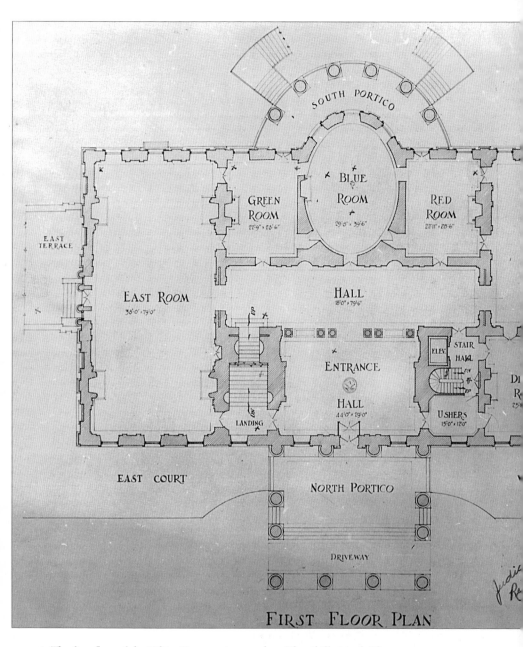

SOUTH PORTICO

BLUE ROOM
29'6" x 39'6"

GREEN ROOM
22'9" x 28'6"

RED ROOM
22'11" x 28'6"

EAST TERRACE

EAST ROOM
36'0" x 79'0"

HALL
18'0" x 79'6"

ELEV. STAIR HALL

DI R

ENTRANCE

HALL
44'0" x 29'0"

USHERS
15'0" x 12'0"

LANDING

EAST COURT

NORTH PORTICO

DRIVEWAY

FIRST FLOOR PLAN

6. The first floor of the White House as it was when Churchill visited. The Blue Room was converted to the current Oval Office (the President's main office) after the war. The Christmas Eve dinner party was held in the Red Room.

7. Though security for the Christmas Eve tree-lighting ceremony was considered heavy at the time, it pales in comparison to measures adopted in the post-9/11 era. Alongside the usual Secret Service complement, a mere thirty six soldiers were detailed to cover the entire White House ground.

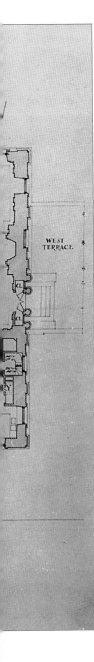

WEST
TERRACE

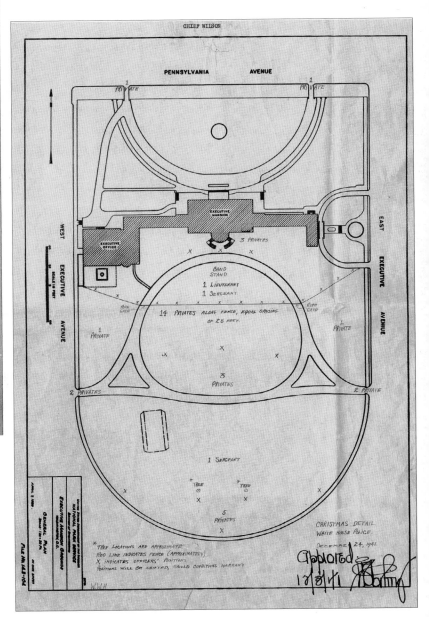

CHIEF WILSON

PENNSYLVANIA   AVENUE

PRIVATE   PRIVATE
1   1

EXECUTIVE
MANSION

EXECUTIVE
OFFICE   3 PRIVATES

WEST   EAST

BAND
STAND

1 LIEUTENANT

1 SERGEANT

EXECUTIVE   EXECUTIVE

14 PRIVATES ALONG FENCE, EQUAL SPACING
OF 25 FEET.

ROAD   ROAD
GATE   GATE

1   1
PRIVATE   PRIVATE

AVENUE   AVENUE

3
PRIVATES

2 PRIVATES   2 PRIVATE

1 SERGEANT

TREE   TREE

5
PRIVATES

* TREE LOCATIONS ARE APPROXIMATE.
RED LINE INDICATES FENCE (APPROXIMATELY)
X INDICATES OFFICERS' POSITIONS
POSITIONS WILL BE SHIFTED, SHOULD CONDITIONS WARRANT

CHRISTMAS DETAIL
WHITE HOUSE POLICE.
DECEMBER 24, 1941

Approved
1/8/41

WWH

UNITED STATES DEPARTMENT OF THE INTERIOR
NATIONAL PARK SERVICE
Branch of Plans and Design

EXECUTIVE MANSION GROUNDS
WASHINGTON, D.C.

GENERAL PLAN
SHEET 1 OF 3 SH.

APRIL 5, 1935

SCALE AS SHOWN

FILE No. 148-704

8. *Unlike Churchill, Beaverbrook was no fan of long sea voyages; he preferred the much shorter discomfort of flight. At the Argentia conference, he flew to meet Churchill and the British party who crossed the Atlantic on the battleship HMS* Prince of Wales.

9. *Churchill appears worn-out arriving at the White House after dark on December 22. He had spent a long day at sea on HMS* Duke of York, *followed by a night flight from Hampton Roads Gate, Virginia, to the Anacostia Naval Air Station just outside Washington. But a long evening of dinner, drinks, and an initial private meeting with FDR still lay ahead.*

10. Churchill and Roosevelt answer questions from the press the day after Churchill's arrival. When asked how long it would take the Allies to win the war, Churchill replied: "If we manage it well, it will only take half as long as if we manage it badly." Everybody laughed.

11. The "press closet," as it was called, was just inside the entrance to the west wing of the White House. David Brinkley recalled that it reeked of "smoke, sweat, whiskey and dust." FDR's black arm band commemorated his mother Sara Delano Roosevelt who had died on September 7, 1941.

12. *On Christmas morning Churchill and FDR went to Foundry Methodist Church accompanied by Lord Beaverbrook (left) and Eleanor (between Beaverbrook and Churchill). FDR observed: "It is good for Winston to sing hymns with the Methodists."*

13. *Churchill maintained only a distant relationship with God. He rarely attended church and religion was not a significant influence in his life. Roosevelt was far more religious.*

14. *Churchill and Roosevelt visit George Washington's tomb at Mt. Vernon, Virginia, on New Year's Day, 1942. Roosevelt is supported by his long-time political advisor Edwin "Pa" Watson. Churchill laid the wreath, tied with red, white, and blue ribbons, against the mausoleum. The act was symbolic of the new "special relationship" forming between the two countries; 1776 lay far in the past.*

15. General George C. Marshall (left), Chief of Staff of the U.S. Army, quickly emerged as the central figure among the American and British chiefs of staff. Here he appears to control the discussion with Admiral of the Fleet Sir Alfred Dudley Pound, First Sea Lord (or commander-in-chief) of the Royal Navy.

16. *"Lighting Up"* *The cartoon was featured in the January 5, 1942 edition of the* Vineland N.J. Journal. *In a less health-conscious age, both men used tobacco products as trademarks. FDR was rarely seen in public without his cigarette and holder held at a jaunty angle; Churchill didn't so much smoke his large Cuban cigars as use several of them a day for props.*

8

CHRISTMAS IN WASHINGTON

THE TINY ISLAND GROUP OF ST. PIERRE AND MIGUELON LIES BUT twelve miles west of Newfoundland's Burin Peninsula. In December 1941 the islands were under the jurisdiction of Vichy France and was a powerful radio station used both for communication with the Vichy Government and for broadcasting Vichy propaganda to the millions of French-speaking Canadians who lived in New Brunswick and Quebec. Virtually every convoy bound for Britain from the east coast of Canada passed to the south of St. Pierre and Miquelon, sometimes in sight of the islands, almost always within range of their fishing boats. There was, therefore, a constant worry on the part of the Allied navies that Britain-bound convoys were being spied on and their course and speed passed on to German U-Boat headquarters. But what to do? The Americans were eager to maintain good relations with the Vichy regime. The British did not want to anger the Americans—or the Free French—by seizing the islands themselves. The Canadians did not want to get anyone angry.

On December 24, 1941, the Free French acted. Admiral Émile Muselier, Free French leader Charles de Gaulle's minister of the marine, led a small force of three corvettes and a submarine from St. John's, Newfoundland, to St. Pierre and Miquelon. They seized the islands at gunpoint. Almost immediately Muselier held a referendum and received overwhelming approval from the islanders for their trans-fer from Vichy to Free French control. Muselier acted on the direct orders of de Gaulle—who had assured his British hosts that he would not move against the islands without their agreement. In fact, however, in de Gaulle's "assertively legalistic, assertively nationalistic mind"[1] he harbored the belief that the fate of St. Pierre and Miquelon was a purely French internal affair despite the wider war. Thus he took "complete responsibility" for the occupation and instructed Muselier not to say a word about it "to the foreigners." Presumably, he meant Canada, Britain, and the United States.

Canadian prime minister William Lyon Mackenzie King was "shocked to hear" that Muselier had "taken possession" of the islands. He worried that the seizure might "prove to be a very critical business" and was "terribly annoyed as well as distressed by it."[2] While the Canadian government almost immediately expressed its official "shock and embarrassment" to Washington, Admiral Georges Robert, the Vichy naval commander at Martinique, demanded that the Free French be evicted at once. Robert was not a man to be trifled with—he had in his possession not only the entire French gold reserve of $384 million (close to $10 billion in 2005 dollars), but also a tidy fleet consisting of an aircraft carrier, a fast cruiser, eight smaller warships, fifteen merchants ships, and 106 American-built aircraft. These assets stood squarely in the path of the Allies' vital supply route of crude oil from Venezuela to Aruba and Trinidad, where it was refined and then transshipped to Britain and the United States. There was a further complication: Admiral William D. Leahy, U.S. ambassador to Vichy France, cabled Washington that Pierre Laval, Field Marshall Pétain's on-and-off-again deputy at Vichy, had been informed by Berlin that the Germans viewed the seizure of St. Pierre and Miquelon "as an argument for the entry of Axis troops into Africa."[3] The seizure took on menacing proportions.

At the heart of what should have been a mere tempest in a teapot in December 1941 was almost universal hatred of Vichy in the United States, rather than support for de Gaulle. A public opinion poll of Americans in December 1941 revealed that fully 63 percent had no idea who he was. But with the capture of he islands, Americans were delighted that someone, somewhere had finally scored a triumph over the Axis. To date the news had been all bad. After Pearl Harbor, the Japanese had taken Guam and Wake Island, Tarawa and Makin; they were about to complete their seizure of Hong Kong; they were advancing down the Malay Peninsula toward Singapore; and they had driven

General Douglas MacArthur off Luzon. Not surprisingly, the press had a field day extolling Muselier's caper. The *Christian Science Monitor* called it a "Beau Geste." The *New York Times* depicted the "bloodless investiture" of the islands as "a display of style and manners in the best tradition of Alexander Dumas." And the *New York Post* spoke of it as bringing "great joy this Christmas Day."[4] But Secretary of State Cordell Hull was furious. Muselier and de Gaulle, in his view, had destroyed the Department of State's complex South American policy in general, and its careful cultivation of Vichy France in particular.

Cordell Hull was Franklin Roosevelt's most senior advisor.[5] Born in a rented log cabin near Brydstown in then Overton (now Pickett) County, Tennessee, on October 2, 1871, the third of five sons of William and Elizabeth Riley Hull, young Cordell grew up with his father's logging business. In the foothills of the Cumberland Mountains, he acquired, in the words of biographer Julius W. Pratt, "a highly effective profane vocabulary" as well as a "rich accumulation of homely anecdotes."[6]

Hull was admitted to the Tennessee bar in 1891 and, after service in the Spanish-American War as a captain of volunteers, was elected to a Tennessee judgeship in 1903. From that time on, he was nicknamed "Judge." But his avocation was politics, and he served in the House of Representatives from 1907 to 1921, and again from 1923 to 1931. In 1917 he married Rosetta Frances Whitney. A champion of President Woodrow Wilson's idealism and progressivism, Hull in 1913 helped engineer the Sixteenth Amendment of the Constitution, empowering Congress to tax incomes. During the Great War, he developed a lifelong hatred of international trade barriers, which, he firmly believed, had caused the war.

Hull was elected to the Senate in 1931, and the next year helped secure the crucial California vote for Roosevelt at the Chicago convention. FDR repaid that favor in January 1933 by offering Hull, by now a powerful leader of the critical Southern wing of the Democratic Party, the post of secretary of state. If Hull lacked experience in foreign affairs, he at least looked the part of a statesman: six feet tall, lean, with sparse white hair, high forehead, large nose, and dark piercing eyes. From the start, he was determined that the State Department would not become "the football of domestic politics." His relations with the president were formal and professional.

By all accounts, Judge Hull was a moralist, an idealist inflexible in his views and stubborn in their execution. He did not take kindly to opposite points of view and did not work smoothly with others. He had a disconcerting habit of speaking in absolutes, which he took to be the essence of foreign policy. He hesitated to move on difficult issues, loved pedantry in his subordinates, and subjected many a staff member to verbose moralizing. Whenever backed into a corner by Roosevelt, he threatened resignation. He never overlooked injuries, real or perceived, and in Washington he developed a strain of "self-pity and querulousness." A workaholic who arrived in the office at nine every day and kept his door open to all callers, Hull each night carried work home to his apartment in the Carlton (and later the Wardman Park) Hotel and worked Sunday mornings as well. The dignified Hull hated the social life of Washington, and he avoided attending the theater, opera, balls, concerts, receptions, formal dinners, cinemas, and even ballparks. His sole diversion from work was croquet, which he liked to play on Secretary of War Henry Stimson's lawn. Tuberculosis dogged him throughout much of his life. More than almost anything else, he disliked the press.

Hull had strongly shared President Wilson's international outlook and had vigorously supported the founding of the League of Nations. As secretary of state, he enunciated a number of "pillars of peace": lowering trade barriers, disarmament, nonaggression, respect for international law, and nonintervention in the internal affairs of other states, to name but a few. He worked hard to shape the Good Neighbor Policy toward Latin America. He stood in the forefront of those who fought to abolish Britain's system of "imperial preferences" as the price for American aid after 1939. He was morbidly suspicious of British imperialism in general and of Winston Churchill's brand of imperialism in particular. On the other hand, convinced that the threatening war would not be "another goddam piddling dispute over a boundary line," but rather an attack on global peace by "powerful nations, armed to the teeth, preaching the doctrine of naked force and practicing a philosophy of barbarism," Hull staunchly favored immediate aid to wartime Britain. For he, the supreme moralist, had to admit, however reluctantly, that power shaped world politics. "I thought for a time, while talking to

Axis diplomats, that they were looking me in the eye," he conceded, "but I soon discovered that they were looking over my shoulder at our armed forces and appraising our strength." His hope of running for the presidency in 1940 was cut short by FDR's decision to seek an unprecedented third term.

Hull's role in shaping national policy decreased as war clouds approached. Roosevelt dominated U.S. foreign policy, especially with regard to Europe, and bypassed his secretary of state by way of a host of special envoys to the Continent's capitals. Hull played little or no role in the destroyers-for-bases deal in 1940 or in the staff conversations with the British in early 1941, and he was not invited to accompany the president to Argentia in August 1941. Left to deal almost alone with Imperial Japan's expansionist ventures in China and against the British, Dutch, and French colonies in the Far East, an angry and tired Hull, now seventy years old, in November 1941 had decided, in his own words, "to kick this whole thing over." In short, he had accepted the risk of war with Japan. And now, in December, the Free French had made a mockery of his foreign policy, enunciated at an inter-American conference in Havana in July 1940, that the U.S. would tolerate no seizure of territory in the Americas by force.

Admiral Muselier's St. Pierre and Miquelon caper attracted no attention at the new Federal Reserve Building on Constitution Avenue on the morning of Christmas Eve 1941. There, at 10:30 A.M., the American and British chiefs of staff gathered in the board room for their second meeting, to formulate a grand strategy to deal with Germany and Japan, not to settle petty squabbles among the French. Above all, they were there to establish more amicable relations than had been evidenced by the Portal-Arnold talks of December 22, and to get down to the specific issues of a developing wartime alliance that had been glossed over at the first meeting of Churchill, Roosevelt, and their respective staffs the day before.

The meeting proceeded cautiously and soon turned into an informal and rambling three-hour review of twenty-two items on the common agenda. The Americans had chosen Admiral Harold "Betty" Stark, U.S. chief of naval operations, to take the lead at the session.

Stark enjoyed both seniority and prestige, and the affection of the president. He was known to prefer compromise to confrontation. He had ample experience working with British leaders, including Churchill, Pound, and the First Lord of the Admiralty, A. V. Alexander. Unlike Admiral Ernest King, he was determined to establish harmonious relations with the British chiefs of staff from the start of the ARCADIA conference.

Stark tried to set a positive note right at the beginning of the meeting by allaying once again British fears that America would concentrate against Japan. Although "much has happened" since the ABC-1 Staff discussions of February–March 1941, Stark stated, "our view remains that Germany is still the prime enemy and her defeat is the key to victory."[7] He went on to describe Britain as "the fortress which must be protected at all cost." But then he slipped: he informed the British chiefs that two Marine Corps observers "had come to the conclusion that [the United Kingdom's defenses] left much to be desired."[8] The atmosphere in the room chilled considerably. However intended, Stark's observation was deeply insulting to the British. After all, they believed, it was the Americans who had been caught napping at Pearl Harbor and then, inexplicably, in the Philippines. John Dill replied icily that "the defences were constantly being improved."

Stark next announced that in future American bombers sent to the United Kingdom would be flown into combat by American crews organized in American formations. "Hap" Arnold of the U.S. Army Air Forces was delighted. Air Marshal Portal objected strenuously. "This had not been the original agreement." His aim, as everyone knew, was to absorb American bombers into the Royal Air Force (RAF). Arnold retorted coldly that the Americans would fulfill whatever commitments they had previously made for individual planes for the RAF, but that was that. The American Army Air Forces were coming.

The naval discussions proceed no more smoothly. The British delighted in pointing out that the U.S. Navy had no destroyers to spare and, in fact, needed to borrow British escorts "for coastal patrol work." They reminded the Americans that Admiral King still refused to adopt a convoy system for their East Coast, Gulf of Mexico, and Caribbean Sea traffic. Even the American promise, at Britain's request, to put troops into Iceland was conditional: the occupation would be only temporary, the U.S. forces to be relieved by British formations as soon as possible.

The discussion then touched on Africa. The Americans agreed to move into North Africa—as the president seemed to want—but only if they could put a large enough formation together and if they could "occupy North Africa without difficulty."[9] It was hardly the ringing endorsement of policy that the British desired. Dill thereupon repeated Churchill's pledge that Britain was ready "to move on 23 days' notice" to put an expeditionary force of 55,000 men into the region and he pressed for an American commitment to the operation, dubbed GYMNAST. General Marshall replied cautiously. In essence, Roosevelt's chief of staff played a delaying game by raising all sorts of American materiel shortcomings from guns to ammunition that stood in the way of a quick landing in North Africa.[10] In his steady, steely way, Marshall was placing himself at the center of the Anglo-American strategic debate.

George Catlett Marshall was born on the last day of 1880 in Uniontown, Pennsylvania, where his father owned a prosperous coking business that supplied the Pittsburgh steel industry. Not particularly good in school in any subject save history, Marshall was denied an appointment to the U.S. Military Academy at West Point and instead at age sixteen went to the Virginia Military Institute. His older brother Stuart had already graduated from VMI and feared that sending George there might disgrace the family name. Undoubtedly encouraged to excel by this grievous cut, George graduated first captain—that is, as the highest-ranking cadet on campus, in the class of 1901. He promptly married his sweetheart, Elizabeth Carter "Lily" Coles.

Thereafter came the usual tours of duty: with the 30th Infantry Regiment in the Philippines, at Fort Reno, at the Infantry and Cavalry School at Fort Leavenworth, at the Army Staff College, with the Massachusetts National Guard, at Forts Roots and Crocket, and back to the Philippines. Then the Great War broke out. Promoted to captain in July 1917, Marshall served with the American Expeditionary Forces (AEF) in France, first as director of training and planning for the 1st Infantry Division, later as chief of staff of the VIII Corps.

Promoted to AEF headquarters at Chaumont, he honed his problem-solving skills during the St. Mihiel operation. As First Army chief of operations, Marshall won the nickname "Wizard" for his logistical brilliance during the Meuse-Argonne campaign, moving 220,000 soldiers out of the western line and replacing them with 600,000 newly trained recruits—mostly by night. When General John J. Pershing berated Marshall's superior for the low level of training for the recently arrived draftees, Marshall informed the commander in chief of the AEF that he had been unfair and harsh in his judgment. Fortunately for Marshall, Pershing not only took the rebuttal well, but promoted Marshall to the rank of colonel in 1918 and appointed him as his aide-de-camp from 1919 to 1924.

The interwar years brought both happiness and sorrow. First, George and Lily was sent to Tientsin, China, where he commanded the 15th Infantry Division and labored to learn Chinese. In 1927 he returned home as instructor at the Army War College. These happy days were shattered by Lily's collapsed and unexpected death after surgery that year. Friends arranged for Marshall to begin a new assignment, that of assistant commandant of the Infantry School at Fort Benning (1927–1932). There, his staff included such future stalwarts as Omar N. Bradley, Joseph W. Stilwell, Matthew B. Ridgway, and Walter Bedell Smith. And there he met an actress and widow, Katherine Boyce Tupper Brown, whom Marshall, at age fifty, married in 1930. He was now the father of three teenage children.

The Great Depression of 1929 brought Marshall into direct contact with poverty—and with relief work. First in South Carolina and then in Washington State, he established work camps as part of Roosevelt's Civilian Conservation Corps (CCC). This would stand him in good stead in later years when he had to work with FDR's "welfare tsar," Harry Hopkins. In October 1936 Marshall was promoted brigadier general; two years later he returned to Washington, DC, as head of the War Plans Division, General Staff. His career prospects were bleak. First, the rules dictated that the head of the Army—Marshall's lifelong dream—could be no older than sixty upon appointment, and George had just turned fifty-eight. Second, he was now seven years from mandatory military retirement. And most discouragingly, thirty other generals, many with higher rank, had announced their candidacy for the top post. The appointment first as deputy chief of staff and then as acting chief of staff seemed to him to be merely marking time until retirement.

But fate intervened. Just as he had tackled Pershing in France in 1917, Marshall now showed his mettle in tackling Roosevelt. When the president raised with senior generals a bold scheme to build 10,000 airplanes for national defense, and even to "lend" them to Britain and France in case of war in Europe, all the Army brass hats present agreed—save one. In what his colleagues saw as a potentially career-ending move, Marshall bravely reminded FDR that he had not set aside the money required for all the related maintenance equipment and that he lacked the pilots for these planes. As they exited the White House, the generals bid fond farewells to Marshall. Five months later, Roosevelt appointed Marshall chief of staff of the United States Army.

George Marshall was sworn in to the top post on September 1, 1939—the day that Adolf Hitler's armies invaded Poland. Marshall commanded but some 200,000 troops; the United States ranked eighteenth militarily in the world. But Marshall brought to the job a sterling reputation for honesty, integrity, and hard work. He led by example and expected others to do the same. When once asked his politics, Marshall responded that his mother was a Republican, his father was a Democrat, and he was an Episcopalian. That disinterest in politics greatly endeared him to Roosevelt.

Marshall, in the words of his biographer Forrest C. Pogue, was a man "capable of burning or freezing anger," which he fought to keep "under strict control." He spoke with candor and frankness, was "impatient of verbiage," and had little patience for commanders who displayed what he called "localitis"—that is, blindness to the needs of theaters other than their own. Dwight D. Eisenhower appreciated Marshall's constancy: the chief of staff, he announced, "stood like a rock." Dean Acheson lauded the general's "immensity of integrity" and the "loftiness and beauty of his character." And Pogue, after writing a four-volume biography, left a sketch of Marshall as a "leader with great self-certainty, born of experience and self-discipline, an ability to learn, a sense of duty, a willingness to accept responsibility, simplicity of spirit, character in its broadest form, loyalty, and compassion."[11]

Marshall needed every ounce of that sense of responsibility and compassion at ARCADIA. His senior advisor on grand strategy, General Stanley D. Embick, had warned him not to be seduced by British entreaties concerning North Africa. Embick, who had served on the Supreme War Council in 1917–18, saw a North African expedition as being "motivated more largely by political than by sound strategic purposes." Put differently, the British were out to lure the Americans into helping them to conquer North Africa. An American commitment at this time, Embick concluded, "would prove to be a mistake of the first magnitude."[12] Marshall and his planning staff had no desire to change the ABC-1 Staff "Europe-first" strategy into a British "Mediterranean-first" strategy.

The Christmas Eve joint staff meeting adjourned after three hours. Colonel Ian Jacob of the British Ministry of Defence was no more impressed by the American chiefs now than he had been after the first conference. "There was no agenda and the first thing Admiral Stark, who was in the Chair, did was to run through the notes he had made at the previous day's meeting. . . . We of course had our minutes prepared, and it was a complete waste of everyone's time to go all over the ground again." Jacob was dismayed at the disorganized state of the American staff, but worse, at the obvious jealousy they showed in guarding their own bailiwicks.

> Their ideas on organization and ours are wide apart, and they have first to close the gap between their Army and Navy before they can work as a real team with us. . . . The Americans are like we were in the days of [World War I commanders] Jacky Fisher and Kitchener. Personalities each pushing their own ideas, and no real cooperation.[13]

Despite the divisions that had surfaced almost immediately in the staff talks, the American public welcomed Churchill that Christmas Eve like a long-lost relative. "A son returning to his mother's land," crowed the *New York Times*. Carnations and irises arrived for him at the White House, as did hundreds of boxes containing some 8,000 cigars. There was even a six-foot-tall V sign made of lilies. Other gifts deluged the White House mailroom as well as the British Embassy. They included a box of onions, catnip for the Churchill cat, bottles of vintage brandy, gloves, socks, cravats, religious tracts, defense bonds, and the like.[14] In time, the Secret Service decreed that only gifts from specially cleared people would be accepted as there was no way to X-ray the flood of packages for poison injected by syringe.

"This is a strange Christmas eve," Churchill later recorded in his memoirs. The world was locked in a "deadly struggle" with "the most terrible weapons which science can devise"[15] deployed from the gates of Moscow to the walls of Hong Kong. Far off in the Pacific, the American garrison on Wake Island surrendered to the Japanese invasion force. In then still largely Anglo-Saxon, Protestant America, Christmas Eve was a most special and holy day. Above all, the war was far away from Washington, DC. No bombing. No air raid sirens. No blackout. No rationing. At 4 P.M. Franklin and Eleanor Roosevelt received the household staff as well as Crown Prince Olaf and Crown Princess Martha of Norway in the East Room. Each White House employee received an autographed photograph of President and Mrs. Roosevelt. Thereafter, the presidential party moved out onto the South Portico. Some 15,000 to 20,000 Washingtonians had crowded the streets surrounding the White House for the twentieth lighting of the National Community Christmas Tree. FDR pushed a button and the tree broke into a blaze of colorful lights. The Marine Band enhanced the brilliant spectacle by striking up "God Save the King" and "The Star-Spangled Banner."

First to speak that evening was The Most Reverend Joseph Corrigan, rector of Catholic University in northeast Washington. "Hear a united people, girded for battle," he intoned, "dedicate themselves to the peace of Christmas." He asked for special supplications for "all who hold power over human life."[16] The president was up next. He reminded what he called "fellow workers for freedom" as well as nationwide radio listeners of his proclamation that January 1, 1942, be celebrated as a day of prayer, as a day "of asking forgiveness for our shortcomings of the past, of consecration to the tasks of the present, of asking God's help in days to come." In lighting Christmas candles across America, he asked the nation for "particular thoughtfulness of those, our sons and brothers, who serve in our armed forces on land and sea, near and far—those who serve for us and endure for us." Roosevelt then turned the festivities over to Churchill, whom he introduced as "my associate, my old and good friend."[17]

Soon, the familiar defiant tones broke over the White House grounds. Churchill did not disappoint:

> Whether it be the ties of blood on my mother's side, or the friendships I have developed here over many years of active life, or the commanding sentiment of comradeship in the common cause of great peoples who speak the same language, who kneel at the same altars and, to a very large extent, pursue the same ideals, I cannot feel myself a stranger here in the center and at the summit of the United States.

He felt a "sense of unity and fraternal association" with his Anglo-Saxon brethren in the United States, which convinced him that he had "a right to sit at your firesides and share your Christmas joy." He assured them that "no greed for the land or wealth of any other people, no vulgar ambition, no morbid lust for material gain at the expense of others has led us to the field." He asked them just for this night to "cast aside" the "cares and dangers" of the moment, so that the children could enjoy "an evening of happiness in a world of storm." He reminded the gathered throng that "formidable years" of strife and sacrifice lay before them so that their children would not be "robbed of their inheritance or denied their right to live in a free and decent world." Above all, Churchill intoned, this was the children's time. "Let the children have their night of fun and laughter. Let the gifts of Father Christmas delight their play."[18] By now it was dark. A crescent moon hung low and a single star glowed in the sky.

As Washingtonians headed home with their last-minute shopping parcels firmly in hand, the presidential party moved back into the White House for tea and toast and cakes at 5:40 P.M. Twenty minutes later, Churchill, Roosevelt, Navy Secretary Frank Knox, Admiral Pound, and Colonel Hollis excused themselves from the social events for a short talk. There was urgent business to discuss.

That day news had at last arrived of the fall of Hong Kong, while American troops on Luzon in the Philippines had been forced back to their secondary line of defense at the Agno River. Churchill had received an urgent message from Field Marshal Archibald Wavell, commander in chief of British forces in the Far East, asking for reinforcements. Wavell wanted a British brigade en route to Colombo, Ceylon, aboard a U.S. Navy transport, the *Mount Vernon*, to be diverted to Singapore. Roosevelt agreed. He then reflected that it was unlikely that the American reinforcements bound for the Philippines via Australia would be able to break through. Thus, the president casually opined, they should be used "in whatever manner might best serve the joint cause in the Far East." He and Churchill instructed their two staffs to meet the following day "to consider what measures should be taken to give effect to his wishes."[19] Colonel Leslie Hollis, secretary to the British chiefs of staff, wrote up his notes of the meeting then sent them to Colonel Walter Bedell Smith, secretary to the War Department general staff, to pass on to Generals Marshall and Eisenhower.

The business of the evening concluded, Lord Beaverbrook and Charles Wilson joined the small social gathering in the Red Room. It had been fully renovated in 1937 in the neoclassical taste of the Federalist era. Red damask covered the walls, on which had been hung presidential portraits. It was sparsely furnished, with one long rose damask sofa and four crimson damask armchairs, all reproductions in mahogany by W. & J. Sloane of New York.[20] Eleanor Roosevelt broke the magic of the moment. Perhaps due to the absence of her children, or to the stress of the Churchill visit, or to the presence of the flirtatious and statuesque Princess Martha (there by the president's personal invitation), she allowed herself to slip into a jealous tiff. Had he called Marguerite "Missy" LeHand at Warm Springs, she asked Franklin. Surely, his former social secretary, confidant, and "surrogate wife," to whom he had given half his estate in a new will just the month before after she had suffered a stroke, was waiting for the sound of his voice wishing her a Merry Christmas. FDR replied, as cold as ice, that he had *not* phoned Missy and that he had no intention of doing so.[21] Deeply hurt, Eleanor later tearfully confessed to her friend, Joseph Lash, that her husband "seemed to have no bond to people. Not even his children. Completely political person."[22]

Churchill, upon entering the Red Room, had immediately sought out his doctor. "It has all been very moving," Wilson recalled Churchill "lisping with excitement." It was a "new war," one with Russia rallying at the gates of Moscow, "Japan in, and America in up to the neck." But Churchill admitted that he had "palpitations" during his speech at the tree lighting ceremony. His pulse was "a hundred and five."[23]

The New York financier Bernard M. Baruch joined the Christmas Eve party in the Red Room for dinner. Henrietta Nesbitt had managed a fine American treat of baked Virginia ham, finished off with crackers and cheese as well as ice cream. Baruch had brought a special bottle of brandy, which the president served after dinner. Churchill teased FDR that "his wings must be sprouting because he was so generous as to share it [brandy] instead of hoarding it for himself." One of the American dinner guests, Percy Chubb, recalled that Roosevelt was in "a buoyant mood." As was Churchill. The prime minister delighted one and all with verbal sallies through great clouds of cigar smoke. He chastised FDR for having sent Britain "too many powdered eggs," which were good only for making Spotted Dick. "Nonsense," Roosevelt charged in reply, "you can do as much with a powdered egg as with a real egg." Chubb then gingerly asked, "How you could fry a powdered egg?"[24] Churchill was triumphant.

"Every night we drink to the health of the United States and Great Britain," "Bertie" Hamlin noted, "and then to the common cause."[25] Churchill, she noted in her diary, had made his way through eight glasses of champagne. After dinner, Wilson joined Harry Hopkins in the Lincoln Bedroom. He was shocked by Hopkins' physical appearance. "His lips are blanched as if he had been bleeding internally, his skin yellow like stretched parchment and his eyelids contracted to a slit." Hopkins gave the appearance of being a "Methodist minister," but then surprised Wilson with a feast of whiskey and oysters.[26] It had been a moving night for all.

Christmas Day 1941 was a mixture of more social events and more hard work. The Thursday morning began for all houseguests and aides with an interfaith service at the Foundry Methodist Church. "It is good for Winston," the president chortled, "to sing hymns with the Methodies." The building chosen was also historically significant. When British forces took Washington in the War of 1812, Henry

Foxhall had vowed that if his cannon-making foundry were spared, he would build a church as an offering of thanks. The present building was the second or third to bear the name Foundry Church. It was a pleasantly warm day with temperatures breaking the sixty-degree mark, more like Easter than Christmas. Company "M" of the 176th Infantry had guarded the grounds of the Foundry Methodist Church since December 22.

The cavalcade motored from State Place to LaFayette and Farragut Squares, up 17th Street to Church Street, all the while "surrounded by bevies of G-men armed with Tommy-guns and revolvers."[27] The president wore a dark business suit, the prime minister a short black coat and striped trousers. The Reverend F. B. Harris gave prayers for the British visitor, leading "his valiant people even through blood and sweat and tears to a new world where men of good will may dwell together, none daring to molest or make afraid." Special altar lilies reminded the worshippers of the recent death on September 7 of the president's mother, Sara Delano Roosevelt. Among the hymns sung was one that was new to Churchill, "O Little Town of Bethlehem." Its middle stanza fit the moment: "Yet in thy dark street shineth; The everlasting light; The hopes and fears of all the years; Are met in thee tonight." The services took Churchill's mind, if only for a moment, from the darkness of the war. "I am glad I went," he confided to Wilson. "It's the first time my mind has been at rest for a long time."[28] At the White House, the prime minister was presented with a traditional Southern treat— broiled sweetbreads and candied sweet potatoes.

The good cheer at 1600 Pennsylvania Avenue was absent at the War Department. There, early in the day, Marshall and his new assistant war plans chief, Eisenhower, had "exploded in wrath" when they received from Bedell Smith what they termed Colonel Hollis' "rather astonishing document" summarizing the "conclusions" that had been reached by Churchill and Roosevelt the night before at the White House. How, they wondered, could the president have agreed to even consider diverting American troop transports from the Philippines to Singapore without consulting his military staff? Obviously, the British were up to their old tricks of first dividing and then exploiting American counsels. Hollis' memorandum only reinforced their suspicion of

British intentions, and their fear of Churchill's ostensive power to charm the president.

Marshall was furious. He had always had to control his quick and fiery temper. Eisenhower was simply overworked to the point of fatigue. Still, there was no time to waste. Marshall at once aired his concerns to Stimson. No one, the secretary of war assured Marshall, had consulted the War Department about this. Stimson was as seized with the apparent British perfidy and FDR's alleged betrayal to it as were Marshall and Eisenhower. Already upset that "sunshine loving American" boys were about to be sent off to "dreary" Iceland to relieve British forces there, he was in no mood for more British conniving. "Extremely angry" over the "astonishing document" by Hollis that the generals had read to him, he spent his lunch hour at home mulling over Marshall's revelation. He grew angrier by the moment. Had FDR untethered another of his infamous "trial balloons"? Or was there real substance to Marshall's claims?

As his rage grew, Stimson decided to call Hopkins at the White House and tell him about the memorandum. If what Marshall had just told him was true, Stimson informed Hopkins, "the President would have to take my resignation." Hopkins, "surprised and shocked" by the secretary's stance, at once consulted both Churchill and Roosevelt. They assured him that no such agreement had been put in place.[29] Roosevelt was no doubt stunned at this revelation of the very thin line that still separated cooperation from deep suspicion in the minds of his military leaders. He would have to deal with this at the first opportunity. He ordered a special meeting of the American chiefs for later that day, right after the joint British-American meeting scheduled for 4:00 P.M.

At the State Department, Judge Hull was also having a bad Christmas Day. He was still incensed over the Free French seizure of St. Pierre and Miquelon the day before. He poured oil on the flames by issuing a statement, drafted by Samuel Reber of the State Department, that "three so-called Free French ships" in "an arbitrary action contrary to the agreement of all parties concerned" had seized the islands.[30] He then lectured an uncaring nation that the Havana Conference of 1940 had specifically outlawed the use of force to affect the transfer of property in the Americas held by belligerent nations. The press reacted with what the stubborn old Tennessee mule called "a violent attack on the State Department and me." Editors turned the "so-called Free French" phrase against him by writing of the "so-called State Department" and the "so-called Secretary of State." The *New York Post* accused him of "treason" by trying to "prop up Vichy against Hitler." Walter Lippmann in his syndicated column spoke of Hull having created a "little, diplomatic Pearl Harbor."[31]

Hull took the slights as personal insults. To date, he had been largely exempted from the vituperations that the press had heaped on Roosevelt, Hopkins, and Treasury Secretary Morgenthau. Now, he had become the "target" of editorials and radio attacks. He accused de Gaulle of being a "marplot" acting against the wishes of the Allies, and Churchill of funding de Gaulle's "propaganda" against the United States.[32] He detected in the entire matter a Canada–Free French conspiracy, tantamount to a personal betrayal. The American ambassador in Ottawa demanded that Canada take back the islands and turn them over to the Vichy French.

That afternoon at Fort Myer the Marshalls entertained the British guests—Lord and Lady Halifax, Lord Beaverbrook, Dudley Pound, "Peter" Portal, and John Dill—at a midday feast. When Katherine Marshall belatedly discovered that December 25 was Dill's birthday, she moved heaven and earth to find a cake. She feared that any produced by her cook "could have sunk the Admirals and the entire British Commission." Thus, she turned the task over to Sergeant Powder, the general's orderly, who found not only a cake at a downtown Washington bakery, but also the last set of American and British flags along with birthday candles at a five-and-dime. After the main course, it was time to cut the cake. Sir John was deeply moved. It was the first time since he was a small boy, he allowed, that anyone had so honored him. When he removed the flags, he discovered to everyone's amusement that on their staffs were stamped the words "Made in Japan!" All the while, the quarters were tightly surrounded by a Secret Service detail. When a messenger from Western Union arrived to deliver a "Happy Birthday to You" singing telegram for Dill, the G-men intercepted him.

In the West Hall of the White House the afternoon of Christmas Day was consumed with "great excitement" as the children of the Norwegian royal couple and Diana Hopkins opened presents wrapped and tied with colorful paper and ribbons. There were games and dolls and boats. Fala ran about the room not knowing what the "noise and confusion" were all about. Churchill and Roosevelt merrily assisted the children in unwrapping the countless gifts. Franklin gave Eleanor Willa Cather's last novel, *Sapphira and the Slave Girl*. The president, for his part, had to open about fifty presents that included pajamas marked with his initials, a leather jacket, sweaters, slacks, slippers, clocks, books, and handkerchiefs. Fala received rubber cats, mice, and balls as well as collars, leashes, and boxes of dog food.

Somehow, FDR found a moment at 2:30 P.M. to compose a brief Christmas message to Clementine Churchill. He sent her "warmest Christmas greetings," informed her what a "joy" it was to have Winston in Washington, and thanked her "for letting him come." By separate cover, he had sent Mrs. Churchill "a box of delicious foods" and what she called "feminine accessories!"[33] Later on, as the president mixed cocktails for the prime minister and his staff chiefs, Churchill read him a passage from "Psalm" 112: "He shall not be afraid of evil tidings: his heart is fixed, trusting in the Lord." Churchill proudly opened a fresh box of cigars that he had ordered up from Cuba. FDR lamented that his finest cigars had to be burned as they were found to have worms in them.

Thereafter, the two leaders attended to business. Having jointly drafted the Atlantic Charter at Argentia, it was now time to craft another joint resolution. Every word had to be weighed carefully. "How to describe all the countries, great and small, conquered or free," Elliot Roosevelt later remembered. Were they "allied" or "associated" powers?[34]

At 4 P.M. on Christmas Day the American and British chiefs of staff huddled in conference once again. Marshall used the previous night's apparent decision by FDR to divert the *Mount Vernon* to Singapore as an entrée to the larger topic of what troops should go where in the Far East. He told the British that there could be no question of diverting reinforcements bound for the Philippines until he had received clarification of the situation there from the local commander, General MacArthur. To this Portal laconically replied that "it was difficult for any man on the spot to make a decision relative to the disposal of his own means," and that the decision needed to be made "here by the responsible group."

Portal's remark gave Marshall an opening to put a completely new idea on to the table:

I express [this] as my personal views and not those as a result of consultation with the Navy or with my own War Plans Division. As a result of what I saw in France and from following our own experience, I feel very strongly that the most important consideration is the question of unity of command. . . . I am convinced that there must be one man in command of the entire theater—air, ground and ships. We cannot manage by cooperation.

By moving toward a system of unified command now, he told his colleagues, "it will solve nine-tenths of our troubles."[35] Portal and the British chiefs were stunned by this abrupt turn of events. Deeply annoyed, Portal lectured Marshall that allocation and disposition of forces needed to be addressed first. Admiral Stark, uninformed about Marshall's planned foray in this matter, remained noncommittal. After a painful silence, Admiral Pound averted further rancor by suggesting that the issue be referred to the staffs' Planning Committee. The meeting broke up after barely eighty minutes. The third plenary session of the joint staffs had gone no better then the first two.

The Americans then met alone with the president at the White House. After a rather routine discussion of the situation in the Far East, Roosevelt, in the words of Secretary Stimson, "as if by aside . . . flung out the remark that a paper had been going round which was nonsense and which entirely misrepresented a conference between him and Churchill." Hopkins soothed matters further by informing Stimson that he had already told Roosevelt to go through proper channels with the British. Marshall seemed satisfied, for now. Stimson summed up the brouhaha in his diary: "I think he [Roosevelt] felt that he had pretty nearly burned his fingers and had called this subsequent meeting to make up for it." There obviously had been a failure to communicate in the American camp. All considered, Stimson noted, "This has been a strange and distressful Christmas."[36]

Their labors were interrupted at 8 P.M. by Eleanor's call to dine. She had organized a formal dinner for sixty people, mostly members of the two branches of the Roosevelt families, as well as Henry and Elinor Morgenthau, Halifax, Olaf and Martha of Norway, and Dill. Betty Hight, one of Eleanor's close friends, was stunned by the magnificence of the setting. "Can you imagine," she wrote her family, "we ate with gold cutlery—that almost floored me."[37] The plates, she recalled, had been designed by FDR. The horseshoe table with square corners had been decorated with "huge bowls of deep red carnations . . . with holly and ivy in between." Gold urns containing fruit were placed "here and there." Each dinner guest had a dish of nuts. After a sauterne wine, champagne was served. To Mrs. Hight's consternation (or delight), "they kept filling the darned glasses." The main course consisted of huge roast turkeys surrounded by sausages, dressing and gravy; dessert, of plum pudding in brandy "with a blue flame all around it." FDR masterfully carved the first bird. Each guest received a small present wrapped in white paper and red ribbon. It was a smashing dinner. "Boy, I really got an eyeful of how the ultra-ultra live," Betty wrote her family, "and I ain't kidding. That gold silverware still amazes me—it's old stuff, too, from [Grover] Cleveland's administration." The gold flatware and gold urns reminded her "of the days before the French Revolution."

Toasts were frequent and eloquent. The president reminded the gathering that the British king and queen had been at the White House two and a half years earlier. That had been the beginning of the coming together of the two English-speaking peoples, which, FDR prophesied, would continue after the war as well. Throughout the meal, Churchill was "silent and preoccupied." British and Canadian forces in Hong Kong had surrendered to the Japanese. Moreover, he was running through his head some "impromptu remarks" for next day's scheduled address to the Congress. Three times he asked to be excused from dinner. He finally took his leave while the dinner party retired to view the film *Oliver Twist*. "I must prepare for tomorrow," were his departing words.

The evening continued without him. Each guest received sheets of music and a "bandmaster" came in and directed carols, starting with "O Come, All Ye Faithful." Next came newsreel films of the two leaders. Eleanor delighted in "baffling" and "mystifing" her British guests with what she called "the complications" of the Roosevelt family relationships. How could she explain to someone, she mused to Beaverbrook, "that the lovely lady sitting opposite him is your husband's half-niece, that she married your first cousin, and that he was her sixth cousin, whereas you are married to your fifth cousin once removed, and are also her sixth cousin?" FDR was in fine fettle that evening. He reminded Wilson of "a schoolboy, jolly and carefree."[38]

Churchill was unusually nervous as he trudged back to his room to finish his speech. Outside a light drizzle fell on Washington. Far to the north a train carrying the Canadian prime minister and his three defense ministers raced through the night to Washington. Mackenzie King had a meeting scheduled for the afternoon of the twenty-sixth with Secretary Hull. No one could be sure how far Hull was going to push his ludicrous insistence that Canada reestablish Vichy control over St. Pierre and Miquelon, nor how much this minor tempest would affect the main talks. Churchill knew well that the meetings between the chiefs of staff were not going well. Each side was probing and testing the other. Suspicion and misunderstanding—as evidenced by the American reaction to the Hollis memorandum—ruled. Not even a hint of a truly joint war effort was beginning to emerge at the all-important operational level. Furthermore, the issue of how Allied war production was to be allocated had not been discussed at all, and it was bound to be highly contentious. Two of FDR's top men, Stimson and Hull, seemed bogged down in anger and confusion over the current state of the talks.

Although the American press and public had embraced Churchill, his biggest test at ARCADIA so far lay on the morrow, when he would face the Congress, with all the (recently converted) isolationists who still sat in it. He was well aware that a strong tide was running in Washington—in the Congress, in the press, and even in some of the highest quarters of the military—to turn in vengeance against Japan and to abandon for the moment the strategy of taking on Germany first. The fate of ARCADIA hung in the balance and a strong burden lay upon Churchill to save it.

9

A PRODIGOUS PACE

A T NOON ON FRIDAY, DECEMBER 26, 1941, A MOTORCADE TOOK Winston Churchill from the back entrance of the White House to Capitol Hill. Franklin Roosevelt remained at the presidential mansion, not wishing to draw attention away from his guest. He would listen to Churchill over the radio in the Oval Room. The American escort captivated Charles Wilson as the prime ministerial party dashed "through the streets with the siren wailing and two G-men on each of the running boards, their pockets bulging with revolvers, ready to jump off in a second if anything happened." In a small waiting room beside the Senate Chamber, Churchill rehearsed his speech. "Do you realize," he asked Wilson, "we are making history?"[1] The prime minister was apprehensive. He knew that among the 531 senators and representatives were countless isolationists, Anglophobes, and Roosevelt haters. How would they receive him?

Standing at the podium of the House of Representatives with his fingertips under the lapels of his coat, the Great Orator at once hit the right note. "I cannot help reflecting that if my father had been American and my mother British, instead of the other way around, I might have got here on my own."[2] Barely had the cheering died down when with passion he asked of, "What sort of people do they [the Japanese] think we are?" This allusion to Pearl Harbor brought the house down. "Is it possible they do not realize that we shall never cease to persevere against them until they have been taught a lesson which they and the world will never forget?" The Congress rose as one and stomped and cheered. It was vintage Churchill. David E. Lilienthal, chairman of the

Tennessee Valley Authority, called the roar "the first sound of blood lust I have yet heard in the war." At times during the passionate speech, Lilienthal noted in his diary, Churchill "made a growling sound that sounded like the British lion!"[3]

But then Churchill slipped. He simply could not help moralizing about America's self-imposed absence from European affairs after 1919. "If we had kept together after the last war, if we had taken common measures for our safety, this renewal of the curse need never have fallen upon us." The cheers turned to polite sporadic applause. And when Churchill continued the history lesson, he was met with stony silence. "Five or six years ago it would have been easy, without shedding a drop of blood, for the United States and Great Britain to have insisted on fulfillment of the disarmament clauses of the treaties which Germany signed after the Great War." But Churchill reclaimed the moment when he promised the Congress that "the task which has been set is not above our strength, its pangs and trials are not beyond our endurance." At 1:05 P.M., after a moment of silence, the *Washington Post* reported, the Congress on its collective feet gave out a mighty "roar."[4] They had witnessed a magnificent drama. When Churchill gave them his famous V sign, they returned the victory salute. The Secret Service reported to Secretary of the Treasury Morgenthau that Churchill spoke at the rate of 108 words per minute and that he was interrupted precisely seven times by applause and laughter.[5]

"Sweating freely," Churchill confided to Wilson that "a great weight" had been lifted off his chest. He had successfully passed his second public inspection in America. Back at the White House and well satisfied with his performance, he paced up and down the garden and crowed, "I hit the target all the time."[6] In Berlin, Hitler was less generous. Churchill's "vulgar-demagogic address" to the Congress, he informed Propaganda Minister Goebbels, was a "prime example of demagogy, a mixture of braggadocio and hidden fear."[7]

Canadian prime minister Mackenzie King missed Churchill's speech. His train pulled into Washington's Union Station shortly after 3:45 P.M. He was met by General Edwin "Pa" Watson, FDR's military aide, and driven to the Mayflower Hotel to rest up before seeing Secretary Hull at the State Department. He was well aware that St. Pierre and Miquelon would be the secretary of state's number one concern.

Mackenzie King had had a warm relationship of sorts with Roosevelt—who called him "Mackenzie"—since the late 1930s. It was by no means a relationship of equals. FDR was somewhat condescending to him though Mackenzie King himself seemed unaware of it. He was awed by Roosevelt, as he was by Churchill, though he took second place to no one when it came to defending Canada against real or perceived slights to independent status. But the Canadian was not a favorite in Washington journalistic or diplomatic circles. He was too circumspect, too noncommittal, too elusive. A popular ditty at the time went, "William Lyon Mackenzie King; never told us a goddamn thing."[8]

Mackenzie King met Judge Hull late in the afternoon before proceeding to the White House for tea with Roosevelt and Churchill. As Mackenzie King noted in his diary, Hull approached the St. Pierre and Miquelon affair carefully. "He suggested that we might appoint a Commission of four, or so many experts, to look after the wireless [on St. Pierre], and that Churchill might put out the Free French, restoring the old order." Hull evidently had been told by his ambassador in Ottawa that there was simply no way Canada was going to do the dirty work he wanted done; maybe Mackenzie King would help him get Churchill to do it. The Canadian wanted no part of such foolishness: "I told him it would not do to have the [Vichy] Governor restored, as he was pro-Axis, and his wife a German. I also mentioned that while we had nothing to do with the [seizure], Canadian feeling was relieved and pleased with the de Gaulle accomplishment." In fact, he told Hull, many Canadians had been very unhappy that Mackenzie King had tolerated the situation on the islands; they had accused him of "leaning too much toward Vichy." "Whatever was done," Mackenzie King made clear, it "[c]ould not appear that we were sacrificing the Free French."[9]

The two men then together went to the White House, where Roosevelt poured tea for himself and the Canadian. Mackenzie King, never a big drinker, had sworn off alcohol for the duration. Churchill had a scotch and soda. After greetings all around and some light banter, FDR turned to St. Pierre and Miquelon. He asked where Émile Muselier had obtained the ships for the attack. Mackenzie King assured the president that the admiral "had come with ships of his own." There was more discussion. At one point Churchill mused that while he endorsed the Free French generally, he was prepared to take de Gaulle "by the neck," tell him that he had "gone too far" this time, and "bring him back to his senses." But Roosevelt and Churchill wanted to be rid of the matter before it developed into a "serious question."[10] FDR hinted that he and Hull might take a crack at some sort of compromise proposal on St. Pierre and Miquelon in which an Allied commission would supervise the radio on the islands.

Before Mackenzie King left the White House, he and Churchill discussed arrangements for a quick visit to Ottawa the following week. Churchill would leave on Sunday, December 28, his railway car attached to the Canadian prime minister's train, and return to Washington on New Year's Day. He would make a speech to the Canadian Parliament, but he did not want too much else placed on his schedule.

Roosevelt and Churchill might have thought Hull was now placated over the St. Pierre and Miquelon affair—but he was not done with it by a long shot. Over the next day or so Hull continued to pester Mackenzie King and tried to push him to get directly involved. At a meeting the next day, Hull told King that

> he thought both the President and Mr. Churchill had yesterday been headed in the wrong direction . . . they had not realized what it would mean if the American Government lost touch with Vichy, and if the South American republics got the idea that the U.S. was countenancing force in any way.[11]

It was extraordinary for Hull to complain to a foreign leader that his president was following the wrong course on a key foreign policy issue—American relations with Vichy France—because he was so miffed about the seizure of the islands. Churchill would later write of the whole episode: "Mr. Hull . . . in my opinion pushed what was little more than a departmental point far beyond its proportions. The President in our daily talks seemed to me to shrug his shoulders over the whole affair. After all, quite a lot of other annoyances were on us or coming upon us."[12]

"The pace here is prodigious," Charles Wilson would note in his diary on Sunday, December 28.[13] With that single sentence he accurately encapsulated the frenetic pace of discussions that took place across Washington in the days between Christmas and Churchill's departure for Ottawa. With the holidays behind them, the British and American chiefs of staff went back to work at the Federal Reserve Building. Having merely sparred at the first three joint-staff talks, it was obvious to all that the time had come to get down to the business of planning and conducting a global war. The subsidiary Joint Planning Committee, working under the direction of U.S. Admiral Richmond K. Turner, labored almost around the clock to deal with all contentious matters referred to it by the chiefs. The Joint Planning Committee, in turn, established a number of subcommittees to hammer out the nitty-gritty details. The mountains of position papers generated by the committees and subcommittees threatened to bury the planners themselves. "What in the world is going to become of all the 'papers' that were written on this war?" Harry Hopkins queried Admiral Pound in January 1942. "I hope I never have to look at one again!"[14]

"Each day in Washington was much like another," Colonel Ian Jacob recalled. "Meetings, telegrams to be dealt with, minutes to do, telephonings to make future arrangements and much traveling hither and thither in a car. The only peaceful time of the day was breakfast." For the British staff, the schedule seemed unrelenting. Up at 7:45 A.M., bathing and dressing before breakfast, then a sally to the office in the British Embassy Annex by 9:15 A.M. The chiefs would invariably meet each morning, sometimes with Churchill, sometimes with the Joint Staff Mission based at the embassy. Then, back to the hotel for lunch. "There is not much difference between British and American food," Jacob observed, "except that there is always too much of the latter. If you ordered meat, you get a slice which spread over the whole plate. The steaks were about 1½ inches thick and wide in proportion. The ice, too, is overdone."

After lunch, the British and American chiefs sometimes met in mid-afternoon; meetings with Churchill and Roosevelt took place at the White House in late afternoon. Jacob later described a typical meeting in the Oval Room: "The President sat at his desk, with the Prime Minister in a chair on his left hand side, and the rest of the company perched in chairs and sofas in a rough semi-circle facing him. No tables or anything, and very awkward for looking at maps or taking notes." The president's Scottish terrier was in the room at the first such meeting and had the temerity to bark in the midst of one of Churchill's orations. Fala was ejected. "I can't think he liked it much," Jacob recalled, not specifying whether he was referring to Fala or to Churchill.[15]

George Marshall shared with his sister a sense of the chaos and anxiety of the times. "We have been very busy during the so-called 'holidays'—a decided mis-nomer this year." Washington, he went on, was "full of all the rank of the British armed forces and we go from conference to conference on the dead run."[16] His assistant chief of the war plans division, Eisenhower, wrote his friend General LeRoy Lutes about the "mad house" that the War Department had become:

> [I]t is now eight o'clock. . . I have a couple hours' work ahead of me, and tomorrow will be no different from today. I have been here about three weeks and this noon I had my first luncheon outside of the office. Usually it is a hot-dog sandwich and a glass of milk. I have had one evening meal in the whole period.[17]

Joseph W. Stilwell, called to Washington by Marshall to command a possible operation at Dakar, on December 26 shared with his wife the chaos that reigned at the War Department:

> My impression of Washington is a rush of clerks in and out of doors, swing doors always swinging, people with papers rushing after other people with papers, groups in corners whispering in huddles, everybody jumping up just as you start to talk, buzzers ringing, telephones ringing, rooms crowded, with clerks all banging away at typewriters. . . . Everybody furiously smoking cigarettes, everybody passing you on to someone else—etc., etc.

How to create order out of chaos? "Vinegar Joe" had the answer: "Someone with a loud voice and a mean look and a big stick ought to appear and yell, 'HALT. You crazy bastards. SILENCE. You imitation ants. Now half of you get the hell out of town before dark and the other half sit down and don't move for one hour'. Then they could burn up all the papers and start fresh." But the general knew the nature of bureaucracies too well to expect change. "Well, to hell with 'em."[18]

One of the most important of the post-Christmas meetings among Roosevelt, Churchill, Beaverbrook, and the chiefs of staff convened at the White House at 4:30 P.M. on December 26. Secretary of War Stimson saw this as "a sort of interim conference to see how the Chiefs of Staff had been getting on in their conferences." He thought "everything [was] going pretty well."[19] It was not. Marshall and Dill opened the meeting by reporting to the president and the prime minister the progress, or lack of it, that the military leaders had made in their discussions about strategic priorities.

On principle, the Americans were not prepared to make recommendations on priorities in Allied strategy. They believed that "limitations on shipping and naval escort vessels made it impossible to carry out the North African plan, and simultaneously relieve the British forces in Ireland and Iceland."[20] Marshall restated what was now the formal American military position: there were simply not enough troops and not sufficient shipping to send an expedition to North Africa while at the same time relieving British forces in Iceland and Northern Ireland. Roosevelt was solidly behind him. The time "was not ripe at present" for North Africa; it most likely was at least "three months away."

Churchill was angry. He made little effort to hide his impatience. The Americans had moved two million doughboys to France in five months during the First World War; why could they not do it again? He was "reluctant to take No for an answer because of shipping." Beaverbrook suggested that the 80,000-ton luxury liners *Queen Mary* and *Queen Elizabeth* be used as troop transports. Churchill intoned that "a large battleship" might carry up to 10,000 men per trip. Roosevelt seemed to make a mockery out of British concerns with his suggestion that the problem be solved by "sending small groups of men, possibly 50 to a boat," with each of the eastbound convoys then plying the waters between the United States and Britain.

The president at once realized that his comment had annoyed the British. Quickly changing the subject, FDR asked what progress had been made on the matter of unity of command in the rapidly deteriorating Southwest Pacific theater. Marshall told Roosevelt that he had raised the matter, but that it had not cropped up again in today's talks. FDR wanted it considered. He did not think the Allies were getting the best use of their forces in the Far East. Churchill seemed to recoil instinctively at the idea of a single commander, on the spot, who would control the American, British, Dominion, and Free Dutch militaries on land, at sea, and in the air. Perhaps he feared American domination; he knew the Americans would insist on taking the lead in the war against Japan. He was almost reconciled that they would. But so soon?

He opened the attack. It simply was not practical. Troops in that theater were in some cases separated by a thousand miles. How could any single person control them? And with what resources would they fight? The war should be controlled from here, from Washington, not there. He tried to move the discussion away from the issue by suggesting that he and the president might talk about it later, in private. But FDR insisted on pushing it. He asked if the Dutch had a good commander out there, perhaps implying that they might take control. Churchill restated his objection. "Unity of command is all right where there is a continuous line of battle, such as existed in France in the [First] World War, but . . . the situation in the Far East is not the same."

Secretary of the Navy Frank Knox disagreed. He thought Churchill was wrong. But Churchill had a secret ally in the American camp. Unknown to Knox or to Marshall at that point, Admiral King, the new U.S. Navy commander in chief, was vigorously opposed to the notion. "I have no intention whatever," he later wrote, "of acceding to any unity of command proposals that are not premised on a particular situation in a particular area at a particular time for a more or less particular period." Above all, he worried that a "single commander" would find it most difficult to reconcile "the various national interests."[21]

The meeting adjourned at 5:30 P.M. The chiefs left the White House; Hopkins, Roosevelt, and Churchill went in for dinner. Roosevelt presided over the customary round of cocktails. Thereafter, the White House kitchen presented rack of lamb with asparagus and cauliflower, pineapple salad, and chocolate pudding. The sumptuous meal, Churchill needled the Americans, reminded him about how the British had found a prepared meal sitting on the White House stoves before they burned it down in 1814! Obviously, Churchill was trying to defuse the tense atmosphere.

After dinner, FDR invited his guests to the upper hall to see the latest Humphrey Bogart movie, *The Maltese Falcon*. Later, he and

Churchill returned to more serious topics. "Last night the President urged upon me to appoint a single officer to command the Army, Navy and Air Force of Great Britain, USA and Dutch," Churchill wired London the next day.[22] "You will be as much astonished as I was to learn that the man the President has in mind is General Wavell."

The idea to raise Archibald Wavell's name had come from Marshall. His reasoning was simple: with mostly British or Commonwealth territory (Australia and New Zealand) at stake in that theater, it would be very difficult for the British to accept an American commander. If the commander must then be British, Wavell was the logical choice. He had tasted both success and failure in Africa and the Middle East. He knew how to command large bodies of troops. He knew India. His appointment would put to rest any fears Churchill might have had that an American might pull troops out from the defense of Singapore.[23]

In fact, FDR much wanted an American, preferably Douglas MacArthur, for the job. At a meeting the following day with Stimson, Marshall, and Arnold, the president argued that the commander of the Far East ought to be an American, because "an American would be accepted more readily by the Australians and the Dutch than any Britisher."[24] He was apparently well aware of the bitter feelings that had developed between Churchill and John Curtin, the recently installed prime minister of Australia, over reinforcements for the region. The British considered Curtin to be taking a "narrow, selfish and at times a craven view of events."[25] How did FDR know this? Churchill was not inclined to discuss Commonwealth family quarrels with Roosevelt, especially at a very important conference where each side looked for advantage over the other. One way FDR could have known about the difficulty was through American interception and decrypting of British diplomatic radio traffic.

Eleanor Roosevelt was never around when these discussions took place. On the night of December 26 she absented herself as the men went in to see *The Maltese Falcon*. She was growing ever more concerned about the developing bond between the president and the prime minister. While she wanted to use the war to both expand and deepen New Deal social programs as well as to extend them beyond America, they wanted simply to win the war. While she thought Churchill to be "loveable & emotional & very human," as she wrote her daughter Anna Boettiger, "I don't want him to write the peace or to carry it out."[26] She worried that Winston was keeping Franklin up far too late into the night, over far too many brandy snifters and cigars. The prime minister had taken over her house, her staff, and now seemingly her husband.

Eleanor expressed her growing fears to several old friends. One was Martha Gellhorn, a journalist who had covered the Spanish Civil War for *Collier's Weekly*. Both she and Eleanor feared Churchill's growing influence on FDR. "I never liked Winston Churchill," Gellhorn wrote. "I always thought nobody enjoyed the war as much as he did." There was too much "derring-do and rushing around" with him, too much the "boys' book of adventure bit." Both she and Eleanor "saw the same thing—theater, lots of glory, having a wonderful time, too. And the President thought that was fun; Winnie was fun; Winnie came to dinner in his boiler suit, which was just as big a fake as possible."[27]

Lorena Hickok, a former aide to Hopkins and a prominent journalist in New York, was Eleanor's most intimate friend. On December 26 Eleanor confided to "Hick" her deepest fears about Churchill—his philosophy, his influence on the president, and his views of the future.[28] "I've talked much with the P.M. He is a forceful personality—but the stress on what the English speaking people can do in the future worries me a little." Churchill reeked too much of power. "I don't trust any of us with too much power," she informed Hickok, "and I want the other nations in too!" Eleanor had listened to Churchill's address to the Congress and admitted that she was "troubled" by the prime minister's repeated calls for an Anglo-Saxon-dominated postwar world.

Eleanor's grandson, Curtis Roosevelt, reported much the same. "She saw in Churchill a male tendency to romanticize war." There seemed to be a parallel with the Roosevelt presidents in the White House. "She had a memory of Teddy Roosevelt caring about the environment and social progress but then getting totally caught up in the Spanish American War."[29] Was the second Roosevelt heading down that same path? Churchill loved war too much for Eleanor's liking. Was Franklin being seduced by Winston's tales of adventure and "derring-do"? Her worst fears were confirmed one day as she passed by the map room. There she spied the two men through the doorway, deeply engaged in military discussions. "They looked like two little boys playing soldier," she lamented. "They seem to be having a wonderful time—too wonderful, in fact. It made me a little sad somehow."[30]

When Churchill went to bed on the night of the twenty-sixth, it was cold outside but hot and stuffy in his bedroom, despite the air-conditioning unit installed in the fireplace. After trying unsuccessfully to sleep, he got up to open the window. It was stuck. He strained to get it to move. He pushed hard. It resisted. He kept pushing, with "considerable force," as he told Wilson the next day. Suddenly, he lost his breath. He noticed a dull pain over his heart, a throbbing down his left arm. He gave up on the window and immediately went back to bed. The pain eased, but he worried about it all night.

It was cool the next morning and the streets of Washington were dry. After breakfast, Wilson took a walk, returning to the hotel at about 10 A.M. There was an urgent message: he was wanted at the White House at once. He took a taxi. Racing up to the second floor, he found the prime minister in bed, looking worried. "It was hot last night and I got up to open the window," Churchill said.[31] "It was very stiff. I had to use considerable force and I noticed all at once that I was short of breath." He then told the doctor about the "dull pain" starting over his heart and flowing down his left arm. "What is it?" Churchill asked. "Is my heart all right? I thought of sending for you, but it passed off." Wilson took out his stethoscope and listened to Churchill's heart. He also did some "quick thinking," knowing that the prime minister would demand blunt answers. Regardless of whether an "electro-cardiograph" examination might reveal a coronary thrombosis, Wilson knew that "his symptoms were those of coronary insufficiency." The medical books called for six weeks of rest for such a case. This, he quickly determined, was out of the question. The press would have a field day announcing to the world "that the P. M. was an invalid with a crippled heart and a doubtful future." Joseph Goebbels would revel in a propaganda coup! Could he keep this to himself? Wilson wondered. What if he did nothing, and Churchill had a second, possibly fatal, heart attack? "The world would undoubtedly say that I had killed him. . . ." America, he thought, needed the prime minister at this critical time. "There is no one but Winston to take her by the hand." But what to tell the prime minister? To gain time, he again listened to Churchill's heart.

"Well, is my heart all right?" Churchill demanded to know. Wilson made a political decision. "There is nothing serious. You have been overdoing things."

Churchill pressed him. "Now, Charles, you're not going to tell me to rest. I can't. I won't. Nobody else can do this job. I must." The prime minister demanded to know what had taken place. "What actually happened when I opened the window? My idea is that I strained one of my chest muscles. I used great force. I don't believe it was my heart at all."

The physician soothed his restless patient. "Your circulation was a bit sluggish. It is nothing serious. You needn't rest in the sense of lying up, but you mustn't do more than you can help in the way of exertion for a little while." At that moment, Hopkins knocked on the door. Wilson slipped out of the bedroom. The world would not learn until Wilson—as Lord Moran—published his memoirs in 1966 that Churchill had suffered from angina pectoris (deficient oxygenation of the heart muscles) the morning of December 27, 1941, in Washington.

Reassured by his physician, Churchill invited Marshall to the White House to talk over the matter of unity of command.[32] Marshall came before noon and found the prime minister "propped up in bed with his work resting against his knees," the "ever-present cigar in his mouth or swung like a baton to emphasize his points." Aware of the psychological height advantage that he thus enjoyed, Marshall paced up and down the bedroom as Churchill growled out his position. A ship was a very special thing, he lectured the general, and thus one could hardly expect the navy to place it under army command. Becoming more belligerent by the minute, Churchill demanded to know what an army officer could possibly know about handling a ship. Marshall, who until now had remained calm and in control, became hot under the collar. "What the devil does a naval officer know about handling a tank," he hurled back. But, Marshall assured Churchill, he was not interested in turning sailors into tank drivers. He had set his sights much higher. "I told him I was not interested in Drake and Frobisher, but . . . in having a unified front against Japan, an enemy which was fighting furiously. I said if we didn't do something right away we were finished in the war." Obviously annoyed at Marshall's persistent strong stance, Churchill rushed off to the bathtub. When he reemerged, glowing pink and wrapped only in a bath towel, he snarled at Marshall that he would have to "take the worst with the best." Fearing the worst, Marshal left.[33]

At least Churchill was delighted at the Americans' "broadminded and selfless" proposal to put Archibald Wavell, commander in chief of the British Army in the Middle East, in command in the Far East.[34] He told Halifax, Pound, Dill, and Portal the next day that "he most strongly desired" Wavell in that job. The British chiefs were not nearly as delighted. As Colonel Ian Jacob noted in his diary, "They foresaw inevitable disasters in the Far East, and feared the force of American public opinion which might so easily cast the blame . . . on to the shoulders of a British general."[35] For the next day or so, Churchill and FDR outrivaled each other in their insincerity about whether an American or a British commander should be appointed. Publicly, Roosevelt insisted that Wavell take the job. Publicly, Churchill insisted that an American do it for fear of possible adverse effect "on American opinion" if that did not happen.

Then, suddenly, Churchill changed his mind about a unified command. There was merit to Marshall's argument. Moreover, Beaverbrook had worked quietly on Hopkins not to let the issue of "unity of command" torpedo the talks. On a White House memo pad, Beaverbrook scrawled, "You should work on Churchill. He is being advised. He is open-minded & needs discussion."[36] Hopkins took his advice. As Jacob later recorded in his diary, "it was hard for the Prime Minister to refuse to back a principle which was undoubtedly attractive in theory and which was to be applied in a way which recognized the pre-eminence in the field of the choice of a British general."[37] But Churchill was far too wily to appear to give in so quickly, and with no quid pro quo. He would continue to dig in his heels for a little while yet.

10

THE CHIEFS COMBINE

I N THESE FIRST DAYS OF ARCADIA THE MEETINGS OF THE AMERICAN and British chiefs of staff produced more heat than light. After the war, George Marshall would recall that in this early period there "was too much anti-British feeling on our side; more than we should have had. Our people were always ready to find Albion perfidious."[1] This was a startling revelation that he surely arrived at only much later. But it was true, and it hurt the prospects of early and easy British-American military cooperation.

One of the most Anglophobic of the American planners was on Marshall's staff. "Vinegar Joe" Stilwell for two weeks ranted and raved about the British, who, he argued, had "completely hypnotized" Franklin D. Roosevelt and sold him "a bill of goods." The presence of Winston Churchill at the White House had a deleterious effect on the "Big Boy," as the general called Roosevelt, as plan after plan was stood up, abandoned, or altered according to the whims and wishes of the prime minister. "We'll do this, we'll do that, we'll do the other," Stilwell complained. "Blow hot, blow cold. And the Limeys have his ear, while we have the hind tit." Above all, he disliked the sudden emphasis on joint operations and unity of command. Japan had attacked America. Germany had declared war on America. Thus, the Republic on its own ought to "rise up and smite these various brands of bastards." He disliked the arrogance of the British staff and accused them of being at loggerheads with each other. "The 'Senior

Service' [Royal Navy] sits disdainfully aloof. Nobody can command *them*—it isn't done. The arrogant Royal Air Force will have none of it." It was all too much for the feisty general. "And to hell with these 'joint things'. I don't like 'em."[2]

Since his first meeting with "Peter" Portal on the night of December 22, Henry Arnold was able to keep a tight rein on his emotions. Colonel Jacob thought of him as "a cherubic little man, with white hair and humourous blue eyes,"[3] but in Arnold's case looks were deceiving. Despite the benign nickname of "Hap" (short for "happy"), Arnold had a mercurial temper as well as a reputation of being a stern taskmaster. Born on June 25, 1886, in Gladwyne, Pennsylvania, one of five children, young Henry entered the U.S. Military Academy at West Point in 1903. He did not excel, graduating in the middle of his class four years later. Looking for adventure and promotion, Arnold in 1911 accepted a posting to Dayton, Ohio, where he received flight training from the Wright Brothers. Arnold grounded himself from 1912 to 1916 after several crashes injured and even killed close friends. In 1913 he married Eleanor A. Pool, the daughter of a Philadelphia banker. Service with the 13th Infantry in the Philippines established contact with George Marshall. When the United States entered the Great War, Arnold was assigned to the Office of Military Aeronautics in Washington, DC, where he trained many of the Army's pilots. Anxious for action, he did not reach France until after the Armistice.

The interwar years brought a succession of postings to the Pacific Coast, to the Civilian Conservation Corps, and to the Army Industrial College. A disciple of General William "Billy" Mitchell, Arnold testified on Mitchell's behalf at the general's court-martial—and was promptly "exiled," as he put it, to Fort Riley, Kansas, to attend the Command and General Staff School. The 1930s found Hap in a variety of command posts at March Field in Riverside, California. There he cultivated close ties with the science faculty at the California Institute of Technology and with the Hollywood film establishment. In 1934 he led a spectacular flight of ten Martin B-10 bombers on a 5,300-mile round-trip from Washington, DC, to Fairbanks, Alaska, thereby demonstrating the potential of strategic bombing. In 1938 he succeeded General Oscar

Westover, who had died in a crash, as chief of the Air Corps; his title changed to chief of the Army Air Forces in July 1941.

Though universally hailed as the father of the modern U.S. Air Force, Arnold was neither a strategist nor an organizer. He continually micromanaged his office, interfering in the affairs of subordinates, and proved unable to organize an efficient staff. He doggedly set out to establish the Army Air Forces as a separate and independent branch of the services. In this, he constantly collided with battleship admirals such as Ernest King. In December 1941 Arnold, who had been with the presidential party at Argentia, Newfoundland, was thrilled that Roosevelt and Marshall included him in what he called "the major leagues"—that is, the service chiefs. Marshall most likely had done so out of political considerations, namely so that Admirals Stark and King could not outvote him.

Arnold, like many American military men, harbored deep suspicions about British military effectiveness. Throughout the summer of 1940, Colonel Carl Spaatz, assistant military attaché (air) in London, had fed Arnold a steady diet of critical observations concerning the Royal Air Force's performance.[4] With regard to heavy bombing, the RAF failed to use weather reconnaissance planes in advance of major raids and called off operations at the first sign of uncertain weather. Many "frank pilots" had doubts about the effectiveness of night attacks, and still others believed that "excessive centralization of control" had robbed the air war of "flexibility in shifting targets in case of weather." Bombing tactics obviously could be improved. "Bombing so far," Arnold wrote in July 1940, "could be termed harassment over a large area rather than bombing for destruction."

In addition to doubts about the efficacy of British heavy bombing, Hap feared what he was certain were British plans to use his Army Air Forces simply as its pool of reservists and replacements. When the RAF mission to Washington suggested that if and when the United States entered the war, its aircraft and pilots should simply be used "to help build up the depleted strength of the Royal Air Force," Arnold not only blew a fuse but in April 1941 headed off to Britain to get a sense of the air war for himself. He got an earful. British pilots complained bitterly that they simply could not do daylight bombings due to German fighter attacks and antiaircraft fire. He was floored when a British air vice marshal expressed his doubts whether American flyers, who were picking out and landing on tiny atolls in the Pacific with routine efficiency, could even be taught navigation. "A shame that your people don't know how to navigate—that you have to use beams and beacons and such gadgets on all your flights when you won't have them in combat." Meeting with Beaverbrook, Arnold was shocked to discover that the British had little idea about American aircraft production, the type of U.S. air forces then in existence, their plans, planes, and capabilities. The RAF was not using the gyro-stabilized Sperry sight that Arnold had sent it. And Portal simply demanded more: more pressure cabins, more longer-range bombers, and more larger bombers.

From the intelligence staff at the Air Ministry, Arnold learned that the RAF was having "abnormal losses" with its night bombers. During a single night mission by twenty-eight Wellingtons, six had crashed (four with the loss of their entire crews) and three others had not returned. On other missions, the loss ratio was even higher. When the first twenty of the long-awaited B-17 Flying Fortresses arrived from America, even this turned into what Arnold called a "fiasco."

The British had been instructed to deploy the new bombers with caution, for the original "Forts" had only four handheld guns for armament, no computing sights, and no tail guns—just a gunner lying on his stomach and firing rearward through a slit in the tail "bathtub." But the RAF ignored Arnold's admonition to use the B-17 in a "close mass of bombers flying under its own protection, bringing to bear on attacking fighters the mutual defensive fire power of all the .50 calibre guns in the tightly stacked formation." Instead, it "used no formation to speak of," sending the Flying Fortresses out by twos and threes. Most were shot down or failed in their mission. The RAF was asking the lumbering "Forts" when attacked to dive into evasive action—against the much faster German Me-109 fighters.

Over the first four months of deploying the new B-17s, 46 percent of all missions were abandoned. Arnold could not help gloating that the Flying Fortresses had been badly mishandled by the RAF. "[I]t was obvious it was their place to learn; and they didn't." The only positive impression that he came away with was the firm conviction of the bomber barons (and of Churchill) that aerial assaults would so cripple Germany "that it might be unnecessary for the ground forces to make a landing."[5] Such thinking was squarely in line with his own air-power theories.

Admiral Ernest Joseph King, like "Vinegar Joe" Stilwell, was a rabid Anglophobe. But like Hap Arnold, he kept a close rein on his passions during ARCADIA. This was a major accomplishment, because both King's Anglophobia and his flash temper were legendary in the U.S. Navy. Born on November 23, 1878 in Lorain, Ohio, the son of a railroad shop foreman, young Ernest entered the Naval Academy in 1897 and, after brief duty in the Spanish-American War, graduated fourth in the class of 1901. Extremely ambitious and impatient with the Navy's slow rate of promotion, King went out of his way to seek the patronage of senior commanders such as Admiral Hugo Osterhaus and Vice Admiral Henry T. Mayo. King accompanied the latter to Europe during the Great War to inspect American naval forces in Britain and to visit the battle-fields in France.

The interwar years brought personnel cutbacks, laying-up of warships, and lack of career prospects. King tried his hand in the submarine service at New London, Connecticut, and then in the naval air service at Pensacola, Florida. He hated shore billets, loathed bureaucrats, and feuded with his superior officers, whom he deemed to be overly cautious in adapting to new tactics and technology. Back at sea in 1938, King as commander of a three-carrier battle force executed a brilliant air strike against Pearl Harbor, in a bizarrely portentous exercise. But his prospects, like those of Marshall, were poor by 1939. He was now past sixty and his dream of ever becoming chief of naval operations (CNO), the Navy's top post, was a distant mirage. It apparently disappeared completely when President Roosevelt that year appointed Admiral Harold R. Stark CNO; King, in his own words, was "retired" to the Navy General Board.

But Ernest King refused to accept "retirement." He used the General Board as a platform from which to criticize what he perceived to be the Navy's lack of readiness. As a result, he was given command of Patrol Forces, U.S. Fleet, Atlantic, in December 1940. When FDR re-created the defunct Atlantic Fleet, he appointed King its commander in chief in February 1941. The Japanese attack on Pearl Harbor propelled King to the post of commander in chief, U.S. Fleet, on December 30, 1941.

Although he quickly developed a good working relationship with Chief of Staff Marshall, King remained difficult. Two common comments about him were: "He was meaner than hell"; and "He was cold blooded." He was gruff and intransigent. He fought a desperate battle with hard liquor and smoked constantly, cigarettes clasped in a long holder. When given the U.S. Fleet in December 1941, he allegedly commented, "Yes, damn it, when they get in trouble they always send for the sons of bitches."[6] Dwight Eisenhower in a confidential part of his diary summed up the feelings of many: "Admiral King is an arbitrary, stubborn type with too much brain and a tendency toward bullying his juniors."[7]

King had very few fans in the Royal Navy. At one point in early 1942, during discussions over naval arrangements in the Southwest Pacific, a senior Royal Navy officer wrote about him:

> King is not a clever man, he is conceited and at the moment on the crest . . . of the wave. With careful handling he may get over his suspicions of the British ("the ancient grudge"): so long as he feels he has the President behind him, he will stick to his guns. . . . He is notoriously rude.[8]

At one of those talks, King unfairly and with sarcastic language criticized the British for having pushed so hard for a North African landing —only to delay the convoying of troops to the United Kingdom. The British, who were suffering an acute destroyer shortage, protested "with some warmth"; Stark and Marshall "were obviously embarrassed."[9]

Ian Jacob had a far more benign view of King. The secretary to the British chiefs of staff thought the admiral "a dominating personality who looks as if he would be the man to inspire the American fleet with a strong and offensive spirit." In Jacob's view, King had already overshadowed Admiral Stark. Though "Betty" Stark sometimes took the chair in the joint meetings at Washington, he "wouldn't go a yard without being sure of King's backing," the colonel observed. Jacob did allow that King might "be easily roused to obstinacy and pig-headedness."[10]

King was convinced in his heart of hearts of British perfidy and nurtured an untrusting view of the new ally. His attitude toward the

Royal Navy, in the words of one historian, developed "from suspicion to profound distrust to near antipathy." He became so infuriated with the "seeming 'helplessness' of our cousins," the British admirals, that he once informed Stark that the "real war" for the British was the one they were conducting against the U.S. Navy. "I am sure that what they wish in their hearts is we would haul down the Stars and Stripes and hoist the White Ensign on all of our ships." King's major asset, in the words of the military commentator Hanson W. Baldwin, was that he was "a man too rare in any age, a man who could not be had."[11] On the first anniversary of Pearl Harbor, *Time* magazine chose him for its front cover, showing a stern King with two heavy naval guns trained on a rising sun lurking above a black swastika.

At 10:10 A.M. on Saturday, December 27, Roosevelt met with Stimson, Marshall, and Arnold to take stock of the conference so far. FDR filled them in on his discussion the night before with Churchill and his offer to accept Wavell as supreme commander for the Far East. Marshall was still under the impression that Churchill was "dead set" against unity of command. The president shared with them Churchill's "surprise" at Wavell's nomination. They agreed to "start out with Wavell with the understanding that he would be replaced later on."

As Marshall and Arnold started to leave, Roosevelt called them back to share a discussion he had had the previous day with Beaverbrook concerning aircraft production. The minister of supply had chastised the Americans for what he considered to be their low output. Britain, with a population of 40 million and with most raw materials having to be imported, was producing more aircraft than the United States, which had a population three times as great and its own supply of raw materials. Arnold tried to deflate the issue with the rather lame observation that Boeing had almost doubled its production of B-17 bombers. "The President seemed to be greatly pleased about that."[12]

There were still significant differences of opinion dividing British from American military leaders when they filed back into the Federal Reserve Building yet again at 3:00 P.M. that Saturday. But this time, due perhaps to propinquity, or the dawning realization that they had no choice but to fight this war as allies, they began to find common ground.

They started to line up not as British or Americans, but as distinct and separate service chiefs—air force with air force, navy with navy, army with army.

The two air force chiefs set the tone in addressing plans drawn up by Admiral Turner's staff for a North African expedition. Portal informed the group that he was simply "horrified" at the vast number of aircraft contemplated for the operation. It would be a dreadful mistake, he went on, to send "such a large number of planes" to a theater of operations where they might not even be deployed. He called for a "spirit of economy," in other words, for planners to be more realistic and to establish "the minimum number" of aircraft required for operations. He lectured Turner's staff that "the large strategy must be the primary consideration, rather than local requirements."

Arnold backed him up. He too "objected to the large number of planes allocated" to a possible move into North Africa and proposed to send the paper back for more staff work. Marshall agreed and pointed out that America's first operation offshore needed to be a success. "Failure in this first venture would have an extremely adverse effect on the morale of the American people."[13] For the first time during the staff talks, there was harmony of interests.

The chiefs then turned to the issue of "unity of command for the Far East," addressing draft instructions that Marshall had laid out. Since this involved the Royal Navy, the usually somnolent Dudley Pound came to life. The admiral testily asked just what the United States meant by the term "unity of command." Marshall explained the broad implications of his scheme. It would be impossible, he allowed, to find a supreme commander with "full technical knowledge of all services." It was not a perfect world, Marshall observed, but surely it was better to appoint a man with good judgment and effective command over all the Allied forces in the theater than "a man with brilliant judgment who must rely [only] on cooperation." Marshall pointed out that in the Far East they were opposed "by an enemy who has unity of command in its highest sense." Should they not follow this example? Moreover, Marshall, with the advice of Eisenhower, had amended his original blanket proposal for supreme theater commanders to the effect that such commanders acknowledge and protect the distinct local sovereign interests of subordinates, be they Australian, Dutch, or French.

It was now time for the British chiefs to concede the point, however unhappily. Churchill recorded simply, "it was evident that we must meet the American view."[14] No doubt he and his generals had thoroughly discussed what position they would take when the matter was inevitably raised at this meeting. He kept them too much under his control not to have done so. The concession came partly for the reason Churchill stated in his memoirs—the Americans were insisting on it—but also because it was a concession that came with a payoff in Wavell's assumption of the Far East command. Giving in on this, Churchill thought, would also set the stage for important American concessions later on in the conference, or the war.

With American endorsement of Wavell, Churchill also had a powerful lever to ensure that Australian prime minister Curtin, and indeed the rest of the Commonwealth, stayed in line behind Britain in supplying men and resources, but with virtually no say in grand strategy. Wavell would command all Australian and New Zealand forces in the theater, as well as the British, American and Dutch. Then too Churchill had privately conceded that the principle did in fact make good military sense. And it might lead to greater unity of purpose in the one matter that the prime minister held almost above all others—the pooling of resources. Another underlying reason was summarized by Charles Wilson several days later:

> Marshall remains the key to the situation. The P.M. has a feeling that in his quiet, unprovocative way he means business, and that if we are too obstinate he might take a strong line. And neither the P.M. nor the President can contemplate going forward without Marshall.[15]

Therewith, the logjam was broken. Reluctant or otherwise, John Dill led the British turnabout. With regard to Marshall's draft, Dill declared, "The proposition formed a good basis to work on." While some of Marshall's restrictions on local commanders might make it "very difficult for the Commander-in-Chief to exercise command," Marshall's safeguards nevertheless might prevent the commander from exploiting one area of his theater (say, the Dutch) at the expense of another (say, the Australian), thus actually crippling overall operations. However awkwardly put, the British had begun to yield on principle. Marshall leaped at the opening. He fully agreed with Dill and asked the chiefs to remember that he had only tried to be a realist in setting out the restrictions. Yet again, ruffled feathers were smoothed. ARCADIA was shaping a joint course.

Admiral King, despite his earlier private doubts about a joint command, now wanted to move ahead on an outline plan to present to the president and the prime minister. Pound not only agreed, but insisted that the issue was urgent, that they had to get to "a conclusion on the matter immediately." When Stark fully backed Marshall and Pound, the issue was settled. The session ended at 4:30 P.M. Marshall later recalled: "The chief of the naval planners [Turner] rushed to the door to shake hands with me and put his arm around me, which surprised me. And Dill followed me and threw his arms around me, and still another one acted explosively."[16] The conference had achieved its first major breakthrough; many other significant logjams remained.

That night Churchill, Hull, Halifax, and Roosevelt discussed the idea of setting up a "supreme war council." Churchill knew that some sort of high-level military body was going to be necessary to give Wavell his orders. It would also eventually coordinate the overall war effort in other theaters of war when their joint commanders were appointed. But, as with Marshall's unity of command idea, he was determined to move slowly and to wring every concession from the Americans that he could. He knew they would insist that such a council be located in Washington. Both its establishment and its location on the other side of the Atlantic were bound to undercut his tight control over the British forces fighting in far-flung theaters.

The other important issue discussed that night concerned the "Joint Declaration" of Allied war aims that Secretary Hull had been drafting since December 14. It was scheduled to be signed by the Allied nations on New Year's Day. Churchill and Roosevelt had agreed to such a future declaration, based on the Atlantic Charter, when they had met off the coast of Newfoundland in August. When Harriman and Beaverbrook went to Moscow to discuss Lend-Lease with Stalin the month after Argentia, they had first raised the declaration. Stalin was distinctly disinterested, especially when he learned that this statement of allied war aims, unlike the Atlantic Charter, might include a guaranty of "freedom of religion." Hull initially bowed to Stalin's wishes and in his first draft left the apparently offending provision out. But Harry Hopkins insisted that it be put back in and FDR agreed. Hopkins then raised a thorny issue for Churchill, the imperialist: he wanted "the British to decide whether or not India should be included [as a distinct signatory], although for the life of me I don't understand why they don't include it."[17]

Churchill would have none of it. He was irritated that Roosevelt had allowed Hopkins even to raise the India question at that juncture. The Americans quickly dropped the matter, at least for now. After a few minor changes in Hopkins' broader proposal, Churchill approved it. Basically, the document reaffirmed Hull's earlier version: each government would pledge its "full resources, military and economic," to defeat the Axis powers and their satellites, and to continue the war and not to make a separate armistice "with the common enemies or any of them."[18] Later that evening, Roosevelt summoned Maxim Litvinov to the White House. He handed the Soviet ambassador the draft "Joint Declaration" and instructed him to send it immediately to Moscow "for comment."

Roosevelt appreciated fully that although the major focus of the ARCADIA meetings was to forge some sort of unified war effort between the United States and Britain on the basis of the previously agreed "Europe-first" policy, the Soviet Union ever loomed in the background. Neither Roosevelt nor Churchill had any illusions about the signal importance of the USSR in the ultimate fate of the Axis. For months after the German attack, very few people in Washington or London gave Stalin much hope to survive beyond the fall of 1941. But by the time Churchill arrived in Washington, a major Soviet winter offensive on the central front appeared to be a harbinger of German defeat. That gave Churchill and the Americans some real hope, as did the much smaller but symbolically important British victories in North Africa. The immediate objective was to keep Stalin on the Allied side and his armies fighting.

When the Nazis had invaded the Soviet Union the previous June, both Churchill and Roosevelt wasted little time deciding to come to the aid of the USSR. FDR extended Lend-Lease to Stalin, then sent Hopkins to Moscow in July 1941 to evaluate Russian chances of survival. Hopkins decided that the Soviets would survive the German onslaughts, despite their terrible initial loses, and Treasury Secretary Morgenthau had extended an initial credit of $100 million to Stalin. That was later increased tenfold. In September, after Argentia, Beaverbrook and Harriman had gone again. Finally, Stalin demanded from Churchill that Foreign Secretary Eden come to Moscow so that direct negotiations might be conducted between the United Kingdom and the USSR regarding Soviet demands of its western Allies. Eden had long argued for a European-centered British foreign policy based on a Soviet-British alliance. He saw Moscow as a natural ally. Stalin was a leader with whom one could do business and a "satisfied" Soviet Union would be a guarantor of the postwar peace.

Eden had arrived in Murmansk on December 13. Three days later he had his first meeting with Stalin. It did not go well. After a sumptuous champagne dinner, "the wiry Gipsy" got down to business. He wanted to restore the borders of June 1941. "He is ruthless in his views of Europe," Oliver Harvey of the British Foreign Office delegation to Moscow commented on this first meeting with the man of steel.[19] In the words of Alexander Cadogan, who accompanied Eden, Stalin wanted not mere "algebra" from these talks, but "practical arithmetic." Greater Germany was to be dismembered. Czechoslovakia was to be restored. Stalin demanded Bessarabia and the Bukovina. Next, he asked for Soviet bases in Finland and in Romania. Bulgaria was to surrender large tracts of land to Turkey, Greece, and Yugoslavia. Hungary was to cede lands to the Czechs and the Romanians.[20] As a carrot, Stalin "offered" London bases in Denmark and Norway. British Ambassador Stafford Cripps encouraged Eden to accept Stalin's terms.

But this was the sort of deal that Churchill wanted no part of, at least at this stage of the war. It could easily unhinge the talks coming up with Roosevelt in Washington. He had given Eden strict instructions neither to bow to Soviet pressure nor to be won over by sweet Soviet entrapments. "Naturally you will not be rough with Stalin [but] we are bound to the U.S. not to enter into secret and special pacts." The map of Russia's future borders with a conquered Germany would be decided by a postwar peace conference, but

all this lies in a future which is uncertain and probably remote. We have now to win the war by a hard and prolonged struggle. To raise such issues publicly now would only be to rally all Germans round Hitler. Even to raise them informally with President Roosevelt at this time would in my opinion be inexpedient.[21]

Churchill later told Eden in a terse telegram from Washington: "We have never recognized the 1941 frontiers of Russia except *de facto*. They were acquired by acts of aggression in shameful collusion with Hitler."[22]

Stalin mounted his last diplomatic effort on Sunday, December 21, the night before Eden's departure. The British delegation was escorted from the National Hotel through heavy snow to the Kremlin. There, Eden, Cadogan, and Harvey were ushered into the Hall of Catherine the Great. Harvey was stunned by its grandeur. The hall was "of magnificent malachite with marble pillars, a vaulted ceiling white and gold, and cream damask walls." Stalin, wearing a gray uniform, "came paddling in, very like a kindly bear." It was the Great Dictator's sixty-second birthday and so the toasts were numerous and heavy. "The old boy was almost genial," Harvey observed. "We drank and drank—pepper Vodka—which is like fire—wines red and white—champagne and brandy. All Russian wine from the Crimea or Caucasus and we had 36 toasts in all."[23] The British delegation staggered home at 5 A.M. As Eden prepared to depart Moscow, he wired Churchill:

> Our work has ended on a friendly note. Final discussions with Stalin were the best and I am sure that the visit has been worth while. We have allayed some at least of the past suspicions. Stalin, I believe, sincerely wants military agreements but he will not sign until we recognize his frontiers, and we must expect continued badgering on this issue.[24]

Was Eden's note a harbinger of how Stalin might react to the proposed Allied declaration of war aims?

When Roosevelt met with Litvinov after dinner on December 27, Churchill gathered with his chiefs. Despite their apparent agreement with Marshall's initiative earlier in the day, there was still some reluctance to fully embrace the idea of a joint command for the Far East. Mostly, they worried that the president was setting Wavell up for a fall. But Churchill, having accepted Marshall's position, would hear no more of it. He angrily informed them that their negative stance "implied doubt of the motives of the President of the United States and he would not stand for it."[25] In the end, Churchill did as he always did—he made the final decision himself. They would go ahead in principle while seeking the views of the War Cabinet as well as of Churchill's principal military advisor, "Pug" Ismay, and, in London, Alan Brooke, Chief of the Imperial General Staff. Churchill wired Clement Attlee: "Things have moved very quickly. The President has obtained the agreement of the American War and Navy Departments . . . and the Chiefs of Staff Committee have endorsed it." He asked Attlee to be ready to inform the prime ministers of Australia, New Zealand, and South Africa—he would tell Mackenzie King of Canada himself—and to signal Wavell that draft terms of reference would soon be on the way.[26]

The reaction in London was almost universally unfavorable. Brooke's immediate thought was that "the whole scheme [is] wild and half baked and only catering for one area of action, namely Western Pacific, one enemy Japan, and no central control." When the military met later in the day to give Attlee their own advice, Brooke recalled, "[The] more we looked at our task, the less we like it." They were even less happy when they finally saw the draft proposals for the new command. "In the first place Burma is included in the Far East command but *not* China," Brooke noted, which was foolish because Burma had to be the forward supply base and entrance to China, given Japan's occupation of virtually all of eastern China. "Second, Australia and New Zealand are not included." They, like Burma, were inevitably going to be the major forward supply and deport areas for the eventual push to retake the Dutch East Indies and the Philippines. Finally, "the wording was such as to restrict the machinery to too slow a cadence for war purposes."[27]

Churchill, as was his habit, did not wait for full and frank reaction from London. He went ahead on his own. On the twenty-eighth he wired Attlee: "I have agreed with President, subject to Cabinet approval, that we should accept his [unity of command] proposals, most strongly endorsed by General Marshall."[28] Brooke noted in his diary, "Cabinet was forced to accept PM's new scheme owing to the fact that it was almost a fait accompli!"[29] Marshall had won all along the line.

Washington: Sunday, December 28, 1941. It was four weeks since Pearl Harbor and the world was engulfed in war. In the fierce cold and snow of the central front west of Moscow, Russian forces were still driving the Germans back. Farther to the south, however, German attacks against Fort Stalin in the Sevastopol region made good progress. Hitler's commanders were confident that the city itself would soon fall.

In the Philippines, General MacArthur had declared his beloved Manila an open city to spare it from the certainty of destruction should the Japanese have to fight for it. He and his family and staff prepared to leave for the island fortress of Corregidor in the mouth of Manila Bay. There, he would set up his headquarters while American and Philippino forces would continue to resist the Japanese on the Bataan peninsula.

In Malaya, British and colonial forces fought a stubborn but losing retreat down the Kra peninsula while the Japanese continued their island-by-island offensive across the Sulu Archipelago. Even in North Africa, where the battle had been going well for the British, General Rommel's tank forces suddenly turned about and launched a strong counterattack, decimating the British 22nd Armoured Brigade.

In the shopping areas south of the Mall, the streets of Washington were practically deserted. It was Sunday. The larger stores were closed, the Christmas shopping long over. People were at home on this cool but fair day, listening to the morning's lineup of radio news programs or going to church. Some readied themselves for afternoon matinees to see *Week-end in Havana*, *A Yank in the RAF*, *Shadow of the Thin Man*, or *Never Give a Sucker an Even Break*. Near the War and Navy Departments, the State Department, the White House, and the Federal Reserve Building, black sedans came and went amidst tan-colored army coupes or light blue Navy trucks with their canvas-covered cargo beds. The majors, the colonels, and the new brigadier generals who were trying to bring some order to this chaos of a great nation suddenly thrust into war vied at the street hot dog vendors with enlisted personnel who were moving typewriters and desks and office chairs into newly refurbished staff rooms. The radio and newspapers had warned Washingtonians to gird for their first blackout that night.

In mid-morning Roosevelt met with Stimson and Navy Secretary Knox as well as his military advisors to review recent developments. He was pleased to note that Churchill had agreed, "after a struggle," to "include sea, land, and air in unity of command." But had he? The prime minister at the last minute had submitted a draft agreement that had Wavell as supreme commander and an American admiral as his deputy commander in control of the British and Dutch naval forces in the Far East. However, the British naval commander in the Far East would only be "directed" to cooperate with the overall plans and policies of the supreme commander. "Directed" did not mean obliged. Obviously, "former naval person" Churchill was still reluctant to place the Royal Navy's top officer in the Far East in the chain of command, even under a British general.

Marshall was livid. Churchill's revisions went against the agreed-upon principle of unity of command with regard to naval forces. The hard work done at the last meeting of the joint chiefs seemed to be coming unglued. He adamantly demanded that Churchill's about-face "not be accepted."[30] Roosevelt appreciated that Marshall had tied his prestige to the principle of "unity of command." And that the British chiefs had conceded the issue. He could not let his chief of staff, who all agreed stood at the center of the staff talks, be disavowed by the prime minister's last-minute shenanigans. The president at once instructed Marshall and Hopkins to recast Churchill's draft cable to the War Cabinet. Stimson happily noted that the Americans—Marshall, Knox, Arnold, King, Stark, and Turner—had "been perfectly strong and loyal" on the issue. Only the admirals of the "recalcitrant" Royal Navy had "kicked like bray steers" as they opposed any and all thought of a unified command. Their "stubborn" American counterparts, with the exception of Ernest King, to Stimson still seemed decimated by Pearl Harbor and required "a pretty thorough spanking" by the president for their "lack of initiative and enterprise."[31]

Given this newfound united American front, Marshall's insistence that all military forces in the Far East theater "operate under the direction of the supreme commander"[32] won the day. The Americans had closed ranks. Marshall quickly pressed his advantage: before the meeting broke up, he mounted another bid to kill the proposal for a speedy North African expedition. In fact, Roosevelt was beginning to have second thoughts about such an operation. He asked his chief of staff what might happen if American troops had to land under fire at Casablanca. Marshall painted a gloomy scene. "This would be a very dangerous operation to attempt because of the hazards involved, especially in meeting an initial reverse, which would have a very detrimental effect on the morale of the American people."[33] FDR broke off the meeting for lunch, gaining time to reconsider Churchill's North Africa initiative.

With the Americans solidly behind Roosevelt and Marshall, and having already committed himself in front of his chiefs of staff, Churchill conceded the point on who would command the Royal Navy in the Far East. It would be General Wavell. Later that day Churchill sent messages to the prime ministers of New Zealand, Australia, and South Africa asking for their "early agreement" to the draft terms of reference that had emerged from Roosevelt's meeting with his military leaders. It was pro forma. They, in fact, had no say in the matter. He and FDR had decided and that was enough. Churchill now informed Wavell that he would "receive his orders from an appropriate joint body, who will be responsible to me as Minister of Defence and to the President of the United States, who is also Commander-in-Chief of all United States Forces."[34] Of course, no such joint body had yet been agreed upon and officially he was still on record as late as the previous evening in opposing such an arrangement. But the deal had been done.

The Allies swiftly moved to put in place unity of command before Churchill departed for Ottawa. They created a vast new single theater called ABDA (American, British, Dutch, Australian), a rough square 3,000 miles on each side containing Burma, Malaya, the Dutch East Indies, and other Pacific islands. They appointed Wavell its supreme commander, with an American, to be named later, as his deputy. Stimson did not spare with giving credit where credit was due: "We have made a good start on it, due largely—most wholly—to Marshall's initiative and vigor."[35] Eisenhower was more prosaic in his observations. On the die-cut appointment pad that served as his diary, he noted: "Unity of command in ABDA area seems assured. Good start! But what an effort. Talk-talk-talk!"[36]

Stimson as well as Marshall knew, of course, that unity of command for ABDA was almost meaningless in terms of the immediate conduct of the war. The Japanese were still running rampant throughout Southeast Asia and there was little prospect that Wavell could put a stop to them. But they understood that the principle involved had to be implemented somewhere for the first time, and that the Pacific theater offered that opportunity. Unity of command under Wavell might mitigate what both feared was a coming year of disasters. But most important, it would set a precedent to be followed elsewhere—especially once the Allies went on the offensive. George Marshall had made one of the greatest contributions toward forging the "grand alliance."

In the late afternoon of Sunday, December 28, 1941, Churchill and his staff departed the White House for Union Station, where the Canadian prime minister's special train waited to take them to Ottawa. Churchill and Mackenzie King would travel in separate cars. Churchill asked Charles Wilson to ride with him to the station. "As we drove out of the [White House] grounds he opened the window of the car," Wilson remembered.

> He was short of breath. "There seems no air," he said, "in this car. Is it a stuffy night, Charles?" And then he put his hand on my knee. "It is a great comfort to have you with me," he said. He has used these words twice in four days; the first time was before the heart attack. This is something new; it has not happened before.[37]

For Roosevelt, Churchill's departure brought some welcome relief. Dinner in the West Hall at 7:30 P.M. that night found neither FDR nor Hopkins present. A butler sent out to find them came back and said, "Theys flat out in bed eating off trays."[38] Eleanor had put her culinary skills to work and made a dish of scrambled eggs.

The White House Usher's Diary, Grace Tully's Appointment Diary, and the Stenographer's Diary all show only occasional brief meetings over the next three days. There were relaxing dinners with Hopkins, early bedtimes, and, of course, far fewer brandies and cigars. Each afternoon FDR checked in with the White House doctor, Admiral Ross McIntire, an ear, nose, and throat specialist, who monitored the president's gradual recovery from the stress and strain of the past week. Eleanor was delighted. As she later admitted, she had always been "frightened of Mr. Churchill." Not surprisingly, she was "always glad when he departed, for I knew that my husband would need a rest."[39]

11

OTTAWA
INTERLUDE

A T PRECISELY 2:15 P.M. ON THE AFTERNOON OF SUNDAY, DECEMBER
28, 1941, the train carrying Winston Churchill to Canada slipped
out of Washington's Union Station. Franklin Roosevelt had lent
Churchill his private car for the trip; Prime Minister William Lyon
Mackenzie King had his own. Churchill took Chief of the Air Staff
Portal, Wilson, his private physician, and about a dozen secretaries,
valets, and military aides with him. Pound and Dill remained in
Washington to continue discussions with the American chiefs. It had
been arranged that Churchill and Wilson would stay at the residence of
the Canadian governor-general, known to Canadians as Rideau Hall,
but to Churchill as Government House. Traveling north, the train rode
the tracks of the Pennsylvania Railroad through Baltimore and
Philadelphia to New York's Pennsylvania Station. The afternoon daylight
soon waned as they moved up the eastern seaboard. It was pitch-dark
as they left New York City for Springfield, Massachusetts, where the
VIP cars were switched to the Vermont Central Railroad.

Outside, the temperature dropped sharply as the train moved
through the low, snow-covered mountain ranges and forests that separated the temperate eastern seaboard from the frozen St. Lawrence
Valley. For the most part, Churchill stayed in his car with Wilson and
a clutch of secretaries and military aides, going through messages
from London and dispatching missives to the far corners of the
Empire. He did not hang about with Mackenzie King as he had with

Roosevelt. His trip to Ottawa was necessary, not to confer with Mackenzie King, but because Canada was a loyal member of the Commonwealth and a staunch ally in war. Canadians were deserving of Churchillian inspiration.

Britain badly needed both the manpower and the resources that the Dominions could contribute to the war effort. Canada, Australia, South Africa, and New Zealand eventually sent 2.5 million men and women, and hundreds of warships and thousands of aircraft to the fight against the Axis. Without these resources, Britain would have been sorely tried even to attempt a rough parity with the United States in the early part of the war. But fighting personnel, ships, and aircraft were only part of the overall Commonwealth contribution to the war. From Canada came the airspace to train more than 100,000 aircrew for the Commonwealth air forces, the uranium that enabled the Manhattan Project to succeed, foodstuffs by the millions of tons, and thousands of guns and vehicles of all kinds. From Australia came the forward bases from which the Allies eventually pushed Japan back to its own borders, as well as enough beef, mutton, grain, and dairy products to feed a small nation. South Africa and New Zealand also made vital contributions in food and raw materials.

Churchill needed the Commonwealth, but with the exception of South African prime minister Jan Smuts, he did not much need or want Commonwealth leaders. Churchill had enjoyed a close and friendly relationship with Smuts for decades. Though Smuts had fought Britain as a general in the Boer War (1899–1902), he and Churchill grew closer as he helped shape the postwar constitution of South Africa. Both men had also served in the Imperial War Cabinet during the First World War. Churchill often sought Smuts' advice and shared things in confidence with him that he would never relay to the other Commonwealth leaders. But whereas Churchill liked Smuts, he despised John Curtin of Australia—and had little regard for Mackenzie King of Canada. These two prime ministers seemed most of all to stand in the way of his ability to deploy Australian and Canadian resources as he, Churchill, deemed fit. He had little patience with what he considered the petty concerns of their own national self-interests. He tolerated their independence— as he had to—but he would just as soon have had it suspended for the duration of the war. He would have liked to have directed the whole

British Commonwealth war effort like the conductor of a symphony, with complete obedience from all the players.

The prime-ministerial train stopped briefly at White River Junction, Vermont, before crossing the border into Canada in the early morning hours of December 29. Then it raced along the track of the Canadian National Railway through the remaining darkness, arriving at Ottawa just after 10:00 A.M. Charles Wilson described the tumult that greeted them: "the big fur-hatted [Royal] Canadian Mounted Police kept back with difficulty the vast, enthusiastic crowds which pushed good-humouredly towards the P.M. and soon enveloped him."[1]

The American ambassador to Canada, J. Pierrepont Moffat, also witnessed Churchill's arrival:

> There was Mr. Churchill standing on the back platform in charac-
> teristic pose, puffing a newly lit cigar and holding up his right hand
> making the sign of V. As the temperature was about zero introduc-
> tions on the platform were made on the double quick and he has-
> tened away to Government House.[2]

After Washington, small and provincial Ottawa struck Wilson as "like Belfast after Dublin."[3]

Ottawa was as excited about this visit as it had been in the summer of 1939 when the king and queen had taken a trip across Canada on the eve of war. Members of Parliament and senators broke their winter holidays and rushed to the city from all parts of Canada. For the first time in history, microphones were installed in the House of Commons so that Churchill's speech could be broadcast via radio to the entire nation. The city was already overcrowded with the burgeoning population of civil servants and military officials trying to manage the greatest war effort in Canadian history. Now, every hotel in town was booked solid for the three days of the prime minister's stay.[4]

Churchill's entourage proceeded through the snow-banked streets. "The Canadians, who are by nature undemonstrative," Moffat recalled, "let themselves go and found in their complete enthusiasm a vent for all their 'pent up' feelings. People traveled from all over the country to get just a glimpse of him in his car as he drove by."[5] At the governor-general's residence, Churchill bathed, and then went quickly to Parliament Hill to meet the War Committee of the Canadian Cabinet. Mackenzie King asked Churchill straightaway what the implications were for Canada of the new arrangement for unity of command that was under discussion in Washington. "He said little beyond that something of the kind had been arranged for the Pacific which would be disclosed later," Mackenzie King noted in his diary. The Canadian leader then asked about the joint statement of Allied war aims. He was clearly miffed that he had learned about it only when he had received it from the British ambassador, who had expressed "the hope that I would accept it as it was, bad grammar, etc. etc." Churchill thereupon launched into one of his patented lengthy discourses on the state of the war thus far. At one point he told Mackenzie King, "things were 3 times better with Japan fighting America, thereby bringing her into the war unanimously." King seemed astonished when Churchill told him that he had "literally danced when he learned that Japan had attacked America."[6]

Churchill tried to give the Canadians the distinct impression that he was getting along famously with Roosevelt, that the president was being very forthcoming, and that his trip to Washington had been well worth it so far. He made no mention of the discussion going on that very day among the chiefs in Washington aimed at creating a joint American-British command structure for all Western Allied forces in the Far East and elsewhere. The arrangement would mean that Canada, with its 1.1 million fighting forces, would have no more say in the higher direction of Allied strategy than would Mexico, which eventually sent a brigade and a fighter squadron to Europe. Nor did he mention that he was still squarely at odds with George Marshall over grand strategy. Churchill simply told the Canadians that he was

> looking forward to '43 to roll tanks off ships at different points all around Europe in countries held by the Germans, getting rifles into the hands of the people themselves, making it impossible for Germany to defend different countries she has overrun. He believed 1943 would be a year of liberation, rescuing the countries that were overrun.[7]

To the Canadians and to Mackenzie King, Churchill was flatter-
ing, reassuring, enthusiastic. But whenever he was alone with Wilson,
he kept asking him to take his pulse. Wilson later wrote:

> I get out of it somehow, but once, when I found him lifting something
> heavy, I did expostulate. At this he broke out: "Now, Charles, you are
> making me heart-minded. I shall soon think of nothing else. I could-
> n't do my work if I kept thinking of my heart." The next time he asked
> me to take his pulse I refused point-blank. "You're all right. Forget
> your damned heart."[8]

Wilson worried that Churchill might not get through his speech
to the Canadian parliament if he continued like this. After the meeting
with the War Cabinet, Mackenzie King hosted a lunch for Churchill at
the Chateau Laurier Hotel. Ambassador Moffatt sat opposite them. He
thought something must have gone wrong in the meeting: "I had the
impression that the session of the War Cabinet . . . could not have been
entirely without incident." For the first three or four minutes, neither
Churchill nor Mackenzie King had spoken at all. "It was only later on
that conversation grew easy and ended up in a love feast."[9]

Nothing had gone wrong. Whereas Churchill tried always to be
outgoing, chatty, charming, and ebullient with Roosevelt, he was no
such thing with Mackenzie King. Wilson later remembered:

> I cannot help noticing Winston's indifference to [Mackenzie King] after
> the wooing of the President at the White House. There the P.M. and
> the President seemed to talk for most of the day, and for the first time I
> have seen Winston content to listen. You could almost feel the impor-
> tance he attaches to bringing the president along with him . . . . And
> when he does say anything it is always something likely to fall pleasantly
> on the President's ear. But here, in Ottawa, he does not seem to bother.[10]

The next afternoon, Churchill met Mackenzie King at the
entrance to the Parliament. The Canadian escorted him into the House
of Commons to tumultuous applause, and then introduced him.
Churchill gripped the lapels of his jacket, faced the microphones, and
began to speak.

It is with feelings of pride and encouragement that I find myself here in the House of Commons of Canada, invited to address the Parliament and the senior Dominion of the Crown. . . . Canada occupies a unique position in the British Empire because of its unbreakable ties with Britain and its ever growing friendship and intimate association with the United States.

He praised the nation's achievements in raising a large army, navy, and air force in such a short time, and noted the tragedy of the fall of Hong Kong, where 1,975 Canadians had been killed, wounded, or captured. They "have crowned with military honour the reputation of their native land." The peoples of the British Empire, he intoned, "do not seek the lands or wealth of any country, but they are a tough and hardy lot. We have not journeyed all this way across the centuries, across the oceans, across the mountains, across the prairies, because we are made of sugar candy." He was frequently interrupted by members of Parliament banging on their desks—a Canadian parliamentary tradition of showing approval for a speaker.

Then Churchill turned to a review of the war thus far, and especially to the fall of France. He had warned the French generals that Britain would not surrender, that it would fight on alone. "Their generals told their Prime Minister and his divided cabinet, 'In three weeks England will have her neck wrung like a chicken.' He paused for a moment. 'Some Chicken! Some Neck!'" More desk banging followed, with roars of approval and laughter. Then finally, the peroration:

Let us then address ourselves to our task, not in any way underrating its tremendous difficulties and perils, but in good heart and sober confidence, resolved that, whatever the cost, whatever the suffering, we shall stand by one another, true and faithful comrades, and do our duty, God helping us, to the end.[11]

The approbation was deafening. Mackenzie King noted, "I felt that the atmosphere had wonderfully cleared, and that his visit had served to put the facts into their right place."[12] Churchill then held a brief press conference. The next day he retraced his route to

Washington. His train arrived at Union Station on the morning of New Year's Day 1942.

Churchill's interlude in Canada did not slow the pace of the chiefs' meetings in Washington. The immediate problem was to create a higher strategy-making body to give General Wavell his orders. Both the Australians and the Dutch government in exile, as Colonel Ian Jacob quickly discovered, "saw this joint body as some kind of special and new politico-military council which would direct the war from Washington," and of course they immediately "put in a claim to be represented on it."[13] Cordell Hull was sympathetic. He still hoped to convince FDR to support his idea for a "supreme war council" that would include representation from all the major Allies.

Stimson vigorously opposed the idea. Roosevelt sided with his secretary of war. The president called Admiral King in for lunch on December 29 and told him in no uncertain terms that he wanted to run the war as a joint American-British operation. He had no intention of sharing decision-making on matters of higher strategy with any other nation. In effect, FDR appointed King to act as his surrogate in this issue to the joint chiefs, to gain their backing. He ordered the admiral to meet them that afternoon, then to report back to him. "The President wanted no further delay," King's biographer Thomas B. Buell wrote, "there was no more time for debate."[14] The longer ARCADIA asked, the more assertive Roosevelt became.

The chiefs duly convened at the Federal Reserve Building on the afternoon of December 29. King was ready to act on the president's orders, but Admiral Pound beat him to the punch. The First Sea Lord declared that they ought not to waste time setting up "a cumbersome machine" to direct Wavell. Churchill had told the War Cabinet in London that Wavell would be issued orders from an "appropriate joint body," Pound reminded them, one that would be responsible both to Churchill as British minister of defence and to Roosevelt as commander in chief of U.S. forces. What more was needed? Wavell was waiting for orders. They were all aware that when Churchill, or Pound, said "joint," they meant Britain and the United States acting together. Other governments would simply be bypassed. Pound then suggested that the

British and American chiefs should, in future, constitute a new "chiefs of staff committee."[15] This was a radical initiative from a most unexpected source.

It caught King totally off guard. He was obviously flustered by Pound's unexpected initiative. It was totally out of character for Pound to advance any new idea on his own. Besides, King wondered, why would the British advocate a scheme that would almost certainly be dominated by the United States once the war effort reached its high point? Instead of forcefully backing Pound's notion, as Roosevelt clearly wanted him to do, King produced his own hastily worked-out plan that proposed the establishment of a South-Western Pacific Council. That council would include a British deputy who would liaise with Roosevelt, as well as a Dutch military representative and an ANZAC (Australian-New Zealand) representative. The council would receive its instructions from the various national chiefs of staff of the ABDA member nations.

This ran completely counter to the president's message to King at lunch. It also ran against Marshall's grain. He intervened immediately. Might it not be better to put this "complicated question" aside for later, Marshall suggested, and just include some phrase in Wavell's instructions that the matter would be "dealt with by such joint machinery as the Associated Powers may hereafter set up?" No, King wanted to tackle the issue right away. In that case, Marshall replied, he was "prepared to accept [Pound's] proposals."

The American camp seemed rife with dissenting views yet again. But this time, unlike Marshall's first initiative to create "unity of command," Admiral Stark rose to the occasion. The chief of naval operations quickly endorsed Marshall's stance. Obviously in the minority, King backpedaled. It would serve no purpose to push the matter further against the wishes of Marshall and Stark and Pound—and Roosevelt. One of the other American admirals put the matter succinctly: "In order to achieve unity of command without delay," some form of machinery "should be agreed upon and established by the British and the United States Governments forthwith." The other Allied governments ought simply to be presented with a "fait accompli" and asked "to notify their acceptance."[16]

Over the next two days, the final draft of the directive to be sent to Wavell was drawn up; the chiefs approved it on New Year's Eve. "It was obvious," King later recalled the president saying, "that with so many participants in the war, decisions could not be made by a show of hands." Those with the greatest stake and effort in the war had to make a stand. "As the United States and Great Britain were financing the war and doing most of the fighting, they should therefore run the war, make the final decisions, and control the military machine." It was realpolitik at its clearest. King swung back into line behind his commander in chief. Salty dog that he was, the admiral appreciated Roosevelt's bluntness. "This is a hard-boiled method bound to cause friction and unhappiness among the smaller nations who thought that they should have a voice in the military decisions," King admitted, "but it is the only way to function effectively."[17]

Regardless of where the Anglo-American Combined Chiefs of Staff would eventually meet, the very establishment of the body was itself a major achievement of ARCADIA; it would run the war in the West until the final defeat of the Axis. Churchill later wrote that the founding of the Combined Chiefs "may well be thought by future historians [to be] the most valuable and lasting result of our first Washington Conference."[18] Still, Judge Hull remained to be placated. Almost as an afterthought, Roosevelt called Hull on December 31 and informed him that he would shelve the secretary of state's various memoranda concerning the creation of a "supreme war council." "It seemed desirable," Roosevelt told Hull, "to work in a cooperative way on a regional basis for the time."[19] To soothe Hull's ruffled feathers, FDR left open the possibility of "eventually" creating such a centralized command.

It would be one committee. But where would it sit? And how would it function? The British began to press almost immediately for two separate venues, one in Washington and one in London. With such a setup, it would be easier for the British to keep watch on their Commonwealth allies and on the Dutch, whose government in exile was located in London. They had no intention of making it easy for anyone but them to talk directly to the Americans. "We have had great difficulties with the Australians and the Dutch," Dill later wrote Wavell,

> in trying to establish a higher direction lay-out. . . . The Australians in particular are pressing to be represented in discussions in

Washington. We regard that as quite unworkable. They can have their say in London where proper machinery exists. The last thing we want to do is to have to battle with them in front of the Americans. The Dutch too can have their say in London where their Government is.[20]

This new disagreement, as Harry Hopkins put it, "kicked up a hell of a row."[21] It seemed that the whole conference through, one major problem was solved only to have another appear.

The British and the Americans remained far apart on the crucial matter of war production. Who would produce what, how much was required, where would it go, and could the war production of the two nations and their chief allies be centrally controlled? If these issues were not resolved, joint Allied theater commanders such as Wavell would have nothing to fight with.

In the words of David Brinkley, America entered the war in December 1941 with "no plan to mobilize war production, no plan to manage the economy, prices, materials, rationing, no plan to prepare the country for war."[22] The British were well aware of this state of affairs. On paper, the American effort seemed prodigious: four *Cimarron*-type tankers were already being converted to auxiliary aircraft carriers and the U.S. Navy was running up a hefty appropriations tab with Congress —$145 million in new funds for the Bureau of Aeronautics, $725 million for the Bureau of Ships, and $70 million for the Bureau of Ordnance.[23] Though the United States was sending a growing flood of trucks, tanks, fighter planes, bombers, and other tools of war to Britain and the Soviet Union, it was but a trickle compared to what was needed, especially given the Republic's productive potential. Beaverbrook's chief role at ARCADIA was somehow to convince the Americans to solve their production bottlenecks and get rolling into a true war economy. He was also there, of course, to claim what he and Churchill thought was Britain's share of that production.

Shortly after Churchill had left for Ottawa, FDR convened a meeting at the White House. Vice President Henry A. Wallace and Beaverbrook attended. In this and subsequent meetings, Beaverbrook continually astonished the Americans with his demands. The United

States, he repeatedly argued, simply had to set "far higher production goals for tanks, anti-tank guns, aircraft, and anti-aircraft guns" than anything yet imagined by Washington. Roosevelt and Wallace were stunned by "what seemed shocking requirements."[24] They were fighting "a resourceful and determined enemy," Beaverbrook reiterated. The Americans "had yet had no experience in the losses of matériel incidental to a war of the kind we are fighting now." Stalin had told him, Beaverbrook allowed, that the Germans in the first half of 1941 had thrown 30,000 tanks against the Red Army, and still had tanks to spare. The current American production goal for 1942 was 30,000 tanks in all, for the entire year. Beaverbrook wanted at least 45,000. He challenged the Americans to find out what was preventing them from producing the tens of thousands of tanks, aircraft, ships, guns, and other necessities of war that he knew they could.[25] He literally demanded a complete overhaul of American production methods and management. Hopkins joked that when Beaverbrook got to heaven, "he [would] be storming about demanding a higher production of harps and angels wings."[26]

The American war production dilemma was perfectly clear to Stimson. On New Year's Day 1942 he confided his concerns to his diary. No secretary of war, he noted, had ever been put in the position of having to fight constantly to make his voice heard to the president on behalf of the United States Army. Too many special advisors, such as Harry Hopkins and Averell Harriman, had the chief executive's ear and were lobbying on behalf of the Allies, especially Britain and the Soviet Union. The difficulty of balancing between "loyalty to my own Army" and "loyalty to those other nation's [sic] armies" constituted "one of the most constant, heavy strains that I have upon me."[27]

In fact, no issue provoked more heated debate during ARCADIA than that of war production and allocation. It was political to the core. It aroused suspicions on both sides that each was holding back production figures and allocation plans from the other. It was the only issue debated along purely nationalistic lines, American and British. The Americans feared what they considered to be yet another British attempt to use the Republic's great industrial and manpower potential to prop up the Empire. The British, for their part, feared that every ship, tank, and aircraft sent to the Philippines was one less for the defense of the British Isles and the proposed landing in North Africa.

A significant part of the blame for the sorry state of American war production at the time of Pearl Harbor falls squarely on Roosevelt's shoulders. The president simply was reluctant to entrust anyone, civilian or military, with sweeping production powers. Thus, in 1939 he had appointed Edward Stettinius, Jr., chairman of U.S. Steel, Walter Gifford, president of American Telephone and Telegraph, and General Robert E. Wood, chairman of Sears, Roebuck & Co., to a War Resources Board. But no sooner had he announced the appointments than he had second thoughts. The isolationist Congress disliked any "War" board and preferred instead a "Defense" board. For his part, the president began to fear that he had handed too much power over to a trio of anti-New Deal businessmen. He thanked them for their willingness to serve the nation—and sent them home.

But the issue would not go away. What was shaping up as a global war would demand massive production of war materials on a scale hitherto unimagined. Thus, in January 1941 FDR created the Office of Production Management, or OPM. In typical Roosevelt fashion, he appointed two men who could not possibly work together to head the new agency: William Knudsen, former president of General Motors, and Sidney Hillman, president of the Amalgamated Clothing Workers Union. The president admired Knudsen's work ethic. The Danish immigrant had worked his way up the corporate ladder, first at Ford and then at Chevrolet, before heading General Motors. Most important, Knudsen had no political ambitions. Hillman was an immigrant from Lithuania who, after working in the clothing industry, had gone into socialist and union politics. At a press conference, the president proudly announced that he had appointed a "single, responsible head. His name is Knudsen and Hillman."[28] The press had a field day referring to the new head of OPM as "Mr. Knudsenhillman." By September 1941, the agency was in disarray, unable to handle the flood of Lend-Lease orders.

FDR acted again, in a fashion. He neither disbanded nor reformed the OPM, but instead created yet another new agency—the Supply, Priorities and Allocation Board. He also found a new director, Donald Nelson. After spending three decades as a buyer for Sears, Roebuck & Co., Nelson had risen to the post of vice president. Patient, slow moving, methodical, and easygoing, Nelson worked "efficiently if not spectacularly." He spoke in folksy language. He has been described as being "overweight, balding, [and] smoked a pipe said to smell like a sulfur sink in Yellowstone National Park."[29] But the scope of the effort needed to put the country on a full war footing was too much for one man to handle. The military as well as the press clamored for the appointment of Bernard M. Baruch, whom President Woodrow Wilson had chosen to head the War Industries Board in 1918, as "war production czar." But FDR would have no grand "Poobah," as he put it, run the nation's war industries.

At this point, December 29, 1941, Lord Beaverbrook approached Roosevelt with a possible way out of the war productions dilemma. Why not appoint Hopkins boss of American war production, "with full powers and entire authority"?[30] FDR's first political instinct was to reject the idea. For years, he had refused to name a "supreme boss" for American industrial production, thereby arousing the ire of many members of Congress. They would now howl not only that he had caved in on the issue—and to the British, to boot—but that he had appointed to the post "that spendthrift liberal, that power-lustful Machiavellian, that Rasputin-like White House manipulator, Harry Hopkins!"[31] In addition, both the War Department and the Navy Department were hostile to civilian control of "end weapons." Thus, Roosevelt equivocated. For days, he debated the issue with Hopkins. At one point, the president even suggested somewhat desperately that he might recall Justice William O. Douglas from the Supreme Court, and hand the job to him. But Douglas had no desire to abandon a safe sinecure for a political hornets' nest. The problem of managing America's war production continued to fester. Still, Churchill would soon return from Ottawa and FDR was fully aware that "the prime" would then push his plan to have two productions committees, one in London and one in Washington. Something had to be done.

New Year's Day was a dismal, rainy Thursday in Washington. After breakfast, Franklin sent word to Eleanor and her houseguests in the West Wing that he would like them to meet Churchill at the front door. The prime minister would be arriving momentarily from Union Station. They were all to motor through the Virginia countryside. At 10:45 A.M. FDR led a procession that included Eleanor, Churchill, and Lord and

Lady Halifax across the Lee Bridge and down Memorial Drive to services at Christ Church in Alexandria.[32] The moment was rich with history. The church had been founded in 1767 and its famous parishioners had included George Washington and Robert E. Lee. It was sited up a gently sloping hill from Old Town, where Hessians in the pay of England had built streets made of cobblestones. U.S. Marines now stood guard on each side of the street, about twenty-five feet apart. The Secret Service and church elders had handpicked and certified 250 parishioners—presumably those who had been most faithful in attendance—to join in the services. Eight young men from Christ Church that morning had aroused many a sleepy Washingtonian to "invite" them for services at 11 A.M. A light rain continued to fall on the leafless trees. Word about the services had somehow leaked out, and by the time the motorcade made its way to Christ Church, people lined Washington Street in Alexandria to catch a glimpse of the famous worshipers.

FDR, leaning on the arm of "Pa" Watson, his personal military advisor, entered the church first. Crimson and purple light dimly glowed through the stained glass windows. Roosevelt and Churchill chatted with the Reverend Edward R. Welles and then inspected the historic building. Thereafter, they took their seats in the squat box-like pew at the front of the church, the one that the Squire of Mount Vernon had once occupied, at the then tidy rental fee of $200 per year. The services began with the hymn "God of Our Father," and then continued with a thunderous rendition of "The Battle Hymn of the Republic." Its words, set against the backdrop of another crisis in American history, were pregnant with meaning for the present moment:

> Mine eyes have seen the glory of the coming of the Lord,
> He is trampling out the vintage where the grapes of wrath were stored;
> He hath loosed the fateful lightning of His terrible swift sword,
> His truth is marching on.

The Reverend Welles delivered a militant sermon pledging that the United States would not sheath its "terrible swift sword" until God had granted it victory over the Axis.[33] The president, Eleanor's friend Joseph Lash recalled, took "roguish delight" by having Churchill pray in Washington's church, where the official prayer was *George Washington's*

Prayer for the United States. "Tommy" Thompson fished a $20 bill out of his pocket and handed it to Churchill for the collection plate, but there was no collection that day.

After services, the motorcade made its way down the Mount Vernon Memorial Highway, built in 1932 to commemorate the bicentennial of the birth of the Republic's first president. After the cars passed through the gate at Mount Vernon, they slowly proceeded downhill toward the Washington Tomb. The rain came down more heavily. Churchill and Roosevelt passed through the Tomb's steel-barred gate. The prime minister placed a wreath of red-brown chrysanthemums and blue iris, tied with a red-white-and-blue ribbon, against the sarcophagus. At the mansion, the two leaders signed the guest book. Neither the symbolism nor the irony of the moment could have escaped either one. There on the page for all to see was written expression of the newfound Anglo-American "special relationship." The year 1776 lay far distant in the past.

The Churchill-Roosevelt bonhomie that day was almost too much for Eleanor. Throughout the trip, Winston had kept up a steady refrain of "After the war we've got to form an Anglo-Saxon alliance to meet the problems of the world." FDR had just kept nodding his head in agreement. "Yes, yes, yes!" To Eleanor, Churchill's bantering was just more of the "old British colonialism in new form." She deeply distrusted Churchill's vision of that "Anglo-Saxon alliance." It had all too much to do with empire, and all too little with democracy. Finally, she could take no more. "You know, Winston," she blurted out, "when Franklin says yes, yes, yes it doesn't mean he agrees with you. It means he's listening."[34] Churchill scowled for the remainder of the journey back to the White House.

But few people ever got the best of Winston Spencer Churchill. He simply bided his time and took his revenge a few days later over lunch. When Eleanor asked him what Mrs. Churchill was doing during the war years, the prime minister with great delight informed her how wonderful it was that his wife, and indeed the wives of all his Cabinet colleagues, did not engage in public activities, but stayed at home! Not wishing to cross swords with the master of the English language, Eleanor took Winston's barb in stride and, as Samuel Rosenman, the president's speechwriter, noted, never "batted an eyelash."[35]

12

THE UNITED NATIONS

WINSTON CHURCHILL WAS IN PRIME FORM AT LUNCH ON NEW Year's Day. Eleanor Roosevelt's intellectual companion, Joseph Lash, sitting next to the prime minister, was duly impressed. "The language poured out of him. He is an exuberant, rich personality, exciting, temperamental, his phrases redolent of the most vigorous period of English literature, witty, resourceful in summoning up apt lines of poetry. His talk was full of imagery."[1] Churchill rambled on about the joys of bathtubs, which the Americans had "foisted upon the British." It was simply grand, he announced, "lying back and kicking one's legs in the air like a bird." As he transferred a poached egg and hash to his plate, the egg slipped off the spoon, but landed on the plate. Triumphantly, Churchill put it back on the corned beef hash, "on its throne," as he announced to Eleanor. He was delighted that Hitler had sounded "awfully anxious" in his New Year's message, and that the Führer had even invoked Almighty God. "But we have a preemption on the Deity," Churchill roared. Then he needled Franklin Roosevelt about the never-ending St. Pierre-Miquelon mess. "You're being nice to Vichy. We're being nice to [Charles] de Gaulle." It was a fair division of labor, Churchill thought. To the president's less than amused reply that the issue should be left to Secretary Hull and Ambassador Halifax to sort out, the prime minister shot back cheekily, "Hell, Hull and Halifax."

After lunch Churchill, Roosevelt, Hull, and Hopkins turned their attention to finalizing the wording of the "Allied Declaration of Unity and Purpose." It was scheduled for release sometime that day. Ambassador Litvinov joined them. The hurdle of possible Soviet opposition to the inclusion of "religious freedom" in the declaration had been overcome in an ingenious way. While it had been part of Roosevelt's list of the "Four Freedoms," it had been left out of the Atlantic Charter, and Roosevelt had taken a good deal of flak over this. He was determined that it be included in the "Allied Declaration of Unity and Purpose." But he also knew that this might cause problems with Stalin. FDR, Sam Rosenman recalled, used an "ingenious argument" with Litvinov. He explained to the Soviet ambassador that he had been seriously criticized and attacked for not having included the concept in the Atlantic Charter, and asked the Russians to help him out of his predicament by including it in the present document, "even though he knew that they might not like it." More, Roosevelt agreed not to use the term "freedom of religion" because it implied that everyone had a religion and that everyone was free to choose the religion they wanted. Instead, he suggested "religious freedom." Surely, this was in line with Article 124 of the Soviet Constitution, which allowed any citizen to have a religion, or not to have a religion, or to oppose religion.[2] Inexplicably, Stalin agreed.

But the Russians were not so pliable on another issue. Churchill wanted the declaration to be signed by both "governments" and "authorities," so that the Free French might be included. Judge Hull tried one last time to head him off, but Roosevelt overruled him and "authorities" carried the day. Litvinov then churlishly informed the group that he, a mere ambassador, had no power to agree to contextual changes in the document. This would have to be referred back to Moscow. More time would be wasted; the deadline might not be met. "Churchill," Hopkins recorded, "became quite angry." He told Litvinov that "he wasn't much of an ambassador if he didn't have the power to even add a word like this; that we were in a war and there was no time for long-winded negotiations." The president was "embarrassed" by the prime minister's outburst, which he thought "bordered on the insulting."[3] Litvinov, whom Churchill secretly thought of as a "mere automaton," was fully aware that both Roosevelt and Churchill desperately wanted the declaration issued that day, in part to offset the mounting bad news from the Far East, but he refused to agree to the change. "Authorities" was deleted from the document.[4] Hull was delighted.

Roosevelt's tolerance for Litvinov was based, in part, on his ignorance of the true nature of the Stalinist regime. Later at dinner, for example, FDR was asked his impression of the Great Dictator. He replied that Stalin had to rule "a very backward people," which explained a good deal about his methods. The Soviet leader reminded him, in fact, of Gutelio Vargas, the Brazilian dictator, in this way. Hopkins, the president stated, had assured him after his visit to Moscow in August 1941 that Stalin had a good sense of humor. FDR added that "Uncle Joe" also had "a sense of proportion." Moreover, the president was certain that Stalin would eventually sign the Atlantic Charter, including a statement on "freedom of religion." FDR told his guests that the Soviet dictator had agreed that the aggressor nations would be compulsorily disarmed at the conclusion of the war, and that a "monopoly of arms" would be left in the hands of Great Britain, the Soviet Union, and the United States.[5]

The name "Allied Declaration of Unity and Purpose" was too cumbersome for a document that would serve as a rallying point for the anti-Axis alliance. For days, Roosevelt had been unhappy about it. Then it came to him: "Declaration of the United Nations." According to Hopkins, the president had been so excited by his sudden inspiration, that he had himself wheeled into the Rose Bedroom to share the good tidings with Churchill. "I've got it! United Nations," FDR announced with pride. It was morning. The prime minister was just emerging from a steaming bathtub, stark naked and flush pink. FDR immediately apologized and promised to come back at a more convenient time. Unflappable as ever, Churchill insisted that there was no need for Roosevelt to leave. "Think nothing of it. The Prime Minister of Great Britain has nothing to conceal from the President of the United States!" Hopkins recounted the story enough times so that it quickly made the rounds in Washington. Canadian Prime Minister Mackenzie King duly recorded it in his diary. When Robert Sherwood, the president's speechwriter, asked Churchill if the story was factual, the prime minister dismissed it as pure "nonsense." He never received the president, Churchill informed Sherwood, without at least a bath towel wrapped around him.[6] But the story was too good to go away.

Eleanor asked Franklin whether the "Declaration of the United Nations" could be read aloud to the group. FDR started to demur, but

Churchill approved. While Hopkins went upstairs to fetch the document, Churchill informed the small group how thrilled he was with the name "Declaration of the United Nations." Lash recorded that Churchill then recited a few lines from Lord Byron's "Childe Harold's Pilgrimage" that seemed to fit the moment:

> Here, where the sword United Nations drew,
>   Our countrymen were warring on that day
> And this is much—and all—which will not pass away.

Hopkins having returned, Churchill read the declaration. It was a short and straightforward document; the body contained less than 200 words. But it was stirring in its simplicity:

> The Governments signatory hereto, Having subscribed to a common program of purposes and principles . . . known as the Atlantic Charter, Being convinced that complete victory over their enemies is essential to defend life, liberty, independence and religious freedom, and to preserve human justice in their own lands as well as in other lands, and they are engaged in a common struggle against savage and brutal forces seeking to subjugate the world, DECLARE: (1) Each Government pledges itself to employ its full resources [to the war]. (2) Each Government pledges itself to cooperate with the Governments signatory hereto and not to make a separate armistice or peace with the enemy.

The dinner discussion then turned back to Russia. Churchill spoke of the parallels between the two world wars. In 1919 he had helped send a British expeditionary force to Russia to fight alongside the Whites against the Bolsheviks, and it had advanced as far as Tula, just south of Moscow. Now, he forgave the Bolsheviks "in proportion to the numbers of Huns they kill." Hopkins mischievously inquired, "Do they forgive you?" To which Churchill had a ready reply: "In proportion to the number of tanks I send."[7]

After dinner, Roosevelt welcomed T. V. Soong, the new Chinese ambassador, to the White House. In the Oval Room the "Declaration of the United Nations" was laid out on the president's desk. Made from the planking of HMS *Resolute*, the desk was stout, with three layers of oak. It had been a gift from Queen Victoria to President Rutherford B. Hayes in 1879, when the ship was broken up. The two leaders then invited Eleanor and some of her dinner guests to view the ceremony from just inside the door to the study. "Bertie" Hamlin later recalled: "The study was hushed and quiet as the statesmen signed. The only sound came from Fala, who was stretched out sleeping heavily, oblivious to the momentous happening."[8] Roosevelt signed first. Perhaps, he mused, he should have signed as "Commander in Chief." "President ought to do!" Hopkins replied dryly. Churchill signed next. When FDR discovered that the prime minister had signed only for England, he chided him: "Hey, ought you not to sign Great Britain and Ireland?"[9] Churchill agreed and corrected his signature. "Four fifths of the human race," he observed, would be represented in the declaration. Litvinov signed next, followed by Soong. Lash was impressed by the gravity of the hour. "In the room there was a sense of Hitler's doom having been sealed."[10]

Roosevelt and Churchill fully appreciated the significance of the moment. When Franklin asked Winston to autograph two of the books Churchill had authored that were in Roosevelt's personal library, "the prime" noted the occasion: "Inscribed by Winston S. Churchill. January 1, 1942, at the moment of signing the Declaration of the United Nations."[11] Around midnight ended what Lash called "quite a historic day." Since it was not a formal "treaty," the "sly squire of Hyde Park" calculated, it did not require Senate approval. Thus, in the words of Assistant Secretary of State Adolf A. Berle, was born "the Charter of the Grand Alliance of the Second World War."[12]

The next day, Berle assembled the representatives of the remaining "associated" or "allied" nations to sign the United Nations declaration. He took malicious delight in the fact that Halifax's notion of having London sign for all of the British Commonwealth of Nations had been rejected by Roosevelt, with "no British nonsense about it." Each nation, including the British Commonwealth Dominions, signed separately in alphabetical order. Roosevelt had insisted that Girja Shankar Bajpai, the Indian representative to the United States, sign for "The Government of India," even though India was still not an independent Dominion like Canada or Australia. In Berle's words, FDR's insistence had effectively "boosted the constitutional status . . . of India." Later, Berle had second thoughts about such American liberties. India was, after all, still a British constitutional matter and the words "Government of" were stricken from "India" in the document.[13]

At the Foreign Office in London, Oliver Harvey had been on pins and needles regarding Churchill's reaction to the inclusion of India as, in effect, a member of the United Nations. "Winston is *au fond* a diehard imperialist," he wrote in his diary, "bad about India (much trouble coming to us here over his refusal to countenance Dominion status)."[14] In fact, Churchill was as opposed to any change in India's inferior constitutional status as ever and his ideas remained hopelessly outmoded. He wired Clement Attlee later in the week:

> I hope my colleagues [in the Cabinet] will realize the danger of raising constitutional issue, still more of making constitutional change, in India at a moment when enemy [Japan] is upon the frontier. . . . The Indian troops are fighting splendidly, but it must be remembered that their allegiance is to the [British] King Emperor and that the rule of the [Indian National] Congress and Hindoo Priesthood machine would never be tolerated by a fighting race. . . . I do not think you will have any trouble with American opinion. All press comments on India I have seen have been singularly restrained. . . .[15]

Harvey was right and Churchill was wrong; the India issue would dog Anglo-American relations for the rest of the war.[16]

Churchill's dressing-down of Litvinov on January 1 gave the Soviet ambassador an opportunity to try to drive a wedge between the Americans and the British. He began with Hopkins. On January 6 he invited "Harry the Hop" for lunch at the Soviet Embassy on Sixteenth Street. Litvinov complained bitterly that Churchill had purposefully shown such "impatience" with him "for some ulterior reason." He told Hopkins that although Churchill was "a great war Prime Minister," he would "not be very useful after the war was over." It would not be Churchill, but Roosevelt who would be "the dominating person at the peace table."[17] Litvinov was a timid man who had barely escaped the great purges of the late 1930s; he had, in fact, been expelled from the Central Committee of the Communist Party and placed "in limbo" before Stalin repatriated him to serve as Soviet ambassador to the United States. It is inconceivable that he would have dared to utter such words without instructions from Moscow. Obviously, Stalin had already set his sights on the "grand alliance" of the two Anglo-Saxon nations.

The signing of the "Declaration of the United Nations" was a great triumph, but it would not yield significant military results for quite some time. On January 2, 1942, the cold light of dawn and the harsh reality of Axis military triumphs once again pervaded the ARCADIA talks. Japanese forces occupied Manila while heavy fighting continued on the Bataan peninsula across Manila Bay. The 12,500 American troops and their 67,500 Filipino allies were running desperately short of food, ammunition, water, and medical supplies. They were killing and eating whatever animals they could find in the thick jungle. General MacArthur's headquarters on Corregidor was being bombed daily. Only the occasional American submarine was able to slip through the Japanese blockade. The position of British forces in Malaya was no less precarious. Pushing south from Thailand, Japanese troops reached Kampar and forced the 15th Indian Division into headlong retreat. They drew closer by the day to Singapore, now virtually cut off.

Incredibly, Secretary Hull continued his temper tantrum over the Free French seizure of St. Pierre and Miquelon. Churchill, in his speech to the House of Commons in Ottawa, had referred to Marshal Pétain and Pierre Laval as men who "fawned" over Hitler and who "lie prostrate at the foot of the conqueror." He had spoken of "some Frenchmen" who "would not bow their knees" and who, under Charles de Gaulle, "continued to fight at the side of the allies." Then, to rub salt into the wound, he had claimed that the Gaullists enjoyed "increasing respect by nine Frenchmen out of every ten throughout the once happy, smiling land of France."[18] The *New York Herald Tribune* trumpeted that with his speech in Ottawa, Churchill had "blown" the seizure of the islands and Hull's reaction to it "through the dusty windows of the State Department."[19] The president, who had listened to Churchill's Ottawa address on his radio, had thought it "grand."

Churchill's celebration of the Free French was for public consumption only. Privately, he had wired de Gaulle the day before his speech in Ottawa:

> Your having broken away from agreement about Miquelon and St Pierre raised a storm which might have been serious had I not been on the spot to speak to the President. Undoubtedly result of your activities there has been to make things more difficult with the United States, and has, in fact, prevented some favourable developments which were occurring. I am always doing my best in all our interests.[20]

Hull, most likely unaware of Churchill's rebuke to de Gaulle, scolded Churchill in front of Roosevelt on January 2 that his comments in Ottawa had been "highly incendiary." He insisted that Churchill issue a statement supporting U.S. policy on Vichy. Churchill refused.[21] FDR then asked Hull to let the matter be, but this only made the old Tennessean more stubborn. His attacks on Churchill, the British, and the Free French grew in intensity over the next few days. He "condemn[ed] the course of the British . . . in the strongest diplomatic terms possible."[22] He charged that Churchill's inflammatory speech in Ottawa had poisoned Anglo-American relations. But Roosevelt refused to pressure the prime minister. The success of ARCADIA could not be jeopardized by a petty quarrel over two barren rocks off Newfoundland. Hull had, in fact, backed himself into a corner. There seemed no honorable way out of the imbroglio but to resign. "I so seriously considered taking this step that I penciled out a note to the President tendering my resignation."[23] In the end, Hull put the note in his desk drawer. But he had his petty revenge. He let almost three years pass before he invited de Gaulle to sign the United Nations declaration.[24]

As Roosevelt, Churchill, Beaverbrook, and Hopkins struggled to step up U.S. war production, American military men desperately tried to find and to direct the means to fight the war. Dwight Eisenhower was one of those men. As assistant chief of the Army's war plans division, it was his job to acquire the shipping to get the men and materials to the various war fronts. Eisenhower's thoughts were welded on the far

Pacific, where the Japanese were driving American troops out of the Philippine Islands. He was desperate to provide reinforcements to General MacArthur and thus concocted a bizarre plan to resupply the American forces on Bataan. In December 1941 Congress had given General Marshall $10 million, which the chief of staff passed on to Eisenhower. With the funds, "Ike" hired what he called "pirates" and their ships and crews in Java, Timor, and New Guinea to run the Japanese blockade of the Philippines. When he found out that his "pirates" refused to accept checks drawn against U.S. funds deposited in a Melbourne bank, Eisenhower literally had bales of cash flown halfway around the world—across Africa, the Middle East, and India —for this purpose. But these were not the legendary buccaneers of the Spanish Main: nearly all of the attempts to get through failed. About fifteen of the mercenary ships were destroyed or captured by the Imperial Japanese Navy. Getting still more desperate, Ike assigned half a dozen overage destroyers to the blockade-running detail. Not one got through.[25]

Eisenhower's often terse entries in the appointment pad on his desk that he used as a makeshift diary convey both the urgency and the chaos of the situation. On January 4, 1942, now chief of the war plans division, he wrote, "Tempers are short! There are lots of amateur strategists on the job—and prima donnas everywhere." Was he perhaps thinking of his commander in chief? One day later, he was exasperated at the news that Brigadier General Wade Haislip at age fifty-two was to get a division. "This War Department is cockeyed!" Suffering from a new bout of what he suspected was shingles, his mood became ever darker. "Two days of feeling bum," he wrote on January 7.[26]

Even at this stage of the ARCADIA conference, with growing agreement at the highest levels on basic war planning, Eisenhower and other American officers still remained suspicious about the British. The old fears and prejudices simply could not be overcome in a week of "jointness." Joseph Stilwell was as rabid in his Anglophobia as ever. On January 6 he complained that Roosevelt, Churchill, Marshall, Stimson, and Dill were still pushing for an invasion of North Africa. The "Limeys" obviously had a "tremendous hold" on Roosevelt. "They shot off their faces as if they were *our* delegates and not theirs." He was suspicious of British plans to have their troops in Northern Ireland replaced by

American Army forces. It would then be, "go home to jolly old England, thank you." And the "Lend-Lease torrent to our British cousins," he bitterly complained, left Americans "without." It was all too political. "The Limeys want us in, committed. They don't care what becomes of us afterward, because they will have shifted the load from their shoulders to ours." Three days later, Stilwell, like Eisenhower, caught the desperate anxiety of the times. "Everybody is shrieking for more men, more guns, more planes, more everything."[27]

The distrust was still mutual. Dill wrote Archibald Wavell:

> As for war, my own belief is that [the Americans] don't know the first thing about it. And yet as you know only too well, they are great critics. How they have the nerve to criticize anyone beats me. However they do. At present our relations with the Americans could not be better, but we are in the honeymoon phase. When we settle down to married life things will, I fear, be very different.[28]

There were signs of that as early as January 2, when Roosevelt and Churchill discussed the critical shipping issue. U.S. Navy Rear Admiral Emery S. Land noted: "As always, the Prime Minister (as well as everyone else) . . . requested more and more merchant ships." FDR was sympathetic, but could offer no succor: "We have reached the bottom of the barrel." Churchill acidly told Roosevelt to "scrape the barrel."[29]

There was better news about potential U.S. aircraft production. On January 4, with the capital in the grips of a heavy snow, "Hap" Arnold made his way to the White House to meet separately with Hopkins, Roosevelt, and Churchill. He told Hopkins that Marshall had signed off on a "1 million man, 115 Group Program" for the U.S. Army Air Forces. Arnold envisaged that by the end of December 1942 he would have on hand 115 groups of heavy bombers, and that he would be able to move 800 heavy bombers to Britain. The only thing holding up the program, Arnold noted, "was approval by the President."

Next, Arnold shared his program estimates with Churchill, who was pleased about the high degree of Anglo-American cooperation in aircraft production. Thereafter, Hap spent forty-five minutes alone with FDR in the Oval Room. The president wanted to know what obstacles there might be in achieving the program, and Arnold repeated what he had told Hopkins. Roosevelt then inquired about the general's relations with his British opposite, Portal. He was delighted with Arnold's brisk reply: "100 per cent." Indeed, Arnold and Portal were about to head off to Florida, for what the American termed "fishing and loafing."[30]

At 5:30 P.M. on January 4 Roosevelt and Churchill met for an hour with their military advisors. North Africa was the major topic of discussion.[31] There were two options on the table: a British invasion of Vichy North Africa without U.S. participation—GYMNAST—and a combined British and American invasion—SUPER GYMNAST. Secretary of War Stimson was very reluctant to support either. In his view, the situation in North Africa was too political. Would Vichy France extend an "invitation" to Washington and London to land forces in North Africa? Would the Spanish government be able to "delay a German invasion of the Iberian Peninsula in sufficient time to permit the occupation to be completed?" When FDR stated that he would discount any idea of Francisco Franco offering opposition to such a German design, Stimson grew even more reticent. The Allies would require "a canopy of air protection" for a successful invasion of North Africa. The Germans already had troops on the ground there and might "quickly establish themselves in the Iberian Peninsula and employ a dangerous force against this operation." And as bad as things were in the immediate future, they would "fade as time goes on." Roosevelt responded that "it would take [the Germans] as long to complete the occupation as it would us." He did not see how the Allies could "stand idly by and permit them to become established." Churchill disliked such musings. He testily interjected that "it had not required the Japs four months to get ashore in Luzon."

Churchill wanted to go into North Africa with as little delay as possible, but it was clear to Roosevelt that "he and Mr. Churchill and the two staffs appeared to know very little about the region." And there remained the "outstanding consideration . . . that the Germans might move into the area first." As far as an "invitation" from Vichy France went, Roosevelt surmised that this was "in the laps of the gods." When Admiral Pound observed that the transfer of American troops to Northern Ireland was supposed to begin in mid-January, everyone soon agreed that the two Allies simply did not have enough ships for both operations. Churchill had to back away from his pet project. "Under no circumstances," he warned, "should we delay [the move to Ireland] going ahead." It was too important "to the morale of the British to have American troops move into Ireland at this time." In the end, he suggested that the chiefs of staff keep their "studies" on hand, and that they all should "meet again within the next few days." FDR agreed and added, "For two men that are in a hurry to get things done, it seems to take a long time." The sun was setting on North Africa.

On January 5, 1942 Churchill flew to Florida, for a brief vacation at the seaside villa in Pompano Beach of a friend of Edward R. Stettinius, Jr. Charles Wilson and "Tommy" Thompson went with him, along with his principal private secretary, John Martin. "The air here is balmy after the bitter cold of Ottawa," Wilson noted in his diary, "oranges and pineapples grow here. And the blue ocean is so warm that Winston basks half-submerged in the water like a hippopotamus in a swamp."[32] Churchill would recall that his American friends "thought that I was looking tired and ought to have a rest."[33] That was no doubt true. But there was also the consideration that the day after Churchill's departure, Roosevelt was scheduled to address Congress. His speaking style was very different from Churchill's, more prosaic, with far less drama and no Shakespearean resonance; there was less likelihood that anyone might draw the comparison with Churchill lying on the sand, far from the press, in the sunny South.

The presidential cavalcade left the White House in bitter cold weather at 12:05 P.M. on Tuesday, January 6. For the second year in a row, Roosevelt had opted to deliver his Annual Address on the State of the Union to the joint session of the Congress in person. Since Thomas Jefferson, no president save Woodrow Wilson had done so, each preferring to have reading clerks intone their messages. It was time for the commander in chief to bring lawmakers up to speed on what steps had been taken since Pearl Harbor, and to allay their fears concerning his closeted discussions with Churchill. The president had rehearsed his speech before Churchill and Beaverbrook in the White House. Some of his staff, most notably Press Secretary Stephen Early, feared that Churchill's address to the joint Congress might have set too high a standard for Roosevelt. They need not have worried.

Franklin Delano Roosevelt took his place at the rostrum at 12:30 P.M. "His face was sharp and stern," presidential speechwriter Rosenman noted. He immediately lauded the high spirit of the American people in their hour of despair: "The Union was never more closely knit together—this country was never more deeply determined to face the solemn tasks before it."[34] It was vintage Roosevelt: no soaring rhetorical heights, no poetic lyrics, just simple talk from the heart. He informed the Congress of the signing of the "Declaration of the United Nations" on New Year's Day and spoke of the "total war effort" to come on the part of its twenty-six nations against Japan's and Germany's "blood-stained course of conquest." Then that resonant, defiant voice addressed the Republic's enemies. "The militarists of Berlin and Tokyo started this war. But the massed, angered forces of common humanity will finish it."

"War costs money," Roosevelt warned the nation's lawmakers. He informed them that in his Budget Message he was asking for $56 billion for war production in the coming fiscal year. Whereas America currently spent only 15 percent on national defense, the new estimates would swallow up more than half the Treasury's annual national income. "That means taxes and bonds and bonds and taxes." He asked Americans to forego "luxuries and other non-essentials." He then revealed absolutely staggering production targets—which he had worked out in consultation with no one but Hopkins. The Republic was to produce 60,000 planes that year and 125,000 in 1943. It was to increase its tank output from 45,000 in 1942 to 75,000 in 1943. Antiaircraft production was to leap from 20,000 that year to 35,000 in 1943. New merchant shipping was to rise from 1.1 million deadweight tons in 1941 to 6 million in the current year and to 10 million by 1943. "The figures," Roosevelt informed a wildly cheering Congress, "will give the Japanese and the Nazis a little idea of just what they accomplished at Pearl Harbor." He asked the nation's industrialists to raise their sights all along the production line. "Let no man say it cannot be done."

Yet again, the president warned the nation that it would be "a hard war, a long war, a bloody war, a costly war." The enemy was "powerful and cunning—and cruel and ruthless." The tasks that lay ahead were daunting. "We must guard against complacency." To allay the fears of his political opponents concerning the daily and nightly discussions with the British leader, Roosevelt informed the Congress that together with Churchill, he had established the machinery to win the war. "Mr. Churchill and I understand each other, our motives and our purposes. Together, during the past two weeks, we have faced squarely the military and economic problems of this greatest world war."

Toward the end of the address, Roosevelt again reminded Congress, and the nation via live radio broadcast, of the moral character of the war. "We are fighting to cleanse the world of ancient ills, ancient evils." The Republic's enemies were "guided by brutal cynicism, by unholy contempt for the human race." America, by contrast, was guided by a Judeo-Christian faith that reached back to the first chapter of the "Book of Genesis": "God created man in His own image." Finally, the president made reference to the unshakable determination of the United Nations to fight the war to the bitter end. "No compromise can end that conflict." He then added eternal words: "There never has been—there never can be—successful compromise between good and evil." He had but one message for Berlin, Rome, and Tokyo. "Only total victory can reward the champions of tolerance, and decency, and freedom, and faith." The vociferous and united roar of approval from the senators and representatives assured the president that he had hit a home run. Secretary of War Stimson called it "the best speech that I have ever heard him make. . . . This knocks the last bottom out of the old isolationist ideas."[35]

Back at the White House, FDR met the press. He was pleased, he led off, to see only a small group of reporters, for the topic was finances and economics. "Of course, very few newspapermen know the difference between a dollar and a dime," he jokingly stated. "But then, on the other hand, very few Presidents do."[36] He informed them that he had presented Congress with the "biggest Budget in the history of the Nation, any time." He was asking steelmakers, for instance, to increase the percentage of "defense steel" from 25 percent in September 1941 to 55 percent in the near future.

Warming to the topic, the president informed the reporters of his talks with the Maritime Commission. In reply to his question concerning present levels of production, they had stated that they were putting out 1 million tons of shipping. "What can you step it up to?" The reply was 5 million tons. "Not enough. Go back and sharpen your pencils."

They did and FDR was happy to report that they had indeed sharpened their pencils. "It will hurt terribly," the members of the Maritime Commission had replied, "but we believe that if we are told to we can turn out six million tons of shipping this year." This was the kind of "can-do" spirit that Roosevelt loved. "Now you're talking." He then turned the screws even tighter. Could the Maritime Commission add another four million tons to the target for 1943? "And they scratched their heads, and came back and said, 'Aye, aye, sir, we will do it'." And then he likewise asked his war productions people to increase aircraft output from 65,000 to 125,000 within a year. And they likewise responded, "Aye, aye, sir. We will do it, sir." Roosevelt was a plunger. He probably had no idea what these figures actually meant in terms of financial investment, plant expansion, labor recruitment, and the like, but he wanted them to be impressive, especially to the Axis. As Hopkins put it, the president "was never afraid of big round numbers."

While Roosevelt regaled reporters with these figures, Congress studied the Annual Budget Message that he had sent up to the Hill the previous day. It was "the budget of a Nation at war in a world at war."[37] Its parameters were truly immense. He had already added $46 billion to the $29 billion defense program of January 3, 1941. Total war expenditures were running to about $2 billion per month, and would soon surge to $5 billion. "Nothing short of maximum will suffice." America had no choice but "overwhelmingly" to outproduce its enemies so that its armies would enjoy a "crushing superiority of equipment" in all theaters of the global war. "I can only say," Roosevelt concluded, "that we are determined to pay whatever price we must to preserve our way of life."

Never in its history had the nation seen such estimates for war production. *U.S. News* informed its readers that FDR's figures "reached such astronomical proportions that human minds could not reach around them." The magazine noted that the president was calling for the production of "a plane every four minutes in 1943; a tank every seven minutes; two seagoing ships a day."[38] Many military and industrial leaders greeted these staggering figures with derision, some with despair. Most blamed Hopkins, a notorious New Deal free-spender, for the illusory goals. But it was Roosevelt, and not Hopkins, who had radically raised even the most optimistic estimates of production on the eve of his State of the Union address to Congress. Indeed, when Hopkins had questioned some of the numbers, FDR had rosily replied, "Oh—the production people can do it if they really try."

Not surprisingly, Churchill was ecstatic. He informed the War Cabinet back home that Beaverbrook had been "magnificent" and Hopkins "a godsend" in bringing about such goals.[39] Secretary of War Stimson was more down to earth. "There is a great tendency," he noted in his diary, "to take the President's enunciations as the law of the Medes and the Persians when as a matter of fact he has put them out by the merest rule of thumb calculations and without taking into consideration the enormous complexities which are involved."[40]

To Roosevelt's delight, his truly astonishing numbers were duly noted in Berlin. Propaganda Minister Goebbels spoke of "hysterically inflated figures." Roosevelt's proposal to build 100,000 aircraft per year, he crowed, was "absolute nonsense." The president's war budget of $56 billion for 1943 was pure illusion. "This man is conducting truly criminal politics." Roosevelt's entire financial and economic house of cards would collapse one day. The good doctor knew, of course, which forces were behind this deception. "Having the Jews as advisers most times will cost a statesman dearly."[41]

The top-secret reports of the *Sicherheitsdienst* were not quite as positive. The SS reported that the public at large did not share Goebbels' propaganda "polemic" against Roosevelt's armaments production "bluff." All too many Germans believed that Goebbels' reports were "colored." All too many were convinced that Britain and the United States could outproduce Germany in war materials. Above all, the "extraordinary material strength" that the Soviets had mounted late in 1941 rendered the propaganda minister's views about the Anglo-Saxon industrial potential suspect.[42]

In a little more than two weeks since Churchill's arrival in Washington, he and Roosevelt, along with their advisors and military staffs, had written a rough draft of the war plan that both nations would follow in the first year or so of the war. They had agreed on a broad strategy to get American troops to Northern Ireland before the end of January and U.S. aircraft to the United Kingdom shortly thereafter. They had established a system of joint theater command and put in place a mechanism—the Combined Chiefs of Staff—that would pull the levers to make that system go. They had hammered out a joint statement of Allied war aims and secured the adherence of the United Nations, as the former "associated" or "allied" powers had heretofore been referred to. And they had disabused American war planners of the notion that anything other than an all-out war production program would suffice to beat the Axis. Their accomplishments to that point were not inconsiderable. But with all that, there were still problems to be resolved—of trust, of priorities, of national pride, and of national interests. Where would the war-allocations committee sit? How would its resources be distributed? Who would decide how much each ally would receive? Who would prioritize the needs of the various war theaters? Again, the devil was in the details. In the last week of the ARCADIA, everything still might suddenly unravel.

13

CHAIN OF COMMAND

Pompano Beach, Florida, 2:00 p.m., January 5, 1942. Two days earlier Alonzo Fields, one of White House Chief Usher Howell G. Crim's most trusted subordinates, and a small staff had been sent to the beachfront house provided by Edward Stettinius and told to prepare for the arrival of "a very important man." Fields had guessed that it would be the president. White House cook Henrietta Nesbitt also knew that something was up, "Atmosphere very tense."[1] Fields was instructed by the Secret Service to prepare a dinner for fifteen to twenty people for the evening of January 5. The important but still unknown guest was to arrive for dinner in just five hours; dinner was set for 8 p.m.

Fields was in a panic. He had with him only $100 in cash. He knew no merchants who might extend him credit; and he suspected that mentioning Franklin Roosevelt's name in what surely had to be a Republican resort would carry little currency. The Stettinius family came to the rescue. They gave him resources enough to buy food and drink for a group of twenty. There was no champagne to be found in Pompano Beach—a requirement for the mystery guest—so the usher sent to Miami for some. It never arrived. At 7 p.m. on the dot, a large contingent of houseguests arrived. Fields recognized Winston Churchill at once. The dinner consisted of a standing roast of beef and Yorkshire pudding, with horseradish and English mustard, Churchill's staple for breakfast, lunch, and dinner.

Churchill was tired from the long flight and went to bed early. The next morning, Fields was in the pantry preparing breakfast when he heard a familiar growl: "I say—Where is everybody?" Entering the dining room, Fields got off a cheerful, "Good morning Mr. Prime Minister." He later recalled the scene: "There he stood in his bare feet, looking like a pudgy, mischievous boy with a smile." Churchill asked the usher to "expedite" his valet and called for the morning papers. He complimented Fields on the magnificent dinner—and slyly told him that the good food and wine had almost helped him forget the lack of champagne. Churchill then toddled off for his customary bath, glass of sherry, and hearty breakfast.

A few minutes later, Churchill rang. "Did you ring for me, sir?" Fields asked. The prime minister answered in the affirmative. "I am sure you are aware that I do not like whistling or talking outside my quarters. May I depend on you to take care of this detail?" Fields well remembered the injunction against whistling and talking from his first meeting with "the prime" at the White House. Estevan Medina, the White House chef who had come down to Florida, had been happily whistling Franz Schubert's *Serenade*. "No more Whistling," Fields instructed his chef. Sometimes, Medina would forget. The bell from the prime minister's bedroom would then summon Fields at once. One time he was called into the library. Churchill scowled at him and asked, "How many stone do you weigh and how tall are you?" Fields confessed that he was not familiar with the English system of weight, but that he weighed 250 pounds and was six-feet-three-and-a-half inches tall. Churchill snapped, "Well, that is good. Don't you think you are big enough to stop that whistling?" With "a voice of humility," Fields, replied, "Oh yes, Mr. Prime Minister, the whistling shall be stopped."

The Florida trip gave Churchill a perfect opportunity to chide Roosevelt about his obsession with secrecy. For all the hush-hush surrounding the journey to Florida, the prime minister took great delight in sending the president a cartoon from one of the local newspapers that showed two elderly, portly men frolicking on the beach. The obvious "Churchill" character pronounced: "Hard work is the thing that will win this war—we must keep at it night and day!" Churchill cabled Roosevelt: "This shows that all the trouble you took about preserving secrecy has been in vain." Tongue in cheek, he added: "Tommy [Thompson, Churchill's private bodyguard] is plainly identifiable."[2]

The Americans took extraordinary precautions to ensure Churchill's privacy and security. John Martin, his private secretary, later recalled: "We were closely guarded by Secret Service men and, though the Press soon scented our presence, we were not molested in any way. The story was put about that a Mr Lobb . . . was staying in the house . . . I was the English butler."[3] If they were not molested, it was not because some of the press did not try every trick and wile. On the third day at Pompano, a car drove up to the villa with two women, obviously reporters. Thompson thought one of the two was especially good looking. The Secret Service men "put them off by saying that someone who had been ill had rented the villa. They hoped the explanation would suffice. I knew it wouldn't." Sure enough, the two reporters soon reappeared "some distance away on the beach" walking toward the villa. Thompson saw one of them stop, poke a beach umbrella into the sand, and sit down. The other one took off her shoes and stockings and began wading toward the villa. She was stopped by a young G-man. "If you can tell me who it is," she offered, "I will go away and just print that and no more." If, however, he might arrange an interview with the stranger in the house, she suggested, "you may spend your nights with me—in case I happen to appeal to you in that way." Thomson heard everything from his perch near an upstairs bedroom: "After a searing inventory of himself, followed by some of the most interesting dialogue I ever heard in America," he recalled, "the Secret Service came through in a fine, but battered show of self-denial."[4]

The villa was about a hundred feet from the beach and Churchill regularly charged into the Atlantic surf. On those occasions, the Secret Service cleared all local residents from the beach for about a mile. But one day, just as the prime minister was emerging from the waves, the G-men were aghast to discover a woman and her dog loitering about. "The prime" was without bathing trunks. Since he was incognito in Florida, the Secret Service did not dare attract attention to him, and so Churchill and the G-men remained in their places until the woman and her dog had moved on. Fields and the staff had a good chuckle over this, "and of course the P.M. never dared to swim in the raw again."[5]

Churchill swam every day. The last day at Pompano it rained but he insisted on taking his daily plunge. Walking down to the water, his party spotted a shark swimming lazily past the beach, "a gentle moving terror if I ever saw one," Thompson recalled. Someone told Churchill that it was a sand shark and not dangerous. Thompson had his doubts:

> In Florida, I discovered that every shark is a sand shark and no sand shark is ever hungry. I told Churchill to stay out of the water; that my usefulness ended at the edge. The shark was big enough to eat a horse. Even Winston was impressed. "Sand shark? I am not so sure about that. I want to see his Identification Card before I trust myself to him." But he went in anyhow, though not far. "Keep sending me bulletins, Thompson . . . keep him classified as inoffensive."[6]

Churchill always worked on his vacations, and Pompano was no exception. In the mornings he conducted business from his bed. Then he would eat a hearty lunch, take a dip in the sea, and return to his usual routine of a full nap and bath before resuming his labors. During the days, couriers would arrive from Washington with papers and telegrams and return with Churchill's latest memos and missives. The phone rang constantly. Churchill made outgoing calls to Washington and elsewhere. There were details to iron out about Archibald Wavell's command, about Soviet claims to the Baltic states, and about the pressure for constitutional reform in India. He was deeply disturbed about the heavy damage done by Italian "human torpedoes" to the two British warships in Alexandria, Egypt. "The Mediterranean battle fleet was for the time being non-existent," he wrote in his memoirs, "and our naval power to guard Egypt from direct overseas invasion in abeyance." He gave direct orders to the Air Ministry and the Royal Navy to reinforce British bomber forces in the eastern Mediterranean, even though it meant pulling aircraft away from the bomber offensive against Germany.[7]

Each evening after dinner, Churchill would retire to the library with his private secretary, his military aide, and sometimes with his physician to deal with the latest war crises. Pacing furiously up and down, with the ever-present cigar clenched between his teeth, he would dictate memos, letters, and responses to urgent matters. During those working sessions, Fields recalled, "the Scotch would evaporate." On one particular evening, when Fields came into the library, he was astonished by the row of empty bottles there. Churchill never missed a beat. "Yes, my man, I need a little more to drink. You see, I have a war to fight and

I need fortitude for the battle." In fact, he had a special favor to ask. "I hope you will come to my defense if someday someone should claim that I am a teetotaler." Fields smiled and assured the prime minister that he could be depended on to defend him against such a claim. At one point, Churchill explained to Fields that when he first went to India, he had discovered that the water was impure and that the only drink fit for human consumption was whiskey.

Over a number of evenings, Churchill composed yet another long memo on the state of the war. Many of his assessments were prescient. News from North Africa had turned bad in the previous days. Rommel was still withdrawing, but in good order and undefeated. Fresh German troops were being sent to North Africa to shore him up. Under the changing circumstances, Churchill suggested that the Allies study possible operations in that theater "more thoroughly" while proceeding with the greatest possible speed to send American troops to Northern Ireland. The main objective, as he saw it, should be "the wearing down by continuous engagement of the German air power." German aircraft production, he was certain, could not stand a prolonged war of attrition against the combined British and American air forces. "We can afford the drain far better that they can." He feared that the most recent Soviet triumphs on the Eastern Front might not last beyond the cold weather. When the "enormous power of the German Army" eventually reasserted itself, Hitler would most likely hold in the North while driving southeast toward the Caucasus and the Baku oilfields that lay just beyond.[8] As usual, he was on the mark.

Mischievously, Churchill had left with his chiefs of staff a highly contentious position paper setting out British ideas about post-ARCADIA collaboration. The British chiefs turned the paper over to their American counterparts on January 8, 1942. The document discussed post-conference planning, intelligence-gathering, troop movements, and war resources production and allocation. It even suggested a new nomenclature to avoid confusion in post-ARCADIA discourses: *joint* would "be applied to Inter-Service collaboration of One Nation," whereas *combined* would be applied "to collaboration between two or more United Nations." Further, Churchill proposed in the paper that John Dill remain in Washington "as representative of the Minister of Defence [i.e. Churchill]" and that he "have contacts with such authorities on the highest level as may be arranged between the President and the Prime Minister." Finally, and most explosively, Churchill's epistle suggested that two "Combined Allocation Committees" be established, one in London and one in Washington, with "each caring for the needs of the Allies for whom [the host nation] has accepted responsibility."[9] Given Churchill's iron grip over his chiefs, there can be little doubt that he was the originator of the British initiative.

The document had the expected effect: for the second time at ARCADIA, George Marshall's famous temper got the best of him. The paper's two main provisions were a direct challenge to his hard-fought-for concept of a single Combined Chiefs of Staff (CCS), sitting in Washington, as the highest military planning and command body for the duration of the war. In Marshall's view, the CCS Committee would take overall political direction directly from the president and the prime minister as the civilian chiefs of both countries' militaries. It would not only set objectives for each war theater and each theater commander, but also coordinate military planning among theaters. This meant that it also had to be in overall control of the distribution of war materiel. There was no point, for example, giving Wavell an order to defend this or attack that while the shipping he would use, or the tanks he would need, were sent to another theater of war. Interposing Dill—as Churchill's personal representative—between the CCS Committee and Roosevelt would invite Churchill to interfere directly in the chain of command. In addition, creating two munitions distributions boards would vastly complicate the CCS Committee's task of coordinating the war. As Churchill romped in the warm Florida surf, Marshall boiled in Washington.

Churchill had carefully crafted the document around the person of John Dill, knowing that the former chief of the imperial general staff had established good relations with Marshall at ARCADIA. Specifically, Churchill wanted Dill to assume leadership of the British Joint Staff Mission, which worked out of the British Embassy. He disliked the idea that whenever some message had to be transmitted to the Americans, or vice versa, it had first to be discussed by the whole mission—a cumbersome "triumvirate of the three services," as Colonel Ian Jacob put it. Rather, Churchill wanted Dill to talk directly to Marshall or Admiral King; or, if need be, directly to Harry Hopkins or Roosevelt.[10] Dill appreciated the centrality of his proposed new role: "[Churchill's] idea is that

I shall be able to talk to the President and others on Military questions in his name without treading on the toes of the Ambassador . . . or the Military Mission." But was the old soldier up to the mission? "I am not yet convinced that I can be very useful as the representative of the Minister of Defence."[11]

There was no arguing with the prime minister on the matter. Churchill had previously cleared his initiative with Britain's permanent military representatives in Washington. And they had emphatically expressed their desire to have a British representative of cabinet rank to head up both their military and supply missions in the United States. Colonel Jacob at once spied trouble with Marshall and the Americans. He believed the prime minister had not fully thought through the implications of naming Dill as a *primus inter pares*, a first among equals, in Washington, "organization not being his strong point."[12] Jacob may have been correct. But Churchill had decided on Dill as a link that would allow him direct access to both the president and the key American chiefs, in effect bypassing the Combined Chiefs of Staff. He may have given in to the Americans on the issue of "unity of command," but he now presented his quid pro quo.

On the afternoon of January 10 Churchill's party motored to Fort Lauderdale for lunch; they then boarded a train for Washington. "The prime" could not resist tweaking FDR yet again about the American obsession with secrecy. The Secret Service had warned him to be extremely careful whenever he used the public telephone system. Thus, when Churchill called Roosevelt to inform the White House that he was heading back, he chided FDR: "I mustn't tell you on the open line how we shall be traveling, but we shall be coming by puff puff."[13] Churchill and party arrived back in Washington at 12:15 P.M. on January 11. It was a bone-chilling 6 degrees in the capital. Fresh snow covered the ground.

Like Churchill, Roosevelt had also needed time off to reflect on the events of the first two weeks of the ARCADIA conference and to gather his strength for its final deliberations. On the evening of Tuesday, January 6, after a strenuous day that had included his Budget Message, his Annual Address to the Congress, and his news conference, the president left the White House. The black bulletproof Capone limousine headed out on Sixteenth Street. It was a bitter cold night with a sharp wind blowing. It was the president's first "blackout trip" since the Republic was at war. There would be no press, no radio, no news, and no mention even that he was leaving the capital. The automobile's immediate destination turned out to be a deserted railroad siding in Silver Springs, Maryland. There was little chance of some stray reporter lingering there.

Shortly after 11 P.M. the special presidential train, the *Ferdinand Magellan*, pulled out of the station. The party onboard included Hopkins; Grace Tully, the president's private secretary; and William D. Hassett, FDR's new public relations secretary. Already on the train were Louise Hackmeister, the White House switchboard operator, and Mike Reilly, commanding an unusually large contingent of sixteen Secret Service men. The conductors were not given the guests' names but only numbers. Since it was night, "Fala the Informer," as the G-men called the president's Scottie, could not give away his master's whereabouts. All too often in the past, Fala had peered out of windows and doors and thus had telegraphed Roosevelt's presence. After a quick snack washed down with FDR's favorite Saratoga Springs water, the presidential party retired.

The *Ferdinand Magellan* steamed through the darkness at its maximum allowable speed of 40 miles per hour. It had the right of way over all other trains, which had to stay clear by at least twenty minutes and to take to sidings to let it pass. "Every trestle, culvert, switch, and crossing," Commander William M. Rigdon, Roosevelt's new White House assistant naval aide, remembered, was "checked carefully in advance and guarded closely."[14]

Apart from the president's car, the train hauled an oversized baggage car, once owned by the Barnum & Bailey Circus, right behind the locomotive. It contained two large sedans and two convertibles for Roosevelt and his Secret Service detail. Next in line came a communications car that contained a diesel-powered radio transmitting and receiving station to keep the president in instant touch with the Signal Corps at the White House Map Room. Then came a Pullman car with four upper and four lower compartment drawing-room sleepers for the radio operators and the railroad staff; a roomette car for the press (empty this trip); a club car with a bar, card tables, and dark green plush armchairs; a dining car; another Pullman roomette car for FDR's personal staff and the G-men; and finally the presidential Pullman. To the engineers in the locomotive, hauling the heavy train was like pulling a fishing line with a lead sinker on the end.

On Wednesday, January 7, the *Ferdinand Magellan* quietly pulled into Highland, New York. It was a "snappy cold morning," Hassett recalled, with FDR "in fine spirits."[15] The presidential party motored across the Hudson River to Poughkeepsie. There, the G-men were lodged at the Campbell House, while Hackmeister and Hassett were billeted at Nelson House. Roosevelt, Hopkins, and Tully proceeded to Hyde Park, where they took quarters at the family mansion, Springwood. When Henry Morgenthau tried to "chisel in on the President," "Hackie" Hackmeister forcefully instructed the secretary of the treasury to communicate only with the White House in Washington. FDR was to be shielded from all outside influences.

The days at Hyde Park continued bitter cold, with sharp, piercing winds. Roosevelt and Hopkins spent the days in the library working over war production figures and staffing for the new production agency, yet to be established. The two also discussed how after the war what the president called the "distributing states" needed to be reestablished in Europe. "Pools of raw and critical material such as steel and foodstuffs must be provided, available to all who need them," Roosevelt announced. Interestingly, he informed Hopkins that "if small states are restored," their existence would have to be "guaranteed by plebiscites every ten years." It was a strange blend of New Deal politics applied worldwide, along with great power constructions. Most important, for Roosevelt, the days spent in near isolation with Hopkins brought back memories of their tempestuous New Deal days.

FDR was pleased with the "complete privacy" of the visit home. No radio and no press had leaked news of the sojourn to Hyde Park. He had once called it "a hole" into which he would crawl, "and pull the hole in after me." To avoid the publicity of his staff housed in hotels in Poughkeepsie, the president mused that in future he would put them all up in the massive Vanderbilt Mansion, three miles north of Springwood, which the Vanderbilt family had turned over to the government in 1940. Hassett took devilish delight at the president, who, in high spirits, stated that "in which event Hackie [Hackmeister] must occupy Mrs. Vanderbilt's Marie Antoinette bedroom (with chicken fence around the bed), sleep under black satin sheets, have black satin negligeé [sic] with blue ribbons, also blue ribbons on bedroom chinaware." Even during these dark days of the war, FDR had not lost his sense of humor.

While at Hyde Park, on January 9 the presidential party learned that Joe Louis, "The Brown Bomber," had knocked out Buddy Baer at 2:56 of the first round at Madison Square Garden in New York. The bout had been the brainchild of Admiral Stark in order to raise money for the Navy Relief Fund; Louis donated his entire purse of $65,200. A few members of Roosevelt's party had brought along F. Scott Fitzgerald's latest novel, *The Last Tycoon*. In Italy, Benedetto Croce had offended the Fascist government with his opus, *History as the Story of Liberty*. For the men of ARCADIA, it was a timely publication.

On Saturday, January 10, the *Ferdinand Magellan* pulled out of Highland at 11 P.M. It was still bitter cold. Nearby Rhinebeck had reported sixteen below. The presidential party reached Silver Springs at 8:30 A.M. the next morning. It was still cold. FDR tipped the conductors the usual five dollars. The party then motored on to the White House "through quiet Sunday-morning streets." The first "blackout trip" of the war had been a complete success. Ahead of Roosevelt lay four days of completing what certainly shaped up to the most contentious work of ARCADIA, the creation of a war allocations committee.

While Roosevelt and Churchill had taken their mid-conference break, the service chiefs, now meeting as the "Combined Chiefs," worked out the precise details of how their new organization might function for the rest of the war. It was decided that the CCS Committee would include the heads of the British Joint Staff Mission in Washington. They would represent their respective British service chiefs—Admiral Pound, Air Chief Marshal Portal, and Chief of the Imperial General Staff Brooke. Dill was to remain in Washington as Churchill's personal representative. But it was not at all clear yet to whom he would report on what had, or had not yet, been determined. The CCS Committee was to meet "weekly, or more often if necessary." (Its first formal post-conference session took place on January 23, 1942, in the Federal Reserve Building. The following month it moved across Constitution Avenue into the former Public Health Service building where it met throughout the war.)

The formation of the CCS Committee forced the Americans to reform their command structure. Realizing that their old Joint Board (with only the Army and the Navy represented) simply was not up to the high organizational standards of the British, the American military established the Joint Chiefs of Staff (JCS). It included Army Chief of Staff Marshall and Commander in Chief U.S. Fleet King. To maintain numerical parity with the British, for whom Portal represented the Royal Air Force, Marshall resorted to what he called a "pleasant subterfuge" and included General Arnold of the Army Air Forces on the JCS, even though there existed no separate and distinct American "air force."

The "Combined Chiefs" quickly discovered that it was easier to establish "combined" machinery than it was to work out common strategy. The British remained firmly focused on the North Atlantic, on getting Lend-Lease supplies to Britain and to Russia, and on ferrying aircraft in large numbers to the Middle East. The Americans, not surprisingly, continued to pine for the fate of the Philippines in general and of Douglas MacArthur in particular. Despite the agreed-upon "Europe-first" strategy, they wanted to get as many men, ships, and planes as possible to the Far East as quickly as possible. And there were continuing divisions over exactly how the CCS Committee would function and what jurisdiction it would have.

On January 10 the chiefs met to discuss the situation in North Africa and the Far East, and specifically China. They were constantly stymied by the shortage of shipping. If too much was sent to one theater, there was not enough to go to another. Which of the disastrous war fronts was the greater disaster? The Allies were hemorrhaging; where to apply the Band-Aid? Toward the end of this meeting, the British chiefs tabled Churchill's highly explosive proposals of January 8. There was only a brief discussion before adjournment. The Americans demanded twenty-four hours to study, and fully comprehend, the deep implications of what the British were now suggesting. Most important, nothing could be done until the presidential party returned from Hyde Park and Roosevelt had a chance to digest Churchill's proposals.

Thus, at two long meetings on January 11 and 12, the chiefs restricted their discussions to the nettlesome problem of how to allocate available sealift. Hour after agonizing hour, they debated the issues.[16] So many threatened fronts, so little sealift. Admiral Stark wondered whether it might not be best to cut the flow of American troops to Northern Ireland and Iceland, and to send the forces thus freed up to the Pacific instead. General Marshall was willing to cut the American contingents going to Europe down to 10,000 soldiers overall, but in the end it was not a question of troops, which were "available for both purposes," he argued, but rather one of finding the "necessary [shipping] tonnage." Portal worried about "a great waste of matériel" should air resources be "poured into the [Far East] without the necessary ground staff to operate and maintain them." He wanted to stick with the original plan to send a large U.S. contingent to Iceland and Northern Ireland. There was still the question of North Africa. And now, with continued Japanese successes and growing domination of the seas and the air to the northeast of Australia and New Zealand, there was the added need to secure the islands that lay between them and Hawaii. If Fiji, New Caledonia, or the New Hebrides fell to Japan, Australia and New Zealand would be isolated from the United States. Should they not be sent the ships, troops, and aircraft to keep them out of Japanese hands?

Almost at the point of despair, the chiefs could only agree to refer the question to American and British shipping experts. Unsurprisingly, the experts came up with a compromise: if the troop convoy to Iceland were cut from 8,000 to 2,500 men and that to Northern Ireland were slashed from 16,000 to 4,000, then some 21,800 soldiers could leave from New York on January 20 for the Far East—a journey of about four weeks. This caused concern for Portal: should 400 aircraft be sent to cover the Far East expeditionary force, would this not cut into American aircraft replacements for the Middle East? Marshall also worried that the diversion of shipping to the Pacific would force a 30 percent cut in Lend-Lease shipments to the Soviet Union. It was, Marshall argued, all a question of priorities. What was more important, he asked rhetorically,

10,000 troops for New Caledonia, or 16,000 for Northern Ireland, or continuing with full Lend-Lease shipments to Russia? Time was of the essence if the ships currently loading in New York were to get away by January 20. In a commendable show of unity, the chiefs accepted Marshall's notion that supplies to Russia were sacrosanct as well as Stark's proposal that relief for Northern Ireland be set back a month. They happily reserved the greater political issue of war materials allocation for Roosevelt and Churchill to decide.

Joseph Stilwell sat in on one of the meetings of the American chiefs over the course of these two anxious days. As ever, his acid pen caught the highly charged mood. "Boy! I got into rarefied atmosphere today. Conference in Stark's office. . . . . Most of the admirals in captivity. My impression was that they were all very conscious of their gold lace, and felt their exalted position greatly. Keenly." The general could not resist another dig at the British. "All agreed on being disgusted with the British hogging *all* the material: quite willing to divide ours with us, but never any mention of putting *theirs* in the pot." Stilwell was fully aware of Marshall's precarious position, having to balance not only British and American views and needs, but also those of his own chiefs. At this all-American meeting, Admiral King demanded that the United States secure at least the line from Hawaii to Samoa. He also wanted New Caledonia, 900 miles east of Australia, to be held at all cost. "Hap" Arnold responded that he did not want to send air reinforcements to that spot, but offered that his heavy bombers could fly over New Caledonia in case the Japanese occupied it. That brought a tart rejoinder from King to the effect that "ships cannot fly." The haggling disgusted "Vinegar Joe" Stilwell. In reply to Marshall's question, "Can you hold Hawaii?" Admiral King had responded with a less than firm, "Can the Army hold it?" To Marshall's follow-up, "If the Army says it can hold it, will the Navy say so?" Stilwell recorded King's "'Yes,' not too emphatically." It was more than he could take: "Imagine. Doubt about Hawaii."[17]

Roosevelt and Churchill, both back in the capital, at once moved to address the critical shipping issue. They convened their military staffs at 5:30 P.M. on January 12, 1942. The president took the lead. He suggested that the status of the North African enterprise be discussed first. Somewhat embarrassed, Churchill conceded that British forces were not doing well in their fight against Rommel. General Claude Auchinleck's British 8th Army, after advancing to El Agheila, had been stopped dead in its tracks by a German counterattack. Auchinleck had to abandon Benghazi and fall back on El Gazala, about 110 miles inside Libya. While Military Intelligence in London kept bragging that "we have Rommel in the can,"[18] Churchill in Washington knew better. "Ultra" codebreaking intercepts revealed that the Afrika Korps was being resupplied with thousands of tons of munitions, food, and water from Tripoli, and, more important, troops, tanks, and vehicles of all sorts from Germany. These could only be for a second counteroffensive. "There will be a battle soon," Churchill prophesied. Even if "the desert fox" were to be defeated, "his defeat would be preceded by a stern chase." The invasion of North Africa might have to be delayed, he conceded with a heavy heart.

Roosevelt then raised the issue of shipping. Marshall told him of the previous day's agreement among the chiefs of staff: 21,800 American troops were to sail from the East Coast on January 20, arriving in the Far East one month later; 10,000 of these would land at New Caledonia. Some twenty cargo ships would carry 250 pursuit planes, 86 medium and 57 light bombers, 220 tons of cargo, and 4.5 million gallons of gasoline. The initial drafts of American troops scheduled for Iceland would be reduced to 2,500 and those for Northern Ireland to 4,000.

Churchill immediately became alarmed by the American plans. He was leery of any move to strengthen the Pacific at the expense of the campaign against Germany, and hence asked what impact these arrangements would have on the shipment of Lend-Lease supplies to Russia. It was not the material he was worried about, it was the ships. The Russians, he stated, would "undoubtedly be disappointed" by cuts at a time when they had just halted the German onslaught at the gates of Moscow. Yet, the list of shipping needs was long and growing daily: ships for the North Atlantic convoy routes, ships to carry Caribbean oil to the United States and to Britain, ships to carry meat and foodstuffs from Latin America to the United Kingdom, ships to carry men and troops to Northern Ireland, Iceland, North Africa, the Far East, the islands linking Australia and New Zealand to the United States, and ships to carry Lend-Lease supplies to Russia.

To be sure, there already were some forty new ships a month coming down the ways at yards in the United States, Britain, and

Canada, but the U-boats were sinking 400,000 tons of Allied shipping every month. Yet again, Hopkins came to the rescue. Since 30 percent of the shipping currently being sent to the Soviet Union translated into but seven ships, the "Lord Root of the Matter" argued, then surely Admiral Land and the Maritime Committee could find these seven ships among an existing inventory of 1,200 merchant ships! Roosevelt and Churchill were delighted with Hopkins' intervention and instructed Land to find the seven ships. Admiral King appreciated Hopkins' critical mediating role. "Hopkins did a lot to keep the President on the beam and even more to keep Churchill on the beam," he later wrote. "I've seldom seen a man whose head was screwed on so tight."[19]

FDR closed the discussions around 6:30 P.M. by approving Marshall's plan to go ahead with the shipping allocations that had been decided the day before, and by having Beaverbrook and Hopkins find the ships for Russia. In Hap Arnold's words, "The President and the Prime Minister felt that it was highly important that there be no indication of reductions in the shipments to Russia."[20] All in all, the day had ended well.

That night Churchill hosted an informal dinner at the British Embassy.[21] He invited the senior American secretaries—Hull (State), Stimson (War), and Morgenthau (Treasury)—as well as Secretary of the Navy Knox, and Hopkins, among others. The British party included Halifax and Beaverbrook. What Stimson called a "very good dinner" in fact became a disastrous free-for-all without Roosevelt to keep a tight rein on his lieutenants.

Knox led off "with his usual vigor and lack of caution," as Stimson put it.[22] The secretary of the Navy attacked the proposal to proceed with the Far East relief operation. He was supported by Beaverbrook, who had a peculiar knack of sometimes siding with those Americans who were most outspoken against Churchill. Everyone around the dinner table knew that the prime minister had supported Marshall's plan in order to maintain unity in decision-making. Why this sudden questioning of difficult decisions already reached? Stimson assumed the role of peacemaker. He "was rather disgusted with Knox's readiness to talk loosely without careful thought," he cruelly remarked. There was no question that the Far East operation was "absolutely necessary," but it would in no way affect "the other main theatres of the war provided only that the Navy would do its part with carriers." That was intended to keep Knox quiet.

Churchill tried to ease the tension by turning the discussions to North Africa. He still favored "immediate action" in that theater. But North Africa was not high on Stimson's list of priorities, and the secretary knew that it was even lower on Marshall's. Hull, sitting beside Churchill, then gave free rein yet again to his pet obsession: imperial preferences and the Ottawa accords of 1932. Surely, now was the time to use Lend-Lease and America's entry into the war, in the words of historian Warren F. Kimball, "as a knife to open that oyster shell, the empire."[23] Churchill was not amused. He refused even to consider Hull's pointed proposal to include in the Lend-Lease contract an "agreement to discard the Empire tariff and trade program." Churchill ended the dinner to head off further discussion. Allies they were becoming—slowly, even grudgingly, in fact as well as in name. But at this critical juncture—with the prime minister scheduled to depart Washington in just forty-eight hours—national self-interest continued to assert itself.

14

ALLIANCE FORGED

THE ISSUE THAT ALMOST WRECKED THE CONFERENCE ON ITS SECOND to last day was the form of post-ARCADIA collaboration Winston Churchill and the British chiefs would leave behind them. The bitter split was occasioned by the introduction into the second-last senior staff conference on January 13 of the memo that the British chiefs had presented to the Americans on January 8, while Churchill was splashing about in the surf in Florida. The Americans by now had read the proposals: John Dill was to stay in Washington as Churchill's personal representative to Franklin Roosevelt and the Combined Chiefs of Staff (CCS) Committee; two Combined Allocations Committees were to be established, one in Washington, the other in London; each of the committees was to care "for the needs of the Allies for whom it has accepted responsibility."[1] The American chiefs were galled at having been presented with an apparent fait accompli on the most critical issue of all, war allocations.

But there was worse to come. The British in effect had divided the world into economic zones, in which London and Washington each would look after the needs of a host of subordinate allies. The British called those client states "protégés." The American protégés were to include the nations of South America, Iceland, and China. The British protégés would encompass all Commonwealth and Empire countries including India, the Free French, and the Nazi-occupied countries of continental Europe whose governments in exile were based in London.

Finally, and probably most objectionable to the Americans, Churchill and his chiefs insisted that both the Washington committee and the London committee would be separate from and independent of the CCS Committee. Soviet needs would be taken care of by way of separate Lend-Lease protocols.

Stimson and Marshall had already registered with Roosevelt their strong opposition to the British proposals. At the staff meeting, Marshall informed the British that he had no problem with Dill being named Churchill's special representative; in fact, he liked Dill. Rather, his objection rested once again on principle. He had no interest, Marshall firmly stated, in interposing an "additional level of authority" between the chiefs of staff and their political leaders.[2] As to the parallel munitions allocation committees, Marshall took a different tack. This time he surprised one and all by stating that he had no objection in principle—provided that both committees were firmly subordinate to the CCS in Washington. Therein lay the crux of the matter.

Marshall knew from his prior experience on General Pershing's staff in the First World War, and from his keen acumen as a military strategist, that there was no sense at all in having munitions allocated by a politically appointed body, reporting directly to Roosevelt and to Churchill. It was, after all, the military that would ultimately use the munitions. Grand strategy consisted of making decisions about the allocation of troops and their weapons—and thus also of their transport. All three were tied together and, in Marshall's view, all three had to be determined by the CCS. He understood inherently that, if implemented, the British scheme would have given Churchill and his military planners in London sole power to allocate American-produced war materials for Europe, Africa, and the Middle East. Marshall saw in the British proposals yet another attempt to undermine his cherished principle of "unity of command."

Despite his deep anger, Marshall held back at the start of the second-to-last CCS meeting. ARCADIA had taught him a good deal about the dynamics of committee work. He let Admiral Stark deliver the initial blow. On the issue of Dill's post-conference status, Stark informed the British that even though the Americans "would rather have Sir John Dill than any one else. . . . They felt strongly . . . that there should be no Military Representative of the British Government above the Chiefs of Staff level." They wanted no such arrangement for themselves in London. The admiral "thought it only right to express the views of the United States Chiefs of Staff quite frankly on this matter, though he realized that the President and the Prime Minister might come to some other agreement on the matter." Dudley Pound at once spied in Stark's last words a possible opening. Replying for the British, the admiral rejoined that they would have to "refer the matter to the Prime Minister as any decision taken on this point would have to be taken on a higher level."[3]

Marshall went next. He straightaway attacked the British proposals about parallel allocations committees not responsible to the CCS Committee. The minutes are prosaic, but Marshall's rising temper is easily discerned: "[T]here could be no question of having any duplication of the Combined Chiefs of Staff organization in Washington and in London," he stated. "[T]here could only be one Combined Chiefs of Staff who [*sic*] would give broad directions on the allocation of matériel." He did not much mind parallel allocation committees in the two capitals, but he lectured the combined chiefs that these would have to be subservient to the CCS Committee in Washington.

The septic minutes of the meeting give no reaction from the other chiefs of staff. There is no doubt that the general's hard line caused mouths to drop and a moment of pained silence to ensue. The chiefs once more were at an impasse. None had any desire to pursue the matter. In the laconic words of the official minutes, the "discussion then turned on the control of shipping." It was brief and formal. They all knew and quickly agreed that the war allocations issue would have to be turned over to Roosevelt and Churchill for resolution.[4] The meeting adjourned. In essence, ARCADIA now hung on a test of will between George Catlett Marshall and Winston Spencer Churchill. No one was quite sure whose side Roosevelt would take.

While the American and British chiefs of staff grappled with the British initiative on war allocations at the Federal Reserve Building, across town at the White House Roosevelt was deeply engrossed in an equally critical issue: the creation of yet another agency to manage U.S. war industries. The president had decided that the head of the Office of Production Management (OPM), William Knudsen, was not up to the task of putting the nation on a war footing. A shake-up was needed. In typical fashion, FDR decided not only to abolish the OPM, but also to cashier its director. Knudsen found out about the radical changes not from Roosevelt, but from his own secretary, who read the news over the wire. "Look here," a stunned Knudsen, holding the paper torn from the ticker, told a coworker on the afternoon of January 13, "I've just been fired."[5]

With Knudsen gone, Washington was full of aspirants for what most likely could be the greatest delegation of power that Roosevelt ever made. Vice President Henry Wallace, chairman of the Supply, Priorities and Allocation Board, hoped to be appointed war production "tsar." Secretary of Commerce Jesse Jones was running hard for the appointment. Justice William Douglas was having second thoughts about having turned down the president's earlier offer to head war productions. Bernard Baruch rushed down from New York, and from his Washington hotel room called in all his markers to get friends and associates to lobby Roosevelt for the job. Secretary of the Treasury Henry Morgenthau, Jr., believed that he, along with Wendell Willkie and Justice Douglas, might head a new war productions troika. And Knudsen still harbored hopes that he might be called back to head up some new agency. Harry Hopkins followed the jockeying for power with roguish mirth, for he had already pressed his choice on the president.

Roosevelt invited Donald Nelson to the White House. He asked the vice president of Sears, Roebuck & Co. what he thought the new war production agency should be called. Nelson suggested "War Production Administration," or WPA. But Roosevelt had called one of his controversial New Deal federal agencies WPA—the Works Progress Administration. That "wouldn't do at all," FDR replied with a hearty laugh. He then put forward his own suggestion, "War Production Board," or WPB. Nelson agreed that those initials sounded better. "I'm glad you approve," Roosevelt informed him, "because *you* are the chairman of the War Production Board."[6] He instructed Press Secretary Stephen Early to prepare an announcement concerning the WPB and

Nelson for next morning, January 14, 1942. Knudsen was consoled with a "3-star" appointment in the Army.

To ease the tension that night, Eleanor Roosevelt invited eleven guests to dinner at the White House. Most received only two hours' notice, but some time previously, she had invited Louis Adamic, a novelist. The first lady had read his recently published book, *Two-Way Passage*, which had already sold 25,000 copies for Harper and Brothers. She had found it so interesting that she had passed it on to Franklin. The story was set on the presidential yacht *Potomac*, anchored in early November 1941 in fog off the coast of Iceland. It consisted of a fictional debate concerning the world situation between "Uncle Sam" and "John Bull"; the latter, "then in no condition to get on his high horse, had all the worst of the argument."[7] She insisted that Franklin give Winston a copy in hopes that it would "add to the interest of the dinner."[8]

It was a crisp, cold evening as Louis and Stella Adamic stepped out of their taxi at the White House's North Gate. "Helmeted soldiers, bayonet fixed on rifle," Louis recalled, "walked post about every hundred yards along the fence surrounding the mansion."[9] Adamic, an immigrant from Yugoslavia, was naturalized in 1918. One can only guess what went through his mind as a White House usher escorted the couple to a small elevator that took them up to the second floor. There stood the first lady, her face lit up with a smile, her hair swept up, dressed in a full-skirted black taffeta gown. Eleanor invited her guests into the president's study for cocktails. Adamic glanced over the Oval Room, with its chintz-covered armchairs, green and yellow curtains, carpeted floor, paintings and prints on the walls. His eyes rested on the massive oak desk, littered with numerous little donkeys, ashtrays, books, a ship's clock, and a tray of cocktail makings. FDR looked "extraordinarily fit, self-possessed, relaxed—on top of the world." As the president flipped the last silver cocktail shaker, Adamic mused that he was "ready to make mischief at the drop of a hat."

Franklin deftly poured his trademark Orange Blossom cocktails to within one-sixteenth of an inch from the brim of each glass. Eleanor passed them out two at a time. Next she handed around a tray of hors d'oeuvres. Fala inspected Louis' shoes and trousers, and then sat back on his haunches. "You pass, you pass," FDR chuckled. When Eleanor reached for a rather heavy armchair, FDR stopped her in her tracks. "We'll save this one for the Prime Minister."

"Is *he* still here?" a stunned Adamic blurted out. It was Eleanor's moment of triumph. She was about to repay Churchill for his cutting comment, in reply to her question about Clementine's role during the war, that his wife did not play a public role but stayed at home. Adamic wondered out loud how the prime minister would react to the last part of *Two-Way Passage*, where Adamic had contrasted "imperial Britain's innate inability to play a constructive role in postwar Europe" to America's "singular opportunity to help European nations move toward a democratic future." Eleanor puckishly replied, "We'll just have to wait and see—."

They did not have long to wait. For "there waddled into the room John Bull himself, in person, alias the Right Honourable Winston Leonard Spencer Churchill," Adamic later wrote. He was surprised by the prime minister's appearance: "a rotund, dumpy figure with short, slight arms and legs, narrow in the shoulders, mostly stomach, chest and head; no neck." He noted the "semi-scowl on his big, chubby, pink-and-white face with its light-blue eyes," and the "long, fat, freshly lit cigar in front of him." As Churchill stepped forward to shake the president's hand, "[h]e moved as though he were without joints, all of a piece: solidly, unhurriedly, impervious to obstacles, like a tank or a bulldozer." His eyes and mouth seemed "shrewd, ruthless, and unscrupulous."

"Had a good nap, Winston?" FDR cheerfully inquired. Churchill muttered something inaudible. Roosevelt offered him an Orange Blossom, which the prime minister, by now used to these strange concoctions, accepted and drank "dutifully." Eleanor got down to business. Purring, she reminded Churchill that Adamic was the author of *Two-Way Passage*. "Yes, yes," Churchill growled. "I'm . . . I'm r-reading it," he stuttered, changing the topic at once by thanking the Roosevelts for all the gifts that Americans had sent to the White House for him.

The group filed out of the study and headed down to the first floor. The private dining room glittered with polished silver service and crystal champagne glasses. A staff of four began to serve dinner. The White House kitchen had outdone itself: broiled filet of flounder and roast beef with Yorkshire pudding and gravy, followed by Stanley cream and cookie trifle.

FDR opened the conversation. "Well, we had a big day today." He had a surprise for them: "I made Donald Nelson head of all war production with full authority and responsibility."

Eleanor immediately changed the subject. "Franklin," she demanded in an agitated voice, "we've simply got to do something about the alien situation." That very day, the first internment of Japanese-Americans had begun. She wanted assurances about the planned future of a million other "aliens," most of them German and Italian. Silence fell over the group. Franklin stared at Eleanor, then at Winston.

"The prime" came to his friend's rescue. In Britain, he said, "We simply separated the goats from the sheep, interned the goats and used the sheep."

Eleanor was not amused. She announced that in the Office of Civilian Defense, which she headed, people were concerned with the spread of unjust suspicion. "We don't want any witch-hunts," she lectured her husband, "such as we had during the last war."

Roosevelt turned to Churchill. "You see Winston, we have a great variety of people in this country. Take almost any football team. Most of the players have Polish, Yugoslav, Scandinavian, Slovak names—even on the Notre Dame team, which is called 'the Fighting Irish'." The president laughed. "And what is true of football is true of our industry. It is the immigrant from Poland or Germany or Bohemia or Italy or the Balkans, or it is the immigrant's son, born here, who mans the machines and gets the coal out of the mines." Churchill lit another cigar. Champagne was served.

As some waiters cleared the main-course dishes and cutlery, others refilled the champagne glasses. The president offered to show the prime minister a new picture of himself in the Cabinet Room. "Which one?" Churchill devilishly asked. "Now look here, Winston, there's only one picture of me in the Cabinet room." It was not hung yet: the artist had been found out by the Secret Service to be a "two-time spy" working for Germany. The portrait was of Roosevelt during one of his famous fireside chats. The fire in the hearth had cast a flame-red glow on one side of the president's face. "Roosevelt in Hell," FDR trumpeted.

Trifle, coffee, and brandy were served. FDR placed a cigarette in his pearl holder and lit it with the customary long wooden match. He was now prepared to hold court more formally. When Stella Adamic started to tell the president about how her husband had come to write *Two-Way Passage*, Roosevelt seized the moment. "You know," he informed her, "my friend over there doesn't understand how most of our people feel about Britain and her role in the life of other peoples." Churchill must have feared the worst. Roosevelt did not disappoint:

> It's in the American tradition, this distrust, this dislike and even hatred of Britain—the Revolution, you know, and 1812; and India and the Boer War, and all that. There are many kinds of Americans of course, but as a people, as a country, we're opposed to imperialism—we can't stomach it.

There, it was out, all of it: 1776 and 1812, India and South Africa. Obviously annoyed with Churchill's memo on war allocations, which had brought the staff talks to a screeching halt that day, the president had decided on payback.

The dinner guests held their breath. Churchill sat "like Budda, a big cigar in his face." Roosevelt, lighting another cigarette, beat the topic into the ground. America's Irish Catholics were anti-British, and for a good reason. Its German element was solidly anti-British. As for himself, the president allowed, he was not anti-British, "now." But there had been a time "in 1889 or '90" when he was a lad of "seven or thereabouts." that his mother had taken him to London and he had seen Queen Victoria ride through the streets in her carriage. "Why, I hated the old woman." He lectured Churchill that "while English is my main strain, I'm also part Scotch and part Dutch." He looked across the table at his guest. "That combination makes one a good bargainer." The prime minister scowled and lit another Corona.

Roosevelt had taken the topic to the edge of permissible limits, if not beyond. On a day when Marshall had demanded of the British chiefs what amounted to primacy for Washington in the conduct of the war, this was adding insult to injury. There was a nasty streak to Roosevelt. He admitted that he had been a "pretty mean cuss" in his early days. He was that again on January 13, 1942. At 10:50 P.M. Eleanor saw the Adamics off. Louis rushed back to his hotel to write down everything he could remember about the evening. In 1946 he published his version of that bizarre night as *Dinner at the White House*.

Eleanor Roosevelt, looking back on the evening a decade later with historian Frank Freidel, referred to it as "the unfortunate dinner in the White House attended by the Adamics." A tragic mistake it had been, she recalled, with Louis Adamic believing that the entire affair had been arranged for him and his book. "Churchill was quite angry over [*Dinner at the White House*]," she stated, "sued in England, and recovered damages."[10] In fact, he never did.

January 14 was to be Churchill's last day in Washington. It was high time to settle the two issues that divided the British from the Americans: the exact definition of John Dill's duties after Churchill's departure, and control of munitions distribution. The first was taken up at the American and British chiefs' meeting at 3:00 P.M. The British had used the intervening twenty-four hours to modify their original proposal regarding Dill, but they had not satisfied the Americans. The latter came back with a draft of their own. It omitted any reference at all to Dill, either as special representative to Churchill or even as a member of the Combined Chiefs of Staff. The British chiefs caved in. The American draft was agreed to and sent to Churchill and Roosevelt for final approval. The matter was still not settled when Churchill left. Colonel Ian Jacob recalled that Churchill "signed Dill's Directive" well after ARCADIA. It appointed Dill head of the British Military Mission in Washington, as well as Churchill's "personal representative" there.[11] Roosevelt and Marshall could live with that.

Leaving Dill in Washington proved to be one of Churchill's best wartime decisions. He served the cause of Allied unity with great patience, humor, and determination until his death of anemia in November 1944. Marshall's biographer, Forrest C. Pogue, wrote of Dill,

[T]he Combined Chiefs of Staff organization worked well because of Marshall's close relationship with Sir John Dill. . . . In an amazing balancing act, Dill was able to represent British wishes to the Americans without antagonizing them and to warn London of the limits of American forbearance without arousing suspicion on the part of his own chiefs that he had become a captive of his hosts.[12]

He did this in part by winning friends in Washington, in part by learning to suppress his earlier contempt for the disorganization he saw in the American command system, and in part because of his cold-eyed appraisal of the shifting balance of power away from Britain and toward the United States as the months and years of the war dragged by.

The munitions allocation question still remained unresolved at 5:00 P.M. when Roosevelt called Marshall and Hopkins to the White House.[13] The last conference with Churchill and the British chiefs was set for 5:30 P.M. The president read Marshall a statement. It proposed a Munitions Assignment Board "divided into two coequal parts, one in Washington, headed by Harry Hopkins, and the other in London, headed by Lord Beaverbrook." The former would report directly to Roosevelt, the latter to Churchill. The Board would be "on a level with and independent of the Combined Chiefs of Staff." Roosevelt then asked his chief of staff for his opinion.

Marshall would not have it. He remained intractable on the issue. The Munitions Assignment Board (or boards) must be under the authority of the CCS Committee. Period. Neither he nor any other chief of staff, Marshall lectured his commander in chief, could plan and conduct military operations if "some other authority, over which he had no control, could refuse to allocate the matériel required for such operations." Hopkins later recalled that Marshall felt so strongly about the matter "that he informed the President that unless the conditions as he stated them were accepted he could not continue to assume the responsibilities of Chief of Staff."

The "climacteric" of ARCADIA had arrived. Roosevelt knew that Marshall, in what Charles Wilson had called his "quiet, unprovocative way," had become the fulcrum of the chiefs of staff deliberations. If he refused Marshall's demand, the conference would undoubtedly end in chaos. He would then have to fire the man who had done more to prepare the Army for war than any other living American—and find a new man to do the job. How could he do that? This was a painful moment for a man who liked to dance around hard decisions if at all possible. True to form, Roosevelt sought counsel. He turned to Hopkins to solicit his opinion. Marshall's heart sank. Surely, Roosevelt must have already discussed this proposal with Hopkins. But he had not! To Marshall's great surprise, Hopkins "supported [me] vociferously." More, Hopkins stated that unless Marshall's position carried the day, he, Hopkins, "could not assume any responsibility" for the Washington allocations committee.

At 5:30 P.M. Churchill, Beaverbrook, Stimson, Secretary of the Navy Knox, and the rest of the British and American chiefs joined the discussion. Roosevelt suggested that two new agencies be created to regulate vital war material: a Raw Materials Board—which would report directly to him and to Churchill—and a Combined Shipping Adjustment Board. Both boards would confer with other Allied nations as needed. On the matter of the Munitions Allocation Committee, Roosevelt informed the British that he now favored "a common pool" for war resources. More, that on the advice of Generals Marshall and Arnold, the board supervising this "common pool" had to "operate as a subcommittee of the Combined Chiefs of Staff Committee." There would be a civilian chairman, with one board operating in London and the other in Washington. And then the final, great decision of ARCADIA: the board would operate under the CCS Committee "in a manner similar to the arrangement for unity of command in the Southwest Pacific area."

The British were stunned by this last-minute hard line. Beaverbrook tried to derail Roosevelt by asking how Russian needs might be taken care of. The president was ready for him: by the CCS. Next it was Churchill's turn to obfuscate. Surely, the two committees could "discuss" matters "through the Chiefs of Staff Committees," that is, through the British chiefs of staff in London and then through the American chiefs of staff in Washington. That interpretation might still leave him in control of British munitions allocation. But Marshall knew the difference between discussion and decision. He stood solid as a rock. The arrangement suggested by Churchill, he firmly interjected, "was not his understanding of the matter." Any allocations committee as well as its civilian chair or chairs could function only as "a subcommittee of the [Combined] Chiefs of Staff Committee." For a second time in less than an hour, Hopkins backed him up. If the combined chiefs did not like the subcommittee's recommendations regarding allocation, Hopkins argued, "they [could] alter them or throw them out."

Sensing that he had the advantage, Marshall pressed on. The purpose of all the discussions, he claimed, "was to set up a command post in Washington." "Strategy is dominated by matériel," he lectured the British, "and any proposal with regard to matériel should come from the same source"—the CCS Committee. When Beaverbrook half-heartedly asked whether "the political viewpoint with regard to certain allocations" would have to be referred to Washington for final decision, a by-now-defiant Roosevelt replied "that it would."

With that, the ball was squarely back in Churchill's court. He had come to Washington with but one objective—to make sure that the Americans remained in what in December 1941 he had called "the harem." Could he jeopardize all that ARCADIA had accomplished so far for the principle of unfettered British allocation of war materials that would, after all, be largely manufactured in the United States? Was this question of "machinery" sufficiently critical to force a break with the Americans? It was obvious that Marshall would not budge, and that Roosevelt was backing his chief of staff to the hilt.

Churchill gave way. The allocation "machinery" proposed by Marshall should "be tried out for a month." If it did not meet expectations, Churchill argued, "there could be a redraft." Beaverbrook and Pound quickly seconded the prime minister's suggestion that Marshall's system should be "given a trial." The matter was decided. Roosevelt was ecstatic. "We will call it a preliminary agreement and try it out that way," he cheerily concluded. The "preliminary agreement," in fact, remained in place for the remainder of the war. The last and most sensitive session of the two leaders and their chiefs of staff at ARCADIA adjourned at 6:30 P.M. FDR had Scotch and soda passed around and the group toasted the coming months and years of mutual accord.

Robert Sherwood, the president's speechwriter and a close friend of Hopkins, was never far from the center of the action during these trying days. He appreciated the stark contrast between the sparse minutes of that last meeting and the powerful emotions present in the room:

> The formal records of this session give little indication of the tension and even embarrassment that prevailed; the historian must read a great deal between the lines to appreciate the fact that herein was the serving of notice on such proud men as Churchill and Beaverbrook that Roosevelt was the Boss and Washington the headquarters of the joint war effort.[14]

Even accounting for a good measure of hyperbole, Sherwood had accurately caught the moment. Hopkins took a broader and more rhetorical view. "There are great and historic days ahead," he wrote Marshall. "I think we have laid the groundwork for final victory."[15]

The closing act of Wednesday, January 14, 1942, was a formal White House dinner. Henrietta Nesbitt presented English lamb pie to honor Churchill. It was the only meal at which minutes were kept. They were terse. The two leaders "wound up the last details of the agreements relative to shipping, raw materials and the allocation board." They agreed that Roosevelt would release "a general statement governing all of them" at some appropriate time after Churchill's departure. They reviewed the work of the past three weeks and initialed several documents. Churchill expressed his "warm appreciation" for the generous welcome he and his delegation had received in Washington as well as his confidence that the machinery established at ARCADIA would prove decisive in the fights to come.[16]

At 9:45 P.M. the president and Hopkins drove with Churchill to the station. It had been arranged that the prime minister and his party would take an overnight train to Norfolk, Virginia, and then fly from there to Bermuda where they would embark on the *Duke of York* for the final leg of the trip back to the United Kingdom. Hopkins sent along a letter for Clementine. "You would have been quite proud of your husband on this trip." The prime minister had been "ever so good natured," had not taken "anybody's head off," and had partaken of food and drink "with his customary vigor."[17] Roosevelt's last words to Churchill were reassuring: "Trust me to the bitter end."[18]

Utterly exhausted by ARCADIA, Hopkins collapsed. He was taken to the Navy Hospital, where for two weeks the doctors ordered a strict regimen of a nutritious diet and proper rest.

Churchill's train arrived at Norfolk in the predawn darkness. Three giant Boeing 314 Flying Boats stood by to carry the British to Bermuda. The one selected for Churchill—RMA (Royal Mail Aircraft) *Berwick*—had a large Union Jack painted on the fuselage just forward of the wings. Its pilot was Captain John Cecil Kelly-Rogers, formerly of the Royal Air Force and Imperial Airways, one of the most experienced flyers on the trans-Atlantic run. *Berwick* was airborne at 6:40 A.M. It was a cold and clear morning, "cloudless with a light surface haze," Kelly-Rogers later remembered.[19]

At some point in the short flight to Bermuda, Churchill asked Kelly-Rogers if the Boeing "clipper" was capable of flying from Bermuda directly to the United Kingdom. He was assured that it was. Churchill began to think about flying home to save time—it would take some twenty hours by air, but at least seven days by sea. With the war situation deteriorating daily in Malaya and North Africa, he wanted to get back to London as quickly as possible. He made his decision at once. Charles Wilson, ever mindful of Winston's heart attack at the White House, and of the need to keep it secret, insisted on accompanying him.

Churchill and his small party reboarded *Berwick* in the late morning of January 16. At regular intervals in the flight, the crew passed around bulletins signed by Kelly-Rogers showing their position, height, speed, time, and distance since departure, time and distance to go, and hours of fuel left. Churchill signed a number of these as souvenirs. At one point the prime minister turned to his physician and said, "Do you realize we are fifteen hundred miles from anywhere?"

Wilson reminded him, "Heaven is as near by sea as by land."

"Who said that?" Churchill asked.

"I think it was Sir Humphrey Gilbert," Wilson replied, referring to a sixteenth-century British sea captain who searched for the Northwest Passage. Beaverbrook did not partake in the levity. He worried about Churchill and the long flight, he told Kelly-Rogers. "If we lose Churchill we lose the war."

They flew into the dawn. Weather reports indicated that Plymouth harbor would be most suitable for a landing. Kelly-Rogers began the flying boat's power descent. All that was visible below was a rolling expanse of fog. To his horror, the navigator reported that they had drifted off their track during the night. *Berwick* was heading toward the coast of German-occupied France! Kelly-Rogers turned northward. Churchill strained for a view of land. Suddenly, the copilot let out, "The coast." Kelly-Rogers began to circle Plymouth harbor, and rested the giant clipper atop the water. He shut the engines down at precisely 8:59 A.M. GMT. Before leaving the aircraft, one of Churchill's secretaries read to him a prepared statement for release to the press: "This morning the

Prime Minister, traveling in a British Airways flying boat, arrived at a West Country port." Churchill interrupted: "To hell with the west country port—say Plymouth."[20]

With his typical flare for the dramatic, Churchill recalled a much different version of the final minutes of the return flight:

> Later on I learnt that if we had held on our course for another five or six minutes before turning north-ward we should have been over the German batteries in Brest . . . [the course correction] had the result, as I was told some weeks later, that we were reported as a hostile bomber coming in from Brest, and six Hurricanes from Fighter Command were ordered out to shoot us down. However, they failed in their mission.[21]

That was not at all Kelly-Rogers' version of events. In his official report, he recorded that Fighter Command had plotted their position every step of the final stages of the approach to England. "The flight had gone very well in all respects."[22]

However real the imminent danger of the last minutes of Churchill's odyssey to ARCADIA and back, the entire journey had been hazardous. He had been away for thirty-six momentous days. At great risk had been the fate of what was to be known to history as the Grand Alliance. Churchill had certainly not achieved all he had sought; it is doubtful if he had even accomplished half of his original objectives. But his three weeks in the New World had brought the Americans and the British onto a convergence course and had established the machinery for the most integrated wartime coalition in history.

EPILOGUE

WINSTON CHURCHILL'S PERSONAL PHYSICIAN, CHARLES WILSON, summed up the ARCADIA conference with a note penned in his diary while accompanying Churchill to Ottawa at the end of December 1941. The prime minister, he noted, had "wanted to show the President how to run the war. It has not worked out quite like that." Instead, George Marshall "in his quiet, unprovocative way" had taken charge of the meetings. "Marshall remains the key to the situation," Wilson presciently observed. Neither Churchill nor Franklin Roosevelt "can contemplate going forward without Marshall."[1]

When Churchill and his staff arrived in Washington, they knew just what they wanted from the Americans. Still reeling from Pearl Harbor, the Americans were not ready for detailed discussion of strategy or of logistics, as Harry Hopkins had suspected. It was General Marshall who took the lead in turning the British aside. From Wilson's perspective, Marshall seemed to embody both Churchill's greatest hope for a combined war effort and his greatest fear of the United States striking out alone. Marshall had quickly become the key man in advancing American ideas about how the war should be organized and in communicating those ideas to both Roosevelt and to Churchill in no uncertain terms. The other American chiefs and Secretary of War Stimson were just as adamant but less important because they lacked Marshall's clear vision and concentrated focus. Hopkins, in his way and at strategic moments—and despite his admiration of, and liking for, Churchill—also pressed Roosevelt to keep American interests uppermost in his mind. But Marshall was the point man.

On the surface, Marshall's sway stemmed from his experience, his personality, his intelligence, and his great political influence in Washington. All those attributes were no doubt important. But Marshall's real effectiveness came from his ability to translate Roosevelt's desire to ensure that American paramountcy quickly emerged from American superiority into a coherent strategic policy.

It is generally held that Roosevelt did not really begin to assume the mantel of leadership of the Anglo-American war effort until a year later—at the Casablanca Conference in January 1943. In fact, he effectively took control at ARCADIA. Churchill failed to secure many of his key objectives at ARCADIA precisely because as disorganized as they were, as amateur as they were, as much as they were neophytes in the real art of war, the Americans assumed control of the conference almost immediately and the British were forced to give way on almost every issue.

On hearing the news of Pearl Harbor, Churchill had thought that the Americans, now "in the harem" as he had put it, would oblige British desires. Once he arrived in Washington, Churchill quickly realized that Roosevelt was well aware that the latent power of the United States gave it the upper hand in deciding what the war's ultimate priorities would be and how much coordination it would tolerate. Much to the consternation of some of the War Cabinet in London, and of Chief of the Imperial General Staff Alan Brooke, the real world as seen from Washington gave Churchill little choice but to defer. From his perch in the White House, he could not risk allowing the Americans to seek their own path to victory, simply forcing Britain and the other Allies to follow. He bowed to reality and, however unwillingly, accepted his new role as second-in-command.

Thus ARCADIA was the moment of transition between the waning global influence of the British Empire and the waxing world power of the United States. At ARCADIA, the United States nudged Britain aside to take overall leadership of the western Allied powers in the war against the Axis. At ARCADIA, the Americans, led by a president who had never heard a shot fired in anger, forced Churchill and Britain to accept the American concept of how the war was to be managed. At ARCADIA, the United States was not yet in a position of either experience or resources to force Churchill to accept its strategic view of the war—or to impose upon the British great risks such as the cross-Channel attack of June 6, 1944—but the means and the mechanisms were created that would eventually allow it to do just that.

America's rise to the status of a great power was rooted in many developments stretching back almost a century before Pearl Harbor. Britain's decline has been dated by some as having commenced with the beginning of colonialism in the 1870s. Certainly, the First World War and its outcome left a new reality in the power balance between the two. After 1918, the United States was the greatest creditor nation in the world, the largest industrial power, the country with the greatest potential to build the most powerful war machine. Britain was virtually bankrupt, its hold on the Empire was slipping, it was dependent for its security on a permanent military alliance with France, and it could not hope to compete with the United States in building a global navy—hence, the Washington Treaty of 1922 that ended once and for all British world naval dominance.

The new alignment of power was not noticeable, however, because the United States did not maintain a globe-spanning empire and chose to withdraw from the dizzying world of European diplomatic maneuvering and to stay aloof from the League of Nations. The Republic certainly played some role in the interwar years in the vain effort to constrain future German ambition by a web of nonaggression pacts, international agreements, and bilateral treaties. But it was neither a leader nor a guarantor of the peacemaking efforts. It never cut its trade ties with the rest of the world and continued to intervene actively in Latin America. It expressed a deep interest in the Far East—a policy that would bring it hard up against both a potential enemy, Japan, and a potential friend, China. The United States was, however, truly isolationist in the one way that really mattered: Europe was far from the minds of Americans and even farther from their concerns.

When war broke out in Poland in September 1939, few Americans understood what implications this new European conflict held for them. They were neither willing nor able to extend a helping hand to Britain and France. When France fell, Britain under Churchill took up the mantel of leadership in the war against Nazism. Churchill pledged to his nation and to the world that the war was to be a death struggle against Hitler's forces. By word in his speeches, by deed in his defiance, by action in his insistence to his service chiefs that Germany be made to bleed whenever and wherever possible, Churchill became the undisputed leader of the forces of freedom. Britain and the Commonwealth stood alone for twelve fateful months between the fall of France and the Nazi attack on the Soviet Union. The real disparity of potential power between the United States and the United Kingdom was thus hidden by the American refusal to play a role in the war.

With Pearl Harbor, the power disparity surfaced dramatically and immediately. Churchill rushed to Washington to bind the American war effort tightly to that of the British. He aimed to achieve three overall goals: maintain the "Europe-first" approach to the war; ensure that the United States fight an all-out war, with no holding back, and get into it as quickly as possible; and try to find a means whereby the war efforts of the two nations could be closely synchronized. He won the first point even before he arrived in the United States. Not only was it the only way to fight the Axis that made any sense, but Germany had willingly obliged him by declaring war on the United States four days after Pearl Harbor. He gained the second because Roosevelt understood the crucial need for a democracy in a very long war to pull the nation solidly behind the war effort. In the long run, American troops engaged in battle against Germans were a much surer guaranty that the nation would support the war over the long haul—and back the emphasis on Germany—than relying on its outraged response to the sneak attack at Pearl Harbor.

Churchill did get the unified, synchronized war effort he sought, but not in the way he had sought it. Given his personal style of command and his close relationship with his military chiefs, he no doubt believed that the best way to coordinate the war was for him and the American president to do it together. Given his experience in war, he might even emerge as Roosevelt's mentor. Certainly, he tried to cast himself in that role. In the end, of course, the leaders did coordinate the war (along with Stalin) at the great conferences held periodically at Casablanca, Teheran, again at Washington, twice in Quebec, and at Yalta. But they did not exercise the more detailed, and less distant, command over their forces to which Churchill aspired. It was the Combined Chiefs of Staff (CCS) who did that. Churchill spent much of the war trying to do end runs around the CCS, or to lobby directly not only with Marshall but also with theater commanders such as Dwight Eisenhower. Nonetheless, the CCS system survived intact and the chiefs took the periodical political direction given them by Roosevelt and Churchill, and turned it into military strategy.

If Churchill's effort to maintain and expand his style of personal control over the armed forces of Britain and, with Roosevelt, the United States failed, so too did some of his other objectives. The president quickly learned to keep his own counsel in war aims and neither sought nor used Churchill's mentorship. Churchill never achieved the goal of a combined and coordinated air offensive against Germany. British and American bomber forces did eventually mount what they dubbed the Combined Bomber Offensive against selected targets such as the German aircraft industry or synthetic oil production, but that air offensive was, as often as not, completely uncombined and subject to petty jealousies, national pride, and the personal interests of the "bomber barons."

Churchill had also sought a concerted and integrated war at sea, in the Battle of the Atlantic. That was very slow in coming. Despite declarations to the contrary, the United States virtually drained the Atlantic of American escort vessels after Pearl Harbor, opening its coastal waters in particular to slashing attacks by German submarines. Almost immediately after ARCADIA, German U-boats in Operation PAUKEN-SCHLAG ("drumroll") ravaged the eastern seaboard of the United States. In what official U.S. Navy historian Samuel Eliot Morison called a "merry massacre,"[2] Admiral Karl Dönitz's "gray sharks" in 184 war patrols sank 609 ships of 3.1 million gross tons in American waters between December 1941 and August 1942—while losing only twenty-two of their own craft. Not until the United States swung its full naval and air support into the war against the U-boats at the Atlantic Convoy Conference in March 1943 did the tide finally turn in the Battle of the Atlantic.

To be sure, the immediate post-ARCADIA period was filled with setbacks and rebuffs. By the end of January 1942, the Japanese hurricane swept south and west, all along the extended lines of General Wavell's Far East command. After the capture of Kuala Lampur, the British position in Malaya rapidly deteriorated. Japanese troops, artillery, and air power decimated the approaches to the British fortress at Singapore and on February 15 the garrison surrendered. It was a blow that Churchill barely survived in the House of Commons. But it was not the last as Wavell prepared himself for the loss of Sumatra and Java as well.

In North Africa, General Rommel's *Afrika Korps* drove the British 8th Army back to eastern Libya, where it prepared a stubborn defense of Egypt. The invasion of North Africa that had so seized discussion at the ARCADIA conference was postponed again and again. Churchill spoke of "obstinate and long delays." On March 3, 1942, the CCS dropped the operation as an immediate possibility.[3] It was primarily through Roosevelt that the invasion was kept on the Allied agenda. Over Marshall's obstinate opposition, the president continued to push for action in North Africa as quickly as possible. Marshall was trying to build an army capable of fighting a global war; Roosevelt was simply trying to keep the American peoples' minds focused on war. On November 9, 1942, Operation TORCH—the forcible seizure of French North Africa—began. The campaign dragged on until spring 1943, with high casualties among Germans and Allies alike. When it ended, however, the Axis threat to completely encircle the Mediterranean had been smashed. The tide of war had turned—at Midway, at Guadalcanal, at Stalingrad—and the Anglo-American Allies stood at the door to Italy and Western Europe.

On February 23, 1942, President Roosevelt in a "Fireside Chat on Progress of the War" sought to assure the nation at a time of continuous defeats and nagging fears what the struggle was all about and how it would be won.[4] Some 61 million adults, the largest audience to date, tuned in their radios to listen to him. It was the day following George Washington's birthday. The historical parallel was clear. Washington had fought a difficult war at a hard time, "a model of moral stamina." He had persevered against "formidable odds and recurring defeats." He had held out against "selfish men, jealous men, fearful men, who proclaimed that Washington's cause was hopeless, and that he should ask for a negotiated peace."

Now, America was again fighting a difficult war. But this time the war extended to "every continent, every island, every sea, every air lane in the world." Roosevelt had asked Americans to have a world map on hand in order to follow his words, and record-breaking map sales had ensued from coast to coast. Now, the president asked his listeners to spread those maps out before them. He asked them to look at the "vast area of China," the "vast area of Russia," the British Isles, Australia, New Zealand, the Dutch Indies, India, the Near East, and the continent of Africa. He asked them to look at North America, Central America, and South America. The very "world-wide lanes of communication" that Alfred Thayer Mahan had preached about to Americans half a century earlier faced a clear and present danger. "We know that if we lose this war," the president warned, "it will be generations or even centuries before our conception of democracy can live again." There was no alternative but to carry the war to the "enemy in distant lands and distant waters." At stake were the ideas of the Atlantic Charter ("disarmament of aggressors, self-determination of Nations and peoples") and the Four Freedoms ("freedom of speech, freedom of religion, freedom from want, and freedom from fear"). In short, Western Civilization itself.

With a voice full of scorn and fury, he hurled in the face of the American people the derision that had been heaped on them by the enemy. "From Berlin, Rome, and Tokyo we have been described as a Nation of weaklings—'playboys'—who would hire British soldiers, or Russian soldiers, or Chinese soldiers to do our fighting for us." He promised the newly founded United Nations "unified command and cooperation and comradeship." He asked of the nation "unified production and unified acceptance of sacrifice and of effort." He closed by citing Thomas Paine's immortal words that George Washington had read to the men of every regiment in the Continental Army: "Tyranny, like hell, is not easily conquered; yet we have this consolation with us, that the harder the sacrifice, the more glorious the triumph." Therewith, the historical parallel to Washington, symbolized by the Roosevelt-Churchill visit to the founder's grave during ARCADIA, was complete. "So spoke Americans in the year 1776!" Roosevelt concluded. "So speak Americans today!" It was one of his greatest speeches.

Franklin Delano Roosevelt's role of war president, as shaped initially by ARCADIA, was one of striking success, at times even of flashing brilliance. 1940 and 1941 were Roosevelt's "lost years." From the fall of France to Pearl Harbor, he had promised more than he could deliver. He had produced rhetoric rather than weapons. He had developed neither a German nor a Russian policy, and had sat on the fence with regard to Vichy France. He had strung Britain along and refused to give his military planners direction. As the war president of ARCADIA, however, he was determined, dedicated, and at times ruthless in seizing the role of organizer of victory. After ARCADIA, he left in his wake broken careers and disappointed ambitions. In the area of war production alone, the list of spurned men included Bernard Baruch, William Douglas, Walter Gifford, Sidney Hillman, William Knudsen, Edward Stettinius, Jr., and Robert E. Wood. Roosevelt promised, then reneged. He promoted, then dismissed. He created, then destroyed. He took seriously and enjoyed his new role as commander in chief.

Roosevelt by his own account could be deceptive, devious, disingenuous, and on occasion "an awfully mean cuss." Whether as the "sly squire of Hyde Park," or as the "sphinx of Pennsylvania Avenue," or as the consummate "juggler" who never let his right hand know what his left hand was doing, he played his cards "close up against [his] belly," as Secretary of the Interior Harold Ickes once put it. He would bend the rules, ignore them, or change them. He broke constitutional precedent by running for a third, and then for a fourth term. He bypassed the State Department by using a regiment of "special envoys" such as Averell Harriman, Harry Hopkins, James Mooney, and Sumner Welles, to name but a few. He was secretive and refused to commit anything to paper that he did not have to by law. He was by nature a manipulator, a fixer, a plunger. He despised all that Hitler and Nazi Germany stood for. He firmly believed that the defense of the United States started at the British Isles. But he never forgot that he was an American. In the end, Roosevelt "navigated the rapids" brilliantly. His optimism, self-confidence and determination, his unshakable belief in the future, his infinite plasticity, and his dedication to decency, to democracy and to freedom, carried all opposition.

During ARCADIA Roosevelt survived three threats of resignation by senior officials—Secretary of State Hull over St. Pierre and Miquelon, Secretary of War Stimson over redirecting U.S. transports bound for the Philippines to Singapore, and General Marshall over war productions and allocations—and one by a senior advisor, Hopkins, again over war production. Still, he kept those senior policymakers on his team. He survived the open animosity that on at least three occasions broke out between his wife Eleanor and Churchill. And when Rooselvelt was shown the errors of his ways, such as by Marshall over his initial preference for decentralized command as well as for independent war productions committees in London and Washington, he had the grace and the wisdom to bow to the better argument. The goals always justified the means to Roosevelt. In the process, he defined the "imperial" presidency. He launched the American century. He cast overboard the American "garrison-state" mentality and replaced it with American globalism. He defined the term "national security" to include both the Atlantic and the Pacific. And he never wavered in his firm belief that the export of American social, economic, and political liberalism to the rest of the world constituted the natural order of things.

Churchill too believed in a natural order of things, but the tide of history was running against him. He was one of the most brilliant war leaders of all time and a renaissance man of inestimable accomplishment. He was a man of destiny who believed in his destiny, and well he might have. His was not a steady rise to the pinnacle of power, as Roosevelt's had been. He had twice fallen from grace, being mocked as too old, too out of fashion, too irrelevant to ever achieve rehabilitation. Indeed, he often despaired for his chances of political recovery. Then, as he had forecast, had come war and as he had feared, defeat. He had willed Britain to survive, much as Abraham Lincoln had once willed the Union to survive. It is no coincidence that he had studied the Civil War and long admired Lincoln as a war president. But his brilliance, oratory, charm, persuasiveness, and accomplishments literary and political, were in the end outweighed by the sheer might of American power. The island kingdom's actual and potential economic strength, historian Kenneth S. Davis has argued, was already smaller than that of Germany and the Soviet Union, "and smaller still against that of the United States."[5] Churchill's choice was to go along as gracefully as circumstance and character would permit, winning as much as he could for Britain and his beloved Empire, or allow personal disappointment to cloud his view of the Allied interest. He made the first choice and it was the right choice.

ARCADIA was never a sure thing. Over the course of the conference, there had been heated, and at times acrimonious, debates between the two sides. Each had a different concept of how to defeat the Axis. Each had its own spheres of interest around the globe. Each had its own postwar priorities. Each had its own notion concerning a postwar international agency. Each was jealous of the other, fearing that every move could bring advantage to the other side. Each was concerned with its own national security interests. And each viewed with suspicion the other's conception of empire, of colonialism.

Yet, there was much to celebrate with the conclusion of ARCADIA. Roosevelt and Churchill laid the groundwork for what was to become the war-winning "grand alliance." They crafted a charter for the United Nations. They appointed the first of many theater commanders—Archibald Wavell—with the then radical new mandate of being in charge of all forces—land, sea, and air—of all the Allies in his theater. They created the Combined Chiefs of Staff to coordinate the war against the Axis. They placed all Allied war production allocation firmly under the control of the military. They assured that Lend-Lease would continue to flow to the USSR and China, despite the need to speed up expansion of the U.S. armed forces. They shocked American industry into setting massive new production goals for ships, tanks, aircraft, and all other manner of war materiel. They set up the Munitions Assignment Board and a combined means to allocate shipping. Food and natural resources boards followed in short order. They positioned themselves to fight a war of attrition and to win it with superior industrial muscle. And they determined the means to ensure that wherever the one had more resources or manpower than the other, that nation would lead locally but follow a global strategy.

"It is fun to be in the same decade with you," Roosevelt, celebrating his sixtieth birthday on January 30, 1942, cabled Churchill in London.[6] No doubt he meant that; Churchill could be the most engaging man in the world with those he saw as his intellectual and political equals. The world will never truly know, however, just what pals they really were. Roosevelt kept his innermost thoughts to himself and left no written legacy of his views, let alone his deep feelings, toward others. We are better endowed with sources when it comes to Churchill's views of Roosevelt. But here too there is room for skepticism. Churchill no doubt respected Roosevelt because he was president of the United States. He also knew from the moment he assumed leadership of the British government that he must pursue him. But he was exasperated with Roosevelt's delays, back-steps, and obfuscations at a time when Britain was bleeding badly and had no prospect of success alone against Hitler. It must have hurt his deep pride to have been the supplicant both before and after Pearl Harbor (though in different ways) no matter how enthusiastic Churchill waxed over Roosevelt and their mutual friendship in his war memoirs.

The world will never truly know what lay at the bottom of the Roosevelt-Churchill relationship. But then no person can ever be truly known by anyone other than possibly the closest "other" in a deep personal and even intimate relationship. Nor does it matter. As intelligent men, Democrats, believers in the cause of freedom and the need to crush the Axis, Roosevelt and Churchill shared common views. So did their military chiefs. That does not mean that they were foreordained to put their personal, service, or national aspirations and jealousies away to serve a common cause. Indeed, those aspirations and jealousies surfaced throughout the war. What the times demanded, however, was a greater allegiance to a larger set of loftier goals, not just to defeat the military threat posed by the Axis, but to build a world of greater hope.

Yet, allegiance alone was not enough. To serve their common interests nations (as with individuals) must operate within structures that they trust. At ARCADIA, two leaders and two nations with different histories, cultures, and strategic needs made a decision to trust each other through the greatest trial in their history.

NOTES

PROLOGUE

1. From William Seale, *The President's House: A History*, 2 vols. (Washington, DC, 1986), vol. 2, pp. 974–75; David Brinkley, *Washington Goes to War* (New York, 1988), pp. 102–03.

2. Ibid., p. 103.

3. Letter of December 19, 1941. Mary Soames, ed., *Speaking for Themselves: The Personal Letters of Winston and Clementine Churchill* (Toronto, 1998), pp. 458–59.

CHAPTER 1

1. This description of Washington is from David Brinkley, *Washington Goes to War* (New York, 1988), ch. 1, "Waiting."

2. Theodore A. Wilson, *The First Summit: Roosevelt and Churchill at Placentia Bay 1941* (Boston, 1969), p. 7.

3. Robert Sherwood, *Roosevelt and Hopkins: An Intimate History* (New York, 1948), pp. 290–91.

4. Kenneth S. Davis, *FDR: The War President, 1939–1943* (New York, 2000), p. 228 and 228n.

5. H. V. Morton, *Atlantic Meeting* (London, 1943), p. 50.

6. Winston S. Churchill, *The Second World War: The Grand Alliance* (London, 1950), p. 431.

7. Cited in Wilson, *The First Summit*, p. 100.

8. Sherwood, *Roosevelt and Hopkins*, p. 351.

9. Morton, *Atlantic Meeting*, p. 97.

10. *Official Papers of Fleet Admiral Ernest J. King*, Reel 1, Correspondence and Memoranda, 1918–1955, Library of Congress, Washington, DC.

11. Cited in Thomas B. Buell, *Master of Sea Power: A Biography of Fleet Admiral Ernest J. King* (Boston and Toronto, 1980), pp. 145–46.

12. Entry for July 3, 1958. Lord Moran [Sir Charles Wilson], *Winston Churchill: The struggle for survival 1940–1965* (London, 1966), pp. 742–43.

13. Forrest C. Pogue, *George C. Marshall: Ordeal and Hope, 1939–1942* (London, 1968), p. 142.

14. See Maurice Matloff and Edwin M. Snell, eds., *United States Army in World War II, Strategic Planning for Coalition Warfare 1941–1942*, 2 vols. (Washington, DC,1953–59), vol. 1, pp. 59–60; Keith E. Eiler, ed., *Wedemeyer on War and Peace* (Stanford, CA, 1987), pp. 12–14, 22–26.

15. General Sir Leslie Hollis, *One Marine's Tale* (London, 1956), p. 82.

16. Morton, *Atlantic Meeting*, p. 114.

17. Two highly sensationalized accounts of the "confrontation" over free trade and the Empire were left by Elliott Roosevelt, *As He Saw It* (New York, 1946), pp. 24–31; and Elliott Roosevelt and James Brough, *A Rendezvous with Destiny: The Roosevelts of the White House* (New York, 1975), pp. 292–95.

18. Wilson, *First Summit*, p. 173.

19. Joseph P. Lash, *Roosevelt and Churchill: 1939–1941: The Partnership that Saved the West* (New York, 1976), p. 260.

20. John Morton Blum, ed., *From the Morgenthau Diaries: Years of Urgency 1938–1941* (Boston, 1965), p. 209.

21. Ibid., pp. 217, 236.

22. David Reynolds, *The Creation of the Anglo-American Alliance 1937–41: A Study in Competitive Co-operation* (London, 1981), pp. 162–64.

23. Ibid.

24. Cited in Warren F. Kimball, *The Juggler: Franklin Roosevelt as Wartime Statesman* (Princeton, 1991), p. 53.

25. Welles' memoranda of August 9 and 11, 1941. *Foreign Relations of the United States: General. The Soviet Union* (Washington, 1958), vol. 1, pp. 345–67. Hereafter cited as FRUS. "Regard" was later changed to "respect."

26. Entry for August 12, 1941. John Harvey, *The War Diaries of Oliver Harvey* (London, 1978), p. 31.

27. Martin Gilbert, ed., *The Churchill War Papers*, vol. 3, *The Ever-Widening War 1941* (London, 1993), p. 1081.

28. James MacGregor Burns, *Roosevelt: The Soldier of Freedom* (New York, 1970), p. 131.

29. Letter to Roosevelt of August 18, 1941. Cited in Max Freedman, ed., *Roosevelt and Frankfurter: Their Correspondence 1928–1945* (Boston and Toronto, 1967), p. 612.

30. Gilbert, ed., *The Churchill War Papers*, vol. 3, *1941*, p. 1081.

31. Frederick W. Marks III, *Wind Over Sand: The Diplomacy of Franklin Roosevelt* (London, 1988), p. 201.

32. Gilbert, ed., *The Churchill War Papers*, vol. 3, *1941*, p. 1125.

33. Sherwood, *Roosevelt and Hopkins*, p. 367.

34. David Stafford, *Roosevelt and Churchill: Men of Secrets* (New York, 200), p. 75.

35. Ibid., pp. 75–76; *British Security Coordination: The Secret History of British Intelligence in the Americas, 1940–1945* (New York, 1998), pp. 276–78. Surprisingly, Christopher Andrew, *For the President's Eyes Only: Secret Intelligence and the American Presidency from Washington to Bush* (New York, 1995), p. 103, sees only "staggering ineptitude" on the American side.

36. Cited in Buell, *Master of Sea Power*, p. 148.

37. Meeting of June 2, 1941. Andreas Hillgruber, ed., *Staatsmännner und Diplomaten bei Hitler. Vertrauliche Aufzeichnungen über Unterredungen mit Vertretern des Auslandes 1939–1941* (Frankfurt, 1967), p. 566.

38. Max Domarus, ed., *Hitler. Reden und Proklamationen 1932–1945* (Munich, 1961), vol. 2, pp. 1747, 1749.

39. Elke Fröhlich, ed., *Die Tagebücher von Joseph Goebbels, Diktate 1941–1945* (Munich, 1996), vol. 1, pp. 235–37.

40. Report of August 18, 1941. Heinz Boberach, ed., *Meldungen aus dem Reich 1938–1945. Die geheimen Lageberichte des Sicherheitsdienstes der SS* (Herrsching, 1984), vol. 8, p. 2659.

CHAPTER 2

1. William E. Leuchtenburg, "Franklin D. Roosevelt: The First Modern President," in Fred I. Greenstein, *Leadership in the Modern Presidency* (Cambridge, MA, and London, 1988), pp. 7–8; Also William E. Leuchtenburg, *The FDR Years: On Roosevelt and His Legacy* (New York, 1995), p. 2.

2. Cited in Warren F. Kimball, *The Juggler: Franklin Roosevelt as Wartime Statesman* (Princeton,1991), p. 7.

3. Earl of Birkenhead, *Halifax: The Life of Lord Halifax* (London, 1965), p. 477.

4. Cited in Michael Beschloss, *The Conquerors: Roosevelt, Truman and the Destruction of Germany, 1941–1945* (New York, 2002), p. 17.

5. Isaiah Berlin, *Personal Impressions* (London, 1980), p. 26.

6. President's Safe Files, Box 159. Franklin D. Roosevelt Library, Hyde Park, New York.

7. Cited in John Charmley, *Churchill's Grand Alliance: The Anglo-American Special Relationship 1940–57* (New York, 1995), p. 11.

8. *Foreign Relations of the United States: The Conferences at Washington, 1941–1942, and Casablanca, 1943* (Washington, 1968), pp. 1–415. Hereafter cited as FRUS.

9. Resa Willis, *FDR and Lucy: Lovers and Friends* (New York, 2004), pp. 38ff.

10. Cited in M. L. Stein, *When Presidents Meet the Press* (New York, 1969), p. 86.

11. David Brinkley, *Washington Goes to War* (New York, 1988), p. 169.

12. Ibid., p. 181. Also, Grace Tully, *F.D.R. My Boss* (Chicago, 1949), pp. 292–93.

13. Frederick W. Marks III, *Wind over Sand: The Diplomacy of Franklin Roosevelt* (Athens, GA, and London, 1988), p. 7.

14. Carlo Levi, *Christ Stopped at Eboli: The Story of a Year* (New York, 1947), p. 122.

15. John Milton Cooper, Jr., *The Warrior and the Priest: Woodrow Wilson and Theodore Roosevelt* (Cambridge, MA, and London, 1983), pp. 358–61. Cooper believes that "Uncle Ted" was the greater influence.

16. Leuchtenburg, "Franklin D. Roosevelt," p. 30.

17. Arthur M. Schlesinger, Jr., *The Coming of the New Deal* (Boston, 1959), p. 528.

18. Stimson diary, November 12, 1941. Henry L. Stimson Papers, Reel 7, vol. 36, Library of Congress, Washington, DC. Hereafter cited as LC; Charmley, *Churchill's Grand Alliance*, pp. 12–13.

19. George Brown Tindall, *America: A Narrative History* (New York and London, 1984), p. 1096.

20. David M. Kennedy, *Freedom from Fear: The American People in Depression and War, 1929–1945* (New York and Oxford, 1999), p. 365.

21. Marks, *Wind over Sand*, p. 148.

22. Cited in ibid., p. 131.

23. Waldo H. Heinrichs, Jr., *American Ambassador: Joseph C. Grew and the Development of the United States Diplomatic Tradition* (Boston and Toronto, 1966), p. 233.

24. *Tagebücher Goebbels*, vol. 7, pp. 333–34.

25. Hillgruber, ed., *Staatsmänner und Diplomaten*, pp. 550–58.

26 Dennis J. Dunn, *Caught Between Roosevelt and Stalin: America's Ambassadors to Moscow* (Lexington, KY, 1998), pp. 2–5.

27. Cited in ibid., p. 80.

28. Note of December 22, 1940. FRUS, *Soviet Union*, pp. 868–69.

29. Cited in Leuchtenburg, *The FDR Years*, p. 295.

30. Cited in Marks, *Wind over Sand*, p. 127.

31. Citations in Norman Moss, *Nineteen Weeks: America, Britain, and the Fateful Summer of 1940* (Boston and New York, 2003), pp. 159, 161.

32. *British Security Coordination: The Secret History of British Intelligence in the Americas, 1940–1945* (New York, 1998), pp. 72–73. The documents pertaining to this subject were destroyed by the British after the war, but a single copy of this summary survived.

33. A listing of July 19, 1940, by Roger S. Greene of the Committee. Benjamin V. Cohen Papers, LC.

34. Cited in Brinkley, *Washington Goes to War*, p. 27.

35. Marks, *Wind over Sand*, pp. 277–87; citation p. 276.

36. Robert Dallek, *Franklin D. Roosevelt and American Foreign Policy, 1932–1945* (New York, 1979), pp. 530, 538.

CHAPTER 3

1. Robert Rhodes James, *Churchill: A Study in Failure* (New York, 1970), p. 334.

2. Robert Rhodes James, ed., *Winston S. Churchill: His Complete Speeches, 1897–1963*, 8 vols. (New York, 1974), vol. 6, p. 6220.i

3. Cited in Violet Bonham Carter, *Winston Churchill as I knew Him* (London, 1965), p. 33.

4. Norman Rose, *Churchill: An Unruly Life* (London, 1994), p. 37; John Keegan, *Winston Churchill* (New York, 2002), p. 15.

5. William Manchester, *The Last Lion: Winston Spencer Churchill; Visions of Glory* (New York, 1983), pp. 29–30.

6. Carter, *Winston Churchill*, pp. 17–18.

7. Isaiah Berlin, *Mr. Churchill in 1940* (London, 1964), p. 16.

8. Ibid., p. 23.

9. All quotes from John Pearson, *The Private Lives of Winston Churchill* (London, 1991), pp. 108–109.

10. Berlin, *Mr. Churchill*, p. 157.

11. Rose, *Curchill*, p. 46.

12. Ibid.

13. John Keegan, *Winston Churchill* (New York, 2002), p. 12.

14. John Lukacs, *Churchill: Visionary, Statesman, Historian* (London, 2002), p. 104.

15. Ibid., p. 105.

16. Cited in Manchester, *Visions of Glory*, p. 12.

17. Lukacs, *Churchill*, pp. 124–25.

18. James, *Churchill: A Study in Failure*, p. 344.

19. Manchester, *Visions of Glory*, p. 13.

20. Carter, *Winston Churchill*, p. 133.

21. Ibid., p. 135.

22. Rose, *Churchill*, p. 84.

23. Ibid., pp. 37–38.

24. Keegan, *Winston Churchill*, pp. 8–9.

25. Carter, *Winston Churchill*, pp. 148–49.

26. Keegan, *Winston Churchill*, p. 12.

27. Rose, *Churchill*, p. 40.

28. Ibid., p. 36.

29. Carter, *Winston Churchill*, p. 148.

30. On the Churchill marriage, see Keegan, *Winston Churchill*, pp. 69–70; Pearson, *Private Lives of Winston Churchill*, pp. 119–21; and especially Richard Hough, *Winston & Clementine: The Triumphs and Tragedies of the Churchills* (New York, 1990).

31. Manchester, *Visions of Glory*, p. 23.

32. Carter, *Winston Churchill*, pp. 15–16.

33. Carlyle citation from http://www.gutenberg.org/text.

34. Manchester, *Visions of Glory*, pp. 692–94.

35. James, *Churchill: A Study in Failure*, p. 353.

36. Andrew Roberts, *Hitler & Churchill: Secrets of Leadership* (London, 2003), pp. 1–2; 167ff.

37. Gilbert, *Winston S. Churchill*, vol. 5, *The Wilderness Years* (London, 1981), p. 62.

38. Cited in Pearson, *Private Lives of Winston Churchill*, p. 227.

39. James, ed., *Churchill: Complete Speeches*, vol. 6, p. 6238.

40. Public Record Office, ADM 223/619, Rear Admiral Sir John Godfrey's unpublished war memoirs.

41. Ibid.

42. Francis L. Loewenheim, Harold D. Langley, and Manfred Jonas, eds., *Roosevelt and Churchill: Their Secret Wartime Correspondence* (New York, 1975), p. 89. Henceforth *Secret Wartime Correspondence*.

43. Churchill, *The Gathering Storm*, p. 441.

44. *Secret Wartime Correspondence*, p. 94.

CHAPTER 4

1. Scott Hart, *Washington at War: 1941–1945* (Englewood Cliffs, NJ, 1970), p. 1.

2. Cited in William Seale, *The President's House: A History*, 2 vols. (Washington, 1986), vol. 2, p. 972.

3. Ibid., pp. 986–87.

4. "Ship Models, Prints, etc. in White House on Second Floor." President's Safe File, FDR Folder, Drawer 4-41, 1941. Franklin D. Roosevelt Library, Hyde Park, New York.

5. Unless otherwise indicated, all menus are from Henrietta Nesbitt Papers, Box 6, folder 2, Daily Menus, Library of Congress, Washington, DC.

6. David Brinkley, *Washington Goes to War* (New York, 1988), p. 87.

7. Robert Sherwood, *Roosevelt and Hopkins: An Intimate History* (New York, 1948), pp. 430–34. As usual, FDR left no detailed record of that day's events.

8. Cited in Brinkley, *Washington Goes to War*, p. 86.

9. Diary entry for December 6, 1941. Beatrice Bishop Berle and Travis Beal Jacobs, ed., *Navigating the Rapids 1918–1971: From the Papers of Adolf A. Berle* (New York, 1973), p. 381.

10. Cordell Hull, *The Memoirs of Cordell Hull*, 2 vols. (New York, 1948), vol. 2, pp. 1095–97; Brinkley, *Washington Goes to War*, p. 87.

11. Grace Tully, *F.D.R. My Boss* (Chicago, 1949), pp. 254–55.

12. Cited in Doris Kearns Goodwin, *No Ordinary Time: Franklin and Eleanor Roosevelt: The Home Front in World War II* (New York, 1994), p. 289.

13. Winston S. Churchill, *The Second World War: The Grand Alliance* (London, 1950), pp. 604–05.

14. Martin Gilbert, ed., *The Churchill War Papers*, vol. 3, *The Ever-Widening War 1941* (London, 1993), p. 1577.

15. Churchill, *The Grand Alliance*, pp. 605.

16. Cited in David Stafford, *Roosevelt and Churchill: Men of Secrets* (New York, 2000), pp. 115–16. Also, *Foreign Relations of the United States: The Conferences at Washington, 1941–1942, and Casablanca, 1943* (Washington, 1968), p. 4.

17. Tully, *F.D.R. My Boss*, p. 256.

18. Frances Perkins, *The Roosevelt I Knew* (New York, 1946), p. 377. Her more detailed recollections of that day are in Oral History Project, Columbia University, New York, vol. 8, pp. 70, 87–88. Also, *The Secret Diary of Harold L. Ickes*, vol. 3, *The Lowering Clouds 1939–1941* (New York, 1954), pp. 661–64.

19. Cited in Stafford, *Roosevelt and Churchill*, p. 123.

20. Tully, *F.D.R. My Boss*, p. 258; John Morton Blum, ed., *From The Morgenthau Diaries: Years of War 1941–1945* (Boston, 1967), p. 2.

21. J. B. West, *Upstairs at the White House: My Life With the First Ladies* (New York, 1973), pp. 35–36.

22. Samuel I. Rosenman, ed., *The Public Papers and Addresses of Franklin D. Roosevelt, 1941 Volume* (New York, 1950), pp. 514–15; Tully, *F.D.R. My Boss*, p. 256.

23. Ibid., p. 261.

24. Rosenman, ed., *Public Papers and Addresses*, pp. 522–30.

25. Martin Gilbert, *Winston S. Churchill* (8 vols., London, 1986), vol. 6, *Road to Victory, 1941–1945*, p. 1.

26. Gilbert, ed., *Churchill War Papers*, vol. 3, *1941*, p. 1585.

27. David Dilks, ed., *The Diaries of Sir Alexander Cadogan* (New York, 1972), p. 417.

28. Max Domarus, *Hitler. Reden und Proklamationen 1932–1945* (4 vols., Munich, 1961), vol. 2, p. 1791.

29. Entry of December 10, 1941. Elke Fröhlich, ed., *Die Tagebücher von Joseph Goebbels*, Part II, *Diktate 1941–1945* (Munich, 1996), vol. 2, p. 464.

30. Entry for December 11, 1941. Ibid., p. 472.

31. Report of December 15, 1941. Bundesarchiv-Koblenz, Germany, R 58 Reichssicherheitshauptamt, pp. 717, 144–94, 1094–96. Also, Heinz Boberach, ed.,

Meldungen aus dem Reich. Die geheimen Lageberichte des Sicherheitsdienstes der SS (Herrsching, 1884), vol. 9, p. 3101. FDR was a thirty-second degree Mason, a member of Holland Lodge No. 8 in New York City.

32. Brinkley, *Washington Goes to War*, pp. 36, 93.

33. Sam Rosenman, *Working with Roosevelt* (New York, 1972), p. 312.

34. Brinkley, *Washington Goes to War*, p. 173.

35. Gilbert, ed., *Churchill War Papers*, vol. 3, *1941*, p. 169.

36. Davis, *FDR: The War President*, p. 354.

37. H. G. Nicholas, ed., *Washington Despatches, 1941–1945: Weekly Political Reports from the British Embassy* (Chicago, 1981), p. 7.

38. Halifax to Churchill, December 9, 1941. Halifax Papers, Reel 4011.

39. Davis, *FDR: The War President*, p. 354.

40. Roosevelt to Churchill, December 11, 1941. Telegram 7967A, Chartwell Estate Papers, 20/46/80–81.

41. Churchill, *The Grand Alliance*, p. 620.

CHAPTER 5

1. Churchill College, Churchill Archives, Cambridge, JACB 1/12, "Sir Ian Jacob's Account of Operation Arcadia." Entry for December 12, 1941. Hereafter cited as Jacob Diary. These materials are also in the Alanbrooke Papers, 6/7/2, Liddell Hart Centre for Military Archives, London.

2. *http://www.spartacus.schoolnet.co.uk/BUbeaverbrook.htm*

3. Robert Rhodes James, ed., *Churchill Speaks: 1897–1963. Collected Speeches in Peace and War* (New York, 1980), p. 326

4. Service Record of Sir Alfred Dudley Pickman Rogers Pound. Public Record Office (hereafter PRO), Kew, ASDM 196/90.

5. John Colville, *Footprints in Time* (London, 1976), p. 189.

6. David Bercuson and Holger Herwig, *The Destruction of the Bismarck* (New York, 2001), pp. 107–09.

7. Colville, *Footprints in Time*, p. 188.

8. Alex Danchev, "'Dilly-Dally' or Having the Last Word: Field Marshal Sir John Dill and Prime Minister Winston Churchill," *Journal of Contemporary History*, January 1987, p. 22.

9. Alex Danchev and Daniel Todman, eds., *War Diaries: 1939–1945, Field Marshal Lord Alanbrooke* (London, 2001), p. 124.

10. Colville, *Footprints*, p. 190.

11. PRO, ADM 53/114155, log HMS *Duke of York*, December 14, 1941.

12. Imperial War Museum, London, 87/35/1. Papers of Lt. R. A. Bennet-Levy.

13. Gilbert, *Winston S. Churchill*, vol. 7, *Road to Victory, 1941–1945*, p. 19.

14. Ibid., p. 13.

15. The memos are in Gilbert, ed., *The Churchill War Papers*, vol. 3, *1941*, pp. 1633–1637, 1639–41, 1642–1644. The minutes of the staff meetings are in PRO, Premier 3/458/2, records of staff conferences held December 18 and 19, 1941.

16. Churchill to Smuts, December 21, 1941. Churchill Archives, Cambridge University, CHAR 20-47-59.

17. PRO Premier 3/458/2, record of staff conference held December 18, 1941.

18. Gilbert, ed., *The Churchill War Papers*, vol. 3, *1941*, pp. 1635, 1643.

CHAPTER 6

1. Hull to Roosevelt, December 14 ,1941. *Foreign Relations of the United States: The Conferences at Washington, 1941–1942, and Casablanca, 1943* (Washington, 1968) p. 12. Hereafter cited as FRUS. Also, *The Memoirs of Cordell Hull*, 2 vols. (New York, 1948), vol. 2, pp. 1114–15.

2. FRUS, p. 37.

3. Diary entry, December 18. 1941. Henry L. Stimson Papers, Reel 7, vol. 36, Library of Congress, Washington, DC. Hereafter cited as LC.

4. Michael Beschloss, *The Conquerors: Roosevelt, Truman and the Destruction of Germany, 1941–1945* (New York, 2002), pp. 88–89; David Brinkley, *Washington Goes to War* (New York, 1988), p. 72.

5. FRUS, pp. 44–47.

6. Ibid., pp. 50–53.

7. Memorandum, December 21, 1941. Henry H. Arnold Papers, Reel 205, White House Conferences, LC. Also, diary entry, December 21, 1941, Henry L. Stimson Papers, Reel 7, vol. 36; ibid.

8. Eleanor Roosevelt Papers, Speech and Articles File, W.S. Churchill Articles 1960. Franklin D. Roosevelt Library, Hyde Park, New York. Hereafter cited as FRDL. She published her account in *The Atlantic*, March 1965, pp. 77–80, for the then princely fee of $1,000.

9. Cited in Doris Kearns Goodwin, *No Ordinary Time: Franklin and Eleanor Roosevelt: The Home Front in World War II* (New York, 1994), p. 300.

10. "My Day," December 24. 1941. Eleanor Roosevelt Papers, Box 3147, FDRL.

11. Henrietta Nesbitt, *White House Diary* (Garden City, NY, 1948), p. 272.

12. Knox to Paul S. Mowrer of the *Chicago Daily News*, December 18, 1941. The Papers of Frank Knox, Box 4, General Correspondence 1941, LC.

13. Brinkley, *Washington Goes to War*, p. 153. For the sake of consistency, all times for FDR's movements have been taken from the Pare Lorentz Chronology, FDRL.

14. "Visit at the White House. November 1941—January 1942." Charles S. Hamlin Papers, Box 358, Folder 15 Miscellany, LC.

15. J. W. Pickersgill, *The Mackenzie King Record*, vol 1, *1939–1944* (Chicago and Toronto, 1960), pp. 317–18.

16. Entry for December 22, 1941. Lord Moran [Sir Charles Wilson], *Winston Churchill: The struggle for survival 1940–1965* (London, 1966), p. 10.

17. Prime Minister to Lord Halifax, 22.12.41. Churchill College, Churchill Archives, Cambridge, CHAR 20/47/69.

18. Walter H. Thompson, *Assignment: Churchill* (New York, 1955), p. 246.

19. Judith R. Cohen, *The Mayflower Hotel: Grand Dame of Washington, D.C.* (New York, 1987), pp. 90ff.

20. Churchill College, Churchill Archives, Cambridge, JACB 1/12, "Sir Ian Jacob's Account of Operation Arcadia," pp. 8–9.

21. Press conference, 10:30 A.M., December 22, 1941. The Stephen Early Papers, Scrapbook No. 12, FDRL; also, *The Washington Post*, December 23, 1941.

22. Diary entry, December 20, 1941. Henrietta Nesbitt Papers, Container 2, LC.

23. Lillian Rogers Parks, *The Roosevelts: A Family in Turmoil* (Englewood Cliffs, NJ, 1981), p. 87.

24. "Some Memories of Franklin D. Roosevelt," Huibertie Pruyn Hamlin. Reminiscences by Contemporaries, Acc. 46-60-1, FDRL; also, Charles S. Hamlin Papers, LC. Small snippets were published by Mrs. Charles Hamlin, "An Old River Friend," *The New Republic*, April 15, 1946, pp. 528–31.

25. "Meeting of President Roosevelt and Prime Minister Churchill with their Military Advisors, December 23, 1941." FRUS, p. 69.

26. Ibid., pp 63–65, reprints Churchill's report of the meeting in *The Second World War: The Grand Alliance* (London, 1950), pp. 663–65.

27. Churchill to Attlee, December 23, 1941. Public Record Office, Kew, CAB 120/28.

28. The Earl of Birkenhead, *Halifax: The Life of Lord Halifax* (London, 1965), p. 536.

29. Entry for December 22, 1941. Lord Moran, *Churchill*, p. 11.

30. Cited in Kearns Goodwin, *No Ordinary Time*, p. 302.

31. Alonzo Fields, *My 21 Years in the White House* (Greenwich, CT, 1961), p. 51.

32. Kearns Goodwin, *No Ordinary Time*, p. 199.

33. William Seale, *The President's House: A History*, 2 vols. (Washington, DC, 1986), vol. 2, p. 974.

34. Nesbitt, *White House Diary*, pp. 266, 274, 276, 289.

35. Parks, *The Roosevelts*, pp. 74, 98–100, 252.

36. Lillian Rogers Parks, *My Thirty Years Backstairs at the White House* (New York, 1961), p. 271.

37. "Setting up Map Room in White House." Admiral John L. McCrae Papers, March 1973, FDRL.

38. "White House Diary" manuscript, p. 340; Henrietta Nesbitt Papers, Box 12, LC.

39. William M. Rigdon, *White House Sailor* (New York, 1962), pp. 7–11; and Seale, *The President's House*, vol. 2, pp. 987–89.

CHAPTER 7

1. Hopkins, Roosevelt and Churchill had lunch together on December 24, 25, 27, 1941, and on January 1, 2, 3, 4, 11, 12, 13, and 14, 1942. The three also shared dinner on December 23, 25, 26, 27, and 28, 1941; and on January 4, 11, and 14, 1942. The Harry Hopkins Papers, Box 308, Book 5. Franklin D. Roosevelt Library, Hyde Park, New York. Hereafter cited as FDRL.

2. Editors' notes. *Foreign Relations of the United States: The Conferences at Washington, 1941–1942, and Casablanca, 1943* (Washington, 1968), pp. 61–63. Hereafter cited as FRUS.

3. David Stafford, *Roosevelt and Churchill: Men of Secrets* (New York, 2000), p. 131.

4. Randall Bennett Woods, *A Changing of the Guard: Anglo-American Relations, 1941–1946* (Chapel Hill, NC, and London, 1990), p. 11. See also George T. McJimsey, *Harry Hopkins: Ally of the Poor and Defender of Democracy* (Cambridge, MA, and London, 1987); and June Hopkins, *Harry Hopkins: Sudden Hero, Brash Reformer* (New York, 1999).

5. Thomas M. Coffey, *Hap: The Story of the US Air Force and the Man Who Built It* (New York, 1982), p. 254.

6. Meeting of Lieutenant General Arnold and Air Chief Marshal Portal, December 22, Evening. FRUS, p. 65; Coffee, *Hap*, p. 242.

7. Arnold's notes, December 22 1941. Henry H. Arnold Papers, Reel 205, White House Conferences, Library of Congress, Washington, DC. Hereafter cited as LC. Also FRUS, pp. 63–65; and General H. H. Arnold, *Global Mission* (London, 1951), p. 165.

8. Forrest C. Pogue, *George C. Marshall: Ordeal and Hope* (New York, 1966), p. 265.

9. Churchill College, Churchill Archives, Cambridge, JACB 1/12, "Sir Ian Jacob's Account of Operation Arcadia," pp. 15ff. Hereafter cited as Jacob Diary.

10. Pogue, *George C. Marshall*, p. 262.

11. Halifax to Churchill, 19 December 1941. Grey Telegrams 1-200. Public Record Office, Kew, CAB 120/28, Operation "Arcadia."

12. John Colville, *Winston Churchill and his Inner Circle* (New York, 1981), p. 187. John Colville, *The Fringes of Power: Downing Street Diaries* (London, 2004) contains a most graphic description of Churchill as war leader; pp. 98–102.

13. Ibid., New York edition.

14. "Visit at the White House. November 1941—January 1942." Charles S. Hamlin Papers, Box 358, Folder 15 Miscellany, LC.

15. Grace Tully, *F.D.R. My Boss* (Chicago, 1949), p. 300.

16. FRUS, pp. 67–68.

17. Brinkley, *Washington Goes to War*, p. 184.

18. The text of the Roosevelt-Churchill press conference is in The Stephen Early Papers, Scrapbook No. 12, FDRL.

19. Samuel I. Rosenman, ed., *The Public Papers and Addresses of Franklin D. Roosevelt, 1941 Volume* (New York, 1950), pp. 585–91; *The Washington Daily News*, December 24, 1941.

20. *The Washington Post*, December 26, 1941.

21. Pogue, *George C. Marshall*, p. 270.

22. This summary is based on Marshall's notes, reprinted in FRUS, pp. 69–71.

23. Ibid., p. 76.

24. Ibid., p. 72; Memorandum of December 23, 1941, Henry H. Arnold Papers, Reel 205, White House Conferences, LC. Also, FRUS, pp. 69–74; Larry I. Bland, ed., *The Papers of George Catlett Marshall*, vol. 3, *"The Right Man For The Job" December 7, 1941—May 31, 1943* (Baltimore and London, 1991), pp. 31–36.

25. "Jacob Diary," p. 15.

26. Diary entry, December 23, 1941. Henry L. Stimson Papers, Reel 7, vol. 36, LC.

27. Diary entries of December 25 and 28, 1941. Elke Fröhlich, ed., *Die Tagebücher von Joseph Goebbels*, part 2, *Diktate 1941–1945* (Munich, 1996), vol. 2, pp. 576–89.

28. Table talk of January 4–5, 1942. Werner Jochmann, ed., *Adolf Hitler. Monologe im Führerhauptquartier 1941–1944* (Munich, 1980), p. 178.

CHAPTER 8

1. Kenneth S. Davis, *FDR: The War President 1940–1943* (New York, 2000), p. 374.

2. National Archives of Canada, Mackenzie King Diary, p. 1190, December 24, 1941.

3. William L. Langer, *Our Vichy Gamble* (New York, 1947), pp. 212–18. William D. Leahy, *I Was There: The Personal Story of the Chief of Staff to Presidents Roosevelt and Truman Based on His Notes and Diaries Made at the Time* (New York, 1950), p. 75, dismisses the entire affair with one laconic sentence. See also Milton Viorst, *Hostile Allies: FDR and Charles De Gaulle* (New York, 1965), pp. 77ff.

4. Davis, *FDR*, p. 376.

5. The following biographical materials are taken from John A. Garraty, ed., *American National Biography*, 24 vols. (New York, 1999).

6. Julius W. Pratt, *Cordell Hull 1933–44*, 2 vols. (New York, 1964), vol. 1, p. 5.

7. Memorandum of December 24, 1941. Henry H. Arnold Papers, Reel 199, Subject File, Arcadia Conference, Library of Congress. Hereafter cited as LC.

8. *Foreign Relations of the United States: The Conferences at Washington, 1941–1942, and Casablanca, 1943* (Washington, 1968), p. 83. Hereafter cited as FRUS.

9. Ibid., p. 85.

10. Admiral King's notes of December 24, 1941. *Official Papers of Fleet Admiral Ernest J. King*, Reel 5, Correspondence and Memoranda, 1918–1955.

11. George C. Pogue, *George C. Marshall: Global Commander* (Colorado Springs, CO, 1968) , pp. 13–19.

12. Cited in Maurice Matloff and Edwin M. Snell, *United States Army in World War II*, The War Department, *Strategic Planning for Coalition Warfare 1941–1942*, 2 vols. (Washington, 1953–59), vol. 1, pp. 104–105.

13. Churchill College, Churchill Archives, Cambridge, JACB 1/12, "Sir Ian Jacob's Account of Operation Arcadia," pp. 15–17.

14. *Washington Evening Standard*, January 11, 1941.

115. David Brinkley, *Washington Goes to War* (New York, 1988), p. 103.

16. Scott Hart, *Washington at War: 1941–1945* (Englewood Cliffs, NJ, 1970), pp. 52–54; *The Washington Post*, December 25, 1941.

17. The President's Personal File, 1933–45, No. 1820, Box 18, Franklin D. Roosevelt Library, Hyde Park, New York. Hereafter cited as FDRL.

18. Speech in ibid.; and The Harry Hopkins Papers, Box 308, Book 5; ibid.

19. The Secretary of the British Chiefs of Staff (Hollis) to the Secretary, War Department General Staff (Smith), FRUS, p. 267.

20. William Seale, *The President's House: A History*, 2 vols. (Washington, 1986), vol. 2, p. 955.

21. Davis, *FDR*, p. 368; "My Day," December 26, 1941, Eleanor Roosevelt Papers, FDRL. Also, Resa Willis, *FDR and Lucy: Lovers and Friends* (New York and London, 2004), p. 102.

22. Diary entry for December 26, 1941. Lash Papers, Lash Diary, Box 31, FDRL; Dorothy Kearns Goodwin, *No Ordinary Time: Franklin and Eleanor Roosevelt: The Home Front in World War II* (New York, 1994), p. 306.

23. Entry for December 24, 1941. Lord Moran [Sir Charles Wilson], *Winston Churchill: The struggle for survival 1940–1965* (London, 1966), p. 12.

24. Martin Gilbert, *Winston S. Churchill*, vol. 7, *Road to Victory 1941–1945* (London, 1986), pp. 27–28.

25. Mrs. Charles Hamlin, "An Old River Friend," *The New Republic*, April 15, 1946, p. 531. See also Edith Benham Helm, *The Captains and the Kings* (New York, 1954), pp. 209–12.

26. Entry for December 24, 1941. Lord Moran, *Churchill*, p. 12.

27. Gilbert, *Winston S. Churchill*, vol. 7, *Road to Victory, 1941–1945*, p. 28; also, *The Washington Daily News*, December 26, 1941.

28. Entry for December 25, 1941. Lord Moran, *Churchill*, p. 13; also Davis, *FDR*, p. 369; and Robert Sherwood, *Roosevelt and Hopkins: An Intimate History* (New York, 1948), pp. 442–43.

29. Stimson Diaries, December 25, 1941. Henry L. Stimson Papers, Reel 7,

vol. 36, LC. Also, FRUS, p. 95; George T. McJimsey, *Harry Hopkins: Ally of the Poor and Defender of Democracy* (Cambridge, MA, and London, 1987), p. 213.

30. Sumner Welles, *Seven Decisions that Shaped History* (New York, 1950), p. 63.

31. Davis, *FDR*, pp. 377–78.

32. *Memoirs of Cordell Hull*, 2 vols. (New York, 1948), vol. 2, pp. 1128–33.

33. Roosevelt to Clementine Churchill, December 25, 1941. President's Safe Files, Diplomatic Correspondence, Great Britain, Box 37, FDRL; Clementine Churchill to Roosevelt, January 31, 1941; ibid.

34. Elliott Roosevelt, *A Rendezvous with Destiny: The Roosevelts of the White House* (New York,1975), p. 309.

35. Memorandum of December 25, 1941. Henry H. Arnold Papers, Reel 199, Subject File, Arcadia Conference, LC. Also, Defense Files, 25 December 1941, FRUS, pp. 90–94.

36. Stimson Diaries, December 25, 1941. Henry L. Stimson Papers, Reel 7, vol. 36, LC. Also, FRUS, p. 95.

37. Betty Hight to family, December 26, 1941. Betty Hight Papers, Acc. 77-79, FDRL.

38. Entry for December 25, 1941. Lord Moran, *Churchill*, p. 14. Also, "My Day," December 27, 1941, Eleanor Roosevelt Papers, Box 3147, FDRL; David Emblidge, ed., *My Day: The Best of Eleanor Roosevelt's Acclaimed Newspaper Columns, 1936–1962* (New York, 2001), pp. 60–61; Kearns Goodwin, *No Ordinary Time*, p. 308; and John Morton Blum, ed., *From the Morgenthau Diaries: Years of War 1941–1945* (Boston, 1967), p. 122.

CHAPTER 9

1. Entry for December 26, 1941. Lord Moran [Sir Charles Wilson], *Winston Churchill: The Struggle for Survival 1940–1965* (London, 1966) , p. 15.

2. Ibid., pp. 15–16; Robert Rhodes James, *Winston Churchill: His Complete Speeches 1897–1963*, 8 vols. (New York, 1974), vol. 6, pp. 6536–41.

3. Doris Kearns Goodwin, *No Ordinary Time: Franklin and Eleanor Roosevelt: The Home Front in World War II* (New York, 1994), p. 309.

4. *The Washington Post*, December 27, 1941.

5. Agent Vincent F. Callahan to Morgenthau, January 7, 1942. The Morgenthau Diaries, Reel 136, No. 403, Franklin D. Roosevelt Library, Hyde Park, New York. Hereafter cited as FDRL.

6. Entry for December 26, 1941. Lord Moran, *Churchill*, pp. 15–16.

7. Entry of December 28, 1941. Elke Fröhlich, ed., *Die Tagebücher von Joseph Goebbels*, Part II, *Diktate 1941–1945* (Munich, 1996), vol. 2, p. 589.

8. Cited in David Brinkley, *Washington Goes to War* (New York, 1988), p. 268.

9. Diary entry for December 26, 1941. National Archives of Canada, Ottawa, Mackenzie King Diary, p. 1197.

10. Ibid., pp. 1197–98.

11. Ibid., p. 1202.

12. Winston S. Churchill, *The Second World War: The Grand Alliance* (London, 1950), p. 667.

13. Entry for December 28, 1941. Lord Moran, *Churchill*, p. 17.

14. Hopkins to Pound, January 14, 1942. The Harry Hopkins Papers, Box 308, Book 5, FDRL.

15. Churchill College, Churchill Archives, Cambridge, JACB 1/12, "Sir Ian Jacob's Account of Operation Arcadia," pp. 30–34. Hereafter cited as Jacob Diary.

16. Letter of December 31, 1941. Larry I. Bland, ed., *The Papers of George Catlett Marshall*, vol. 3, *"The Right Man for the Job" December 7, 1941—May 31, 1943* (Baltimore and London, 1991), p. 45.

17. Letter of December 31, 1941. Alfred D. Chandler, ed., *The Papers of Dwight David Eisenhower: The War Years: 1* (Baltimore and London, 1970), p. 33.

18. *The Stilwell Papers: Joseph W. Stilwell* (New York, 1997), p. 15.

19. Stimson Diaries, December 26, 1941. Henry L. Stimson Papers, Reel 7, vol. 36, Library of Congress, Washington, DC. Hereafter cited as LC.

20. Memorandum of December 26, 1941. Henry H. Arnold Papers, Reel 1999, Subject File, Arcadia Conference, LC. Also, Defense Files, December 26, 1941, *Foreign Relations of the United States: The Conferences at Washington, 1941–1942, and Casablanca, 1943* (Washington, 1968), pp. 96–98. Hereafter cited as FRUS.

21. Robert William Love, Jr., *The Chiefs of Naval Operations* (Annapolis, MD, 1980), p. 145; Thomas B. Buell, *Master of Sea Power: A Biography of Fleet Admiral Ernest J. King* (Boston and Toronto, 1980), p. 164. Curiously, Marshall's biographer writes: "Only King had spoken up for the proposal in its early stages." Forrest C. Pogue, *George C. Marshall: Ordeal and Hope, 1939–1942* (London, 1968), p. 278.

22. Churchill to Attlee, Grey No. 141. Public Record Office (hereafter PRO), Kew, CAB 120/28. This message was received in London on the twenty-eighth, but certainly sent on the twenty-seventh. Martin Gilbert, ed., *The Churchill War Papers*, vol. 3, *The Ever-Widening War 1941* (London, 1993), has correctly dated the message December 27.

23. Pogue, *George C. Marshall*, p. 278.

24. FRUS, p. 110.

25. Gilbert, ed., *Churchill War Papers*, vol. 3, *1941*, p. 1698.

26. Eleanor to Anna Roosevelt, January 4, 1942. Bernard Asbell, ed., *Mother & Daughter: The Letters of Eleanor and Anna Roosevelt* (New York, 1982), p. 141.

27. Martha Gellhorn interview, February 20, 1980. Eleanor Roosevelt Papers, Oral Histories, Box 2, FDRL.

28. Eleanor Roosevelt to Lorena Hickok, September 26, 1941. The Lorena Hickok Papers, Box 8, FDRL.

29. Cited in Kearns Goodwin, *No Ordinary Time*, p. 310.

30. Cited in David Stafford, *Roosevelt and Churchill: Men of Secrets* (New York, 2000), p. 127.

31. Entry for December 27, 1941. Lord Moran, *Churchill*, pp. 16–17.

32. There is confusion over how this meeting came about and when it was held. Lord Moran, *Churchill*, p. 17, claims that Beaverbrook and Hopkins arranged the meeting; Pogue, *George C. Marshall*, p. 279, agrees. Churchill, however, reported to Attlee later that day: "this morning General Marshall visited me *at my request* and pleaded case with great conviction" (italics added); Churchill to Attlee, Grey No. 141, PRO CAB 120/28. Churchill's chronology is accepted here. Pogue has this meeting taking place on the morning of the twenty-eighth. Martin Gilbert, *Winston S. Churchill*, vol. 7, *Road to Victory 1941–1945* (London, 1986), p. 31, places it on the twenty-seventh. So does Churchill in his report to Attlee (Grey No. 141); and FRUS, p. 108.

33. Pogue, *George C. Marshall*, pp. 279–80; Bland, ed., *Papers of George Catlett Marshall*, vol. 2, p. 41; Katherine Tupper Marshall, *Together: Annals of an Army Wife* (New York and Atlanta, 1946), pp. 103–04.

34. Churchill to Attlee, Grey No. 141, PRO CAB 120/28.

35. Jacob Diary, p. 20.

36. Robert Sherwood, *Roosevelt and Hopkins: An Intimate History* (New York, 1948), p. 457.

37. Jacob Diary, p. 20.

CHAPTER 10

1. Cited in Forrest C. Pogue, *George C. Marshall: Ordeal and Hope, 1939–1942* (London, 1968), p. 264.

2. *The Stilwell Papers: Joseph W. Stilwell* (New York, 1997), pp. 16–18.

3. Churchill College, Churchill Archives, Cambridge, JACB 1/12, "Sir Ian Jabob's Account of Operation Arcadia," p. 28. Hereafter cited as Jacob Diary.

4. See, for example, Spaatz's diary for July 16 and 22, and August 5, 1940. Carl Spaatz Papers, Box 7, Diaries, Library of Congress, Washington, DC. Hereafter cited as LC.

5. General H. H. Arnold, *Global Mission* (London, 1951), pp. 141–50, 157–59.

6. Cited in Walter Muir Whitehill, "A Postscript to *Fleet Admiral King: A Naval Record*," *Proceedings of the Massachusetts Historical Society* V (1950–53), p. 219. King later denied having made the statement, "but I wish I had."

7. Cited in Thomas M. Coffey, *HAP: The Story of the U.S. Air Force and the Man who Built it: General Henry H. "Hap" Arnold* (New York, 1982), p. 260.

8. Little to Pound, February 4, 1942. Public Record Office, Kew, ADM 178/1323, Personal letters to Pound, 1942–43. Hereafter cited as PRO.

9. Ibid.

10. Jacob Diary, p. 27.

11. Robert William Love, Jr., ed., *The Chiefs of Naval Operations* (Annapolis, MD, 1980), pp. 140–79.

12. Arnold's notes, December 27, 1941. Henry H. Arnold Papers, Reel 205, White House Conferences, LC. Also, Stimson Diaries, December 27, 1941. Henry L. Stimson Papers, Reel 7, vol. 36, ibid.; and *Foreign Relations of the United States: The Conferences at Washington, 1941–1942, and Casablanca, 1943* (Washington, 1968), pp. 109–10. Hereafter cited as FRUS.

13. Memorandum of December 27, 1941. Henry H. Arnold Papers, Reel 1999, Subject File, Arcadia Conference, LC. Also, FRUS, pp. 113–15.

14. Winston S. Churchill, *The Second World War: The Grand Alliance* (London, 1950), p. 674.

15. Entry for January 1, 1942. Lord Moran [Sir Charles Wilson], *Winston Churchill: The struggle for survival 1940–1965* (London, 1966), p. 20.

16. Cited in Pogue, *George C. Marshall*, p. 279. See also FRUS, pp. 115–17.

17. Ibid., p. 368.

18. Ibid., p. 369.

19. Anthony Eden, *The Eden Memoirs: The Reckoning* (London, 1965) p. 289.

20. John Harvey, ed., *The War Diaries of Oliver Harvey* (London, 1978), pp. 74–75. Also, Steven Merritt Miner, *Between Churchill and Stalin: The Soviet Union, Great Britain, and the Origins of the Grand Alliance* (Chapel Hill and London, 1988), pp. 184–92. Ambassador Litvinov informed the State Department of the gist of the Eden-Stalin discussions. Joseph E. Davies Diary, January 8, 1942. Joseph E. Davies Diary, Box 11, LC.

21. Churchill to Eden, December 12, 1941. PRO CAB 120/28.

22. Cited in Miner, *Between Churchill and Stalin*, p. 195.

23. Harvey, ed., *War Diaries*, pp. 78–79; David Dilks, ed., *The Diaries of Sir Alexander Cadogan 1938–1945* (New York, 1972), pp. 422–24.

24. Eden, *Eden Memoirs*, p. 303.

25. Robert Sherwood, *Roosevelt and Hopkins: An Intimate History* (New York, 1948), p. 457.

26. Martin Gilbert, ed., *The Churchill War Papers*, vol. 3, *The Ever-Widening War 1941* (London, 1993—), p. 1700.

27. Alex Danchev and Daniel Todman, eds., *War Diaries: 1939–1945, Field Marshal Lord Alanbrooke* (London, 2001), pp. 215–16 (italics in original). Hereafter cited as *Alanbrooke War Diaries*.

28. Cited in Pogue, *George C. Marshall*, p. 281.

29. *Alanbrooke War Diaries*, p. 215.

30. Meeting of December 28, 1941. FRUS, pp. 125–31.

31. Stimson Diaries, December 28, 1941. Henry L. Stimson Papers, Reel 6, vol. 36, LC.

32. FRUS, p. 128.

33. Ibid.

34. Ibid., p. 1703.

35. Stimson Diaries, December 29, 1941. Henry L. Stimson Papers, Reel 6, vol. 36, LC.

36. Entry for January 2, 1942. Cited in Kevin McCann, *Man from Abilene* (New York, 1952), p. 44.

37. Entry for December 28, 1941. Lord Moran, *Churchill*, p. 18.

38. "Visit at the White House. November 1941–January 1942." Charles S. Hamlin Papers, Box 358, Folder 15 Miscellany, LC.

39. Eleanor Roosevelt Papers, Speech and Article Files, W.S. Churchill Articles, 1960, FDRL.

CHAPTER 11

1. Entry for December 29, 1942. Lord Moran [Sir Charles Wilson], *Winston Churchill: the struggle for survival 1940–1965* (London, 1966), p. 18.

2. Martin Gilbert, ed., *The Churchill War Papers*, vol. 3, *The Ever-Widening War 1941* (London, 1993—), pp. 1706–07.

3. Entry for December 29, 1941. Lord Moran, *Churchill*, p. 18.

4. *The Washington Post*, December 28, 1941.

5. Gilbert, ed., *Churchill War Papers*, vol. 3, *1941*, pp. 1706–07.

6. Entry for December 29, 1941. National Archives of Canada, Ottawa, Mackenzie King Diary, pp. 1214–17. Hereafter cited as King Diary.

7. Ibid., p. 1215.

8. Entry for December 29, 1941. Lord Moran, *Churchill*, p. 18.

9. Gilbert, ed., *Churchill War Papers*, vol. 3, *1941*, p. 1707.

10. Entry for December 29, 1941. Lord Moran, *Churchill*, pp. 19–20.

11. Gilbert, ed., *Churchill War Papers*, vol. 3, *1941*, pp. 1709–17.

12. King Diary, p. 1222.

13. Churchill College, Churchill Archives, Cambridge, JACB 1/12, "Sir Ian Jacob's Account of Operation Arcadia," p. 21.

14. Thomas B. Buell, *Master of Sea Power: A Biography of Fleet Admiral Ernest J. King* (Boston and Toronto, 1980), p. 168.

15. Memorandum of December 29, 1941. Henry H. Arnold Papers, Reel 199, Subject File, Arcadia Conference, Library of Congress, Washington DC. Hereafter cited as LC. Also, *Foreign Relations of the United States: The Conferences at Washington, 1941–1942, and Casablanca, 1943* (Washington, 1968), p. 138. Hereafter cited as FRUS.

16. Ibid., p. 139.

17. From Buell, *Master of Sea Power*, p. 169.

18. Winston S. Churchill, *The Second World War: The Grand Alliance* (London, 1950), p. 686.

19. FRUS, pp. 149–50.

20. Dill to Wavell, January 9, 1942. Dill/Wavell Papers. Public Record Office, Kew, CAB 106/1209.

21. Robert Sherwood, *Roosevelt and Hopkins: An Intimate History* (New York, 1948), p. 469.

22. David Brinkley, *Washington Goes to War* (New York, 1988), p. 63.

23. Diary entries of December 20 and 26, 1941. The John H. Towers Papers, LC.

24. FRUS, pp. 98–99.

25. Donald M. Nelson's memorandum, December 30, 1941. FRUS, p. 136; also ibid., pp. 334–39.

26. Hopkins to Air Chief Marshal Sir Charles Portal, January 14, 1942. The Harry Hopkins Papers, Box 308, Book 5, Franklin D. Roosevelt Library, Hyde Park, New York. Hereafter cited as FDRL.

27. Stimson Diaries, January 1, 1942. Henry L. Stimson Papers, Reel 7, vol. 36, LC.

28. Brinkley, *Washington Goes to War*, p. 63.

29. Ibid., p. 68.

30. Sherwood, *Roosevelt and Hopkins*, p. 470.

31. Kenneth S. Davis, *FDR: The War President 1940–1943* (New York, 2000), p. 390.

32. The following is from Scott Hart, *Washington at War: 1941–1945* (Englewood Cliffs, NJ, 1970), pp. 58–59; and Joseph Lash, *Roosevelt and Churchill 1939–1941* (New York, 1976), pp. 15–20.

33. The special service and the sermon are in The President's Personal File, 1933–45, File 7887, FDRL.

34. Cited in Doris Kearns Goodwin, *No Ordinary Time: Franklin and Eleanor Roosevelt: The Home Front in World War II* (New York, 1994), p. 311.

35. Samuel Rosenman, *Working with Roosevelt* (New York, 1972), p. 320.

CHAPTER 12

1. The lunch description for January 1, 1942, is in The Joseph Lash Papers, Lash Diary, Box 31, Franklin D. Roosevelt Library, Hyde Park, New York. Hereafter cited as FDRL.

2. Samuel I. Rosenman, *Working with Roosevelt* (New York, 1972), p. 316. Also, Adolf A. Berle's memorandum, January 6, 1942. The Adolf A. Berle Papers, Diary Box 213, FDRL.

3. Joseph E. Davies diary, January 8 ,1942. Joseph E. Davies Diaries, Box 11, Library of Congress, Washington, DC. Herafter cited as LC; Robert Sherwood, *Roosevelt and Hopkins: An Intimate History* (New York, 1948), p. 449.

4. Hopkins Papers, January 1, 1942, FDRL; *Foreign Relations of the United States: The Conferences at Washington, 1941–1942, and Casablanca, 1943* (Washington, 1968), pp. 151–52. Herafter cited as FRUS.

5. Joseph P. Lash, *Roosevelt and Churchill 1939–1941: The Partnership That Saved the West* (New York, 1976), pp. 16–17.

6. Sherwood, *Roosevelt and Hopkins*, pp. 442–43; Doris Goodwin Kearns, *No Ordinary Time: Franklin and Eleanor Roosevelt: The Home Front in World War II* (New York, 1994), p. 312; Kenneth S. Davis, *FDR: The War President 1940–1943* (New York, 2000), p. 372; Elliott Roosevelt and James Brough, *A Rendezvous with Destiny: The Roosevelts of the White House* (New York, 1975), p. 310; J. W. Pickersgill, *The Mackenzie King Record*, vol. 1, *1939–1944* (Chicago and Toronto, 1960), pp. 429–30.

7. Roosevelt and Brough, *A Rendezvous with Destiny*, p. 311; Lash, *Roosevelt and Churchill*, p. 18.

8. Mrs. Charles Hamlin, "An Old River Friend," *The New Republic*, April 15, 1946. She erroneously gave the date as January 2, 1942.

9. Cited in Kearns Goodwin, *No Ordinary Time*, p. 313.

10. Lash, *Roosevelt and Churchill*, p. 20.

11. Warren F. Kimball, ed., *Churchill & Roosevelt: The Complete Correspondence*, vol. 1, *Alliance Emerging October 1933–November 1941* (Princeton, 1984), p. 310.

12. Memorandum of January 1, 1942. Berle Papers, Diary Box 213, FDRL.

13. Entries for January 1 and 3, 1942. Beatrice Bishop Berle, ed., *Navigating the Rapids 1918–1971: From the Papers of Adolf A. Berle* (New York, 1973), pp. 392–94.

14. Entry for January 8, 1942. John Harvey, ed., *The War Diaries of Oliver Harvey* (London, 1978), p. 86.

15. Churchill to Attlee, January 7 1942. Public Record Office, Kew, CAB 120/29. Hereafter cited as PRO.

16. Entry for September 20, 1942. Harvey, ed., *War Diaries of Oliver Harvey*, p. 159.

17. FRUS, pp. 170–71.

18. Cited in William L. Langer, *Our Vichy Gamble* (New York, 1947), p. 219.

19. Cited in Sherwood, *Roosevelt and Hopkins*, p. 483.

20. Martin Gilbert, ed., *The Churchill War Papers*, vol. 3, *The Ever-Widening War 1941* (London, 2000), p. 1705.

21. Hull to Roosevelt, January 2, 1942. Map Room Papers, Roosevelt-Churchill Strays, File 4, FDRL; also, FRUS, pp. 156–57.

22. Memorandum of Conversation, January 5, 1941. Cordell Hull Papers, Reel 21, Correspondence, LC.

23. *The Memoirs of Cordell Hull*, 2 vols. (New York, 1948), vol. 2, p. 1137.

24. Milton Viorst, *Hostile Allies: FDR and Charles de Gaulle* (New York, 1965), p. 83.

25. Davis, *FDR: The War President*, p. 382; and Kenneth S. Davis, *Soldier of Democracy: A Biography of Dwight Eisenhower* (New York, 1952), pp. 268–69.

26. Cited in Kevin McCann, *Man from Abilene* (Garden City, NY, 1952), pp. 44–46.

27. *The Stilwell Papers: Joseph W. Stilwell* (New York, 1997), pp. 22–23.

28. Dill to Wavell, January 9, 1942. Dill/Wavell Papers, PRO CAB 106/1209.

29. FRUS, p. 157.

30. General H. H. Arnold, *Global Mission* (London, 1951), pp. 167–68; Arnold Papers, January 4, 1942, LC; FRUS, pp. 159–61.

31. Memorandum of January 4, 1942. Arnold Papers, Reel 205, White House Conferences, LC. Also, Stimson Diaries, January 4, 1942. Stimson Papers, Reel 7, vol. 35, LC; and FRUS, pp. 161–70.

32. Entry for January 5, 1942. Lord Moran [Sir Charles Wilson], *Winston Churchill: The struggle for survival 1940–1965* (London, 1966), p. 21.

33. Winston S. Churchill, *The Second World War: The Grand Alliance* (London, 1950), p. 691.

34. From Samuel I. Rosenman, ed., *The Public Papers and Addresses of Franklin D. Roosevelt*, 13 vols. (New York, 1938–1950), vol. 11, pp. 32–42; and Rosenman, *Working with Roosevelt*, pp. 323–24.

35. Stimson Diaries, January 6, 1942. Stimson Papers, Reel 7, vol. 35, LC.

36. Rosenman, *Working with Roosevelt*, pp. 20–24.

37. Ibid., pp. 6–9.

38. Cited in Kearns Goodwin, *No Ordinary Time*, p. 313.

39. Sherwood, *Roosevelt and Hopkins*, pp. 473–74.

40. Stimson Diaries, January 12, 1942. Stimson Papers, Reel 7, vol. 36, LC.

41. Diary entry for January 8, 1942. Elke Fröhlich, ed., *Die Tagebücher von Joseph Goebbels*, part 2, *Diktate 1941–1945* (Munich, 1994), vol. 3, pp. 69–70.

42. Report of January 12, 1942. Bundesarchiv-Koblenz, Germany, Bestand R 58 Reichssicherheitshauptarchiv, pp. 717, 144–94, 1094–96. Also, Heinz Boberach, ed., *Meldungen aus dem Reich. Die geheimen Lageberichte des Sicherheitsdienstes der SS* (Herrsching, 1984), vol. 9, pp. 3151–54.

CHAPTER 13

1. From Alonzo Fields, *My 21 Years in the White House* (Greenwich, CT, 1961), pp. 53ff.

2. Churchill to Roosevelt, January 6, 1941. Map Room Papers, Box 2, Franklin D. Roosevelt Library, Hyde Park, New York. Hereafter cited as FDRL.

3. Cited in Martin Gilbert, *Winston S. Churchill*, vol. 7, *Road to Victory 1941–1945* (London, 1986), p. 37.

4. W. H. Thompson, *Assignment: Churchill* (New York, 1955), pp. 259–60.

5. Fields, *My 21 Years*, p. 58.

6. Thompson, *Assignment: Churchill*, p. 261.

7. Winston S. Churchill, *The Second World War: The Grand Alliance* (London, 1950), pp. 692–93.

8. Ibid., pp. 702–03.

9. *Foreign Relations of the United States: The Conferences at Washington, 1941–1942, and Casablanca, 1943* (Washington, 1968), pp. 217–19. Hereafter cited as FRUS.

10. Churchill College, Churchill Archives, Cambridge, JACB 1/12, "Sir Ian Jacob's Account of Operation Arcadia," p. 40. Hereafter cited as Jacob Diary.

11. Dill to Wavell, January 9, 1942. Public Record Office, Kew, CAB 106/1209 Dill/Wavell Papers.

12. Jacob Diary, p. 41.

13. Cited in Gilbert, *Winston S. Churchill*, vol. 7, *Road to Victory*, p. 38.

14. William M. Rigdon, *White House Sailor* (Garden City, NY, 1962), pp. 18, 19–20.

15. The following is from William D. Hassett Papers, Diary January 6, 1941–November 2, 1943, Box 21, FDRL. Also William D. Hassett, *Off the Record with F.D.R. 1941–1945* (New Brunswick, NJ, 1958), pp. 1 ff.

16. Memoranda of January 11 and 12, 1942. Henry H. Arnold Papers, Reel 205, White House Conferences, Library of Congress, Washington, DC. Hereafter cited as LC. Also, FRUS, pp. 175–80, 182–85, 229–30, 262–65.

17. *The Stilwell Papers: Joseph W. Stilwell* (New York, 1997), p. 24.

18. F. H. Hinsley, *British Intelligence in the Second World War: Its Influence on Strategy and Operations* (4 vols., London, 1981), vol. 2, p. 335.

19. Cited in Thomas B. Buell, *Master of Sea Power: A Biography of Fleet Admiral Ernest J. King* (Boston and Toronto, 1980), p. 172.

20. FRUS, pp. 185–95.

21. Ibid., pp. 195–96.

22. Stimson Diaries, January 12. 1942. Henry L. Stimson Papers, Reel 7, vol. 36, LC.

23. Warren F. Kimball, *The Juggler: Franklin Roosevelt as Wartime Statesman* (Princeton, 1991), p. 49.

CHAPTER 14

1. *Foreign Relations of the United States: The Conferences at Washington, 1941–1942, and Casablanca, 1943* (Washington, 1968), p. 219. Herafter cited as FRUS.

2. For this, see Forrest C. Pogue, *George C. Marshall: Ordeal and Hope, 1939–1942* (London, 1968).

3. FRUS, p. 198.

4. Ibid., pp. 199–200.

5. Cited in Doris Kearns Goodwin, *No Ordinary Time: Franklin and Eleanor Roosevelt: The Home Front in World War II* (New York, 1994), p. 315.

6. Cited in Kenneth S. Davis, *FDR: The War President 1940–1943* (New York, 2000), p. 398.

7. Louis Adamic, *Two-Way Passage* (New York, 1941).

8. Eleanor Roosevelt, *This I Remember* (New York, 1949), p. 245.

9. Louis Adamic, *Dinner at The White House* (New York, 1946), pp. 1–139. His reconstruction is based "on very detailed notes written immediately after the dinner." Ibid., p. 116.

10. Freidel interview with Eleanor, September 3, 1952. Oral History Interviews, Franklin D. Roosevelt Library, Hyde Park, New York. Hereafter cited as FDRL.

11. Churchill College, Churchill Archives, Cambridge, JACB 1/12, "Sir Ian Jacob's Account of Operation Arcadia," p. 42.

12. Pogue, *George C. Marshall*, p. 284.

13. The following is from Robert Sherwood, *Roosevelt and Hopkins: An Intimate History* (New York, 1948), pp. 471–72; and Defense Files, January 14, 1942, FRUS, pp. 203–08.

14. Sherwood, *Roosevelt and Hopkins*, p. 472.

15. Cited in George McJimsey, *Harry Hopkins: Ally of the Poor and Defender of Democracy* (Cambridge, MA, and London, 1987), p. 222.

16. Hopkins' memorandum, January 15, 1942. The Harry Hopkins Papers, Box 3008, Book 5, FDRL.

17. Hopkins' memorandum, January 15, 1942, FRUS, p. 209. The various agreements initialed by Roosevelt and Churchill are in ibid., pp. 359–62. Also, Sherwood, *Roosevelt and Hopkins*, p. 478.

18. Cited in David Stafford, *Roosevelt and Churchill: Men of Secrets* (New York, 2000), p. 128.

19. House of Lords, London, Beaverbrook Papers, BB D/123, "Report by Captain Kelly-Rogers of Prime Minister's Journey in 'Berwick'," n. d.

20. All citations are from "Report by Captain Kelly-Rogers of Prime Minister's Journey in 'Berwick'."

21. Winston S. Churchill, *The Second World War: The Grand Alliance* (London, 1950), pp. 710–11.

22. "Report by Captain Kelly-Rogers of Prime Minister's Journey in 'Berwick'."

EPILOGUE

1. Entry for January 1, 1942. Lord Moran [Sir Charles Wilson], *Winston Churchill: The struggle for survival 1940–1965* (London, 1966), p. 20.

2. Samuel Eliot Morison, *The Battle of the Atlantic: September 1939—May 1943* (Urbana and Chicago, 2001), p. 128.

3. Maurice Matloff and Edwin M. Snell, *The War Department: Strategic Planning for Coalition Warfare 1941–1942,* 2 vols. (Washington, D C, 1953–59), vol. 2, pp. 175–76.

4. Samuel I. Rosenman, ed., *The Public Papers and Addresses of Franklin D. Roosevelt 1942 Volume* (New York, 1950), pp. 105–16.

5. Kenneth S. Davis, *FDR: The War President 1940–1943* (New York, 2000), p. 141.

6. Roosevelt to Churchill, January 30, 1942. Map Room Papers, Box 2, Franklin D. Roosevelt Library, Hyde Park, New York. Also, Moran, *Churchill*, pp. 25–28.

A NOTE ON SOURCES

As of this writing, the Library of Congress lists more than 1,000 books in English by or about Winston Churchill, Franklin Roosevelt, or their relationship. They cover just about every aspect of their lives and careers, their family lives, their friends and colleagues, and virtually all the events and people with which they were associated. This note on sources includes only those books and archival collections which were used in the writing of this book.

WINSTON S. CHURCHILL

There are dozens of biographies of Churchill, single and multi-volume, long and exhaustive, short and interpretive. The most important of these is Martin Gilbert's eight-volume biography, *Winston S. Churchill* (London, 1966–1988). The two volumes covering Churchill's life from the outbreak of the Second World War to the end of the ARCADIA conference are: *Finest Hour: Winston S. Churchill, 1939–1941* (London, 1983), and *Road to Victory: Winston S. Churchill, 1941–1945* (London, 1986). William Manchester's two-volume study, *The Last Lion*, covers Churchill's life to 1940. The first is *Visions of Glory: 1874–1932* (Boston, 1983); the second is *Alone: 1932–1940* (Boston, 1988). Other more recent biographies include Norman Rose, *Churchill: An Unruly Life* (London, 1994), and Roy Jenkins, *Churchill: A Biography* (New York, 2001). John Keegan's *Winston Churchill* (New York, 2002) and John Lukacs' *Churchill: Visionary, Statesman, Historian* (London, 2002) are both short and impressionistic works. One of the best political biographies is that by Robert Rhodes James, *Churchill: A Study in Failure* (New York, 1970), which ends with the outbreak of the Second World War. One recent book has contrasted Churchill to his archenemy: Andrew Roberts, *Hitler & Churchill: Secrets of Leadership* (London, 2003).

Churchill's personal life is the subject of books by Violet Bonham Carter,

Winston Churchill As I Knew Him (London, 1965); Robert Hough, *Winston & Clemetine: The Triumphs and Tragedies of the Churchills* (New York, 1990); Mary Soames' collection of her parents' correspondence, *Speaking for Themselves: The Personal Letters of Winston and Clementine Churchill* (Toronto, 1998); and John Pearson, *The Private Lives of Winston Churchill* (London, 1991).

Several authors have published Churchill's speeches, letters, and other primary sources. Robert Rhodes James compiled eight volumes of *Winston S. Churchill: His Complete Speeches, 1897–1963* (New York, 1974), while Martin Gilbert to date has produced three volumes of *The Churchill War Papers* (London, 1993–2002).

CHURCHILL'S CONTEMPORARIES

The diaries, collected letters, and biographies of Churchill's contemporaries give a picture of embattled Great Britain and reveal the impressions that Churchill's political colleagues had of him and his wartime leadership. Those used were: Harold Nicolson, *Diaries and Letters 1907–1964*, ed. Nigel Nicolson (London, 2004); Hugh Dalton, *The Fateful Years: Memoirs, 1939–1945* (London, 1957); Sir Anthony Eden, *The Eden Memoirs: The Reckoning* (London, 1965); David Dilks, ed., *The Diaries of Sir Alexander Cadogan, 1939–1945* (New York, 1972); General Sir Leslie Hollis, *One Marine's Tale* (London, 1956); The Earl of Birkenhead, *Halifax: The Life of Lord Halifax* (London, 1956); John Harvey, *The War Diaries of Oliver Harvey* (London, 1978); Alex Danchev and Daniel Todman, eds., *War Diaries: 1939–1945, Field Marshal Lord Alanbrooke* (London, 2001); and Andrew Roberts, *"The Holy Fox": A Biography of Lord Halifax* (London, 1991). Lord Moran [Sir Charles Wilson], *Winston Churchill: The struggle for survival, 1940–1965. Taken from the Diaries of Lord Moran* (London, 1966), John Colville, *Footprints in Time* (London, 1976) and *Winston Churchill and His Inner Circle* (New York, 1981), John Colville, *The Fringes of Power: Downing Street Diaries* (London, 2004) and Walter H. Thompson, *Assignment: Churchill* (New York, 1955) are all personal accounts by men who worked directly with Churchill.

THE BRITISH WAR

There are many books on the British war effort from September 3, 1939, to Pearl Harbor. The essential ones used here were the first three volumes of Churchill's *The Second World War*. They are: *The Gathering Storm* (Boston, 1948), *Their Finest Hour* (Boston, 1949), and *The Grand Alliance* (Boston, 1950). Other books used include Isaiah Berlin, *Mr. Churchill in 1940* (London, 1964); John Lukacs, *Five Days in London: May 1940* (New Haven, 1999); Edward Spears, *Assignment to Catastrophe*, vol. 2, *The Fall of France, June 1940* (London, 1954); and Phillip Zeigler, *London at War* (Toronto, 1994). *The Ironside Diaries, 1937–1940* (Westport,

CT, 1962) presents Sir Edmund Ironside's views on Chamberlain's ineffective war leadership. The Battle of Britain and the early air war against Germany are covered in John Terraine, *The Right of the Line: The Royal Air Force in the European War, 1939–1945* (London, 1985), and Denis Richardson, *The Hardest Victory: RAF Bomber Command in the Second World War* (London, 1994).

CHURCHILL AND ROOSEVELT

The Anglo-American relationship—and, more specifically the birth of that relationship under Churchill and Roosevelt in the Second World War—continues to fascinate scholars and journalists. In writing *Christmas in Washington*, the following books were consulted: Francis Loewenheim, et al., *Roosevelt and Churchill: Their Secret Wartime Correspondence* (New York, 1975); David Stafford, *Roosevelt and Churchill: Men of Secrets* (New York, 2000); Theodore A. Wilson, *The First Summit: Roosevelt and Churchill at Placentia Bay 1941* (Boston, 1969); H.V. Morton, *Atlantic Meeting* (London, 1943); Joseph P. Lash, *Roosevelt and Churchill 1939–1941: The Partnership That Saved the West* (New York, 1976); David Reynolds, *The Creation of the Anglo-American Alliance 1937–41: A Study in Competitive Co-operation* (London, 1981); Randall Bennett Woods, *A Changing of the Guard: Anglo-American Relations, 1941–1946* (Chapel Hill and London, 1990); John Charmley, *Churchill's Grand Alliance: The Anglo-American Special Relationship 1940–57* (New York, 1995); Warren F. Kimball, *Forged in War: Roosevelt, Churchill, and the Second World War* (New York, 1997); Norman Moss, *Nineteen Weeks: America, Britain, and the Fateful Summer of 1940* (Boston and New York, 2003); and Jon Meacham, *Franklin and Winston: An Intimate Portrait of an Epic Friendship* (New York, 2003). British intelligence operations in the United States were largely ignored by F. H. Hinsley, *British Intelligence in the Second World War*, vol. 2, *Its Influence on Strategy and Operations* (London 1981); but they have survived miraculously (despite the destruction of original documents after the Second World War) in British Security Coordination, *The Secret History of British Intelligence in the Americas, 1940–1945* (New York, 1998).

FRANKLIN D. ROOSEVELT

Critical collections of published primary materials include Samuel I. Rosenman, ed., *The Public Papers and Addresses of Franklin D. Roosevelt*, 13 vols. (New York, 1938–1950); *Complete Presidential Press Conferences of Franklin D. Roosevelt, 1933–1945*, 25 vols. (New York, 1972); Elliott Roosevelt, ed., *F.D.R. His Personal Letters*, 2 vols. (New York, 1950); Max Freedman, ed., *Roosevelt and Frankfurter: Their Correspondence 1928–1945* (Boston and Toronto, 1967); and Warren F. Kimball, *Churchill and Roosevelt: The Complete Correspondence*, 3 vols. (Princeton, 1984). The ARCADIA Conference records were published in *Foreign Relations of* the United States: The Conferences at Washington, 1941–1942, and Casablanca, 1943 (Washington, DC, 1968).

Especially useful for Roosevelt and America's entry into the war were more recent books by Waldo Heinrichs, Threshold of War: Franklin D. Roosevelt and American Entry into World War II (New York and Oxford, 1988); and David Reynolds, From Munich to Pearl Harbor: Roosevelt's America and the Origins of the Second World War (Chicago, 2001). Most critical of Roosevelt is Frederick W. Marks III, Wind over Sand: The Diplomacy of Franklin Roosevelt (Athens, GA, 1988). Not to be overlooked is an older classic: Robert Dallek, Franklin D. Roosevelt and American Foreign Policy, 1932–1945 (New York, 1979). Roosevelt as commander-in-chief is detailed in James MacGregor Burns, Roosevelt: The Soldier of Freedom (New York, 1970); and Kenneth S. Davis, FDR: The War President 1940–1943 (New York, 2000). A good collection of essays has been provided by Warren F. Kimball, The Juggler: Franklin Roosevelt as Wartime Statesman (Princeton, 1991). On Franklin and Eleanor Roosevelt, see Joseph P. Lash, Eleanor and Franklin: The story of their relationship, based on Eleanor Roosevelt's private papers (New York, 1971); and especially Doris Kearns Goodwin, No Ordinary Time: Franklin and Eleanor Roosevelt: The Home Front in World War II (New York, 1994). A selection of Eleanor Roosevelt's newspaper columns has been edited by David Emblidge, in My Day: The Best of Eleanor Roosevelt's Acclaimed Newspaper Columns, 1936–1962 (New York, 2001). Mrs. Roosevelt has also left a detailed memoir, This I Remember (New York, 1949). Elliott Roosevelt has left two passionate accounts of his father's life: As He Saw It (New York, 1946); and, with James Brough, A Rendezvous with Destiny: The Roosevelts of the White House (New York, 1975). For the broader topic of Roosevelt and the Americans, see David M. Kenney, Freedom from Fear: The American People in Depression and War, 1929–1945 (New York and Oxford, 1999).

ROOSEVELT'S CONTEMPORARIES

Many of Roosevelt's closest aides left valuable records. For the State Department, these include The Memoirs of Cordell Hull, 2 vols. (New York, 1948); Sumner Welles, Seven Decisions that Shaped History (New York, 1950), and The Time for Decision (London, 1944); Beatrice Bishop Berle and Travis Beal Jacob, eds., Navigating the Rapids: 1918–1971: From the Papers of Adolf A. Berle (New York, 1973); W. Averell Harriman and Elie Abel, Special Envoy to Churchill and Stalin 1941–1946 (New York, 1975); and George F. Kennan, Memoirs 1925–1950, 2 vols. (Boston and Toronto, 1967–1972). For an interventionist at the Department of the Interior, see The Secret Diary of Harold L. Ickes, vol. 3, The Lowering Clouds 1939–1941 (New York, 1954). For Roosevelt's neighbor from the Hudson Valley, Secretary of the Treasury Henry Morgenthau, see John Morton Blum, ed., From the Morgenthau Diaries: Years of Urgency 1938–1941 (Boston, 1965); From the Morgenthau Diaries: Years of War 1941–1945 (Boston, 1967). Roosevelt's close political advisor, Samuel I. Rosenman, produced a defense of his boss: *Working with Roosevelt* (New York, 1972).

Harry Hopkins assumed a special position in diplomatic affairs. See Robert Sherwood's essential works: *The White House Papers of Harry L. Hopkins*, 2 vols. (London, 1948 and 1949); and *Roosevelt and Hopkins: An Intimate History* (New York, 1950). Also, Henry H. Adams, *Harry Hopkins: A Biography* (New York, 1977); George McJimsey, *Harry Hopkins: Ally of the Poor and Defender of Democracy* (Cambridge, MA, and London, 1987); and June Hopkins, *Harry Hopkins: Sudden Hero, Brash Reformer* (New York, 1999). A brief assessment of Hopkins is in Patrick Anderson, *The Presidents' Men: White House Assistants of Franklin D. Roosevelt, Harry S Truman, Dwight D. Eisenhower, John F. Kennedy and Lyndon B. Johnson* (Garden City, NY, 1968). Also relevant are the memoirs of FDR's secretary William D. Hassett, *Off the Record with F.D.R. 1941–1945* (New Brunswick, NJ, 1958). Less important but still useful are those of Roosevelt's chief of staff Fleet Admiral William D. Leahy, *I Was There: The Personal Story of the Chief of Staff to Presidents Roosevelt and Truman Based on His Notes and Diaries Made at the Time* (New York, London, Toronto, 1950).

THE AMERICAN MILITARY AT THE OUTSET OF WAR

Records for the American military must begin with Henry L. Stimson and McGeorge Bundy, *On Active Service in Peace and War* (New York, 1947). George C. Marshall played a key role in December 1941, as related in: Larry I. Bland, ed., *The Papers of George Catlett Marshall*, vol. 3, *"The Right Man for the Right Job" December 7, 1941–May 31, 1943* (Baltimore and London, 1991); Forrest C. Pogue, *George C. Marshall: Ordeal and Hope* (New York, 1966); and Katherine Tupper Marshall, *Together: Annals of an Army Wife* (New York and Atlanta, 1946). Joseph Stilwell left behind trenchant observations of Washington on the brink of war: *The Stilwell Papers: Joseph W. Stilwell* (New York, 1997). For behind-the-scenes operational planning, see Alfred D. Chandler, Jr., ed., *The Papers of Dwight David Eisenhower: The War Years I* (Baltimore and London, 1970); Kevin McCann, *Man from Abilene* (Garden City, NY, 1952); and Kenneth S. Davis, *Soldier of Democracy: A Biography of Dwight D. Eisenhower* (New York, 1952). Formal planning studies are in Maurice Matloff and Edwin M. Snell, *Strategic Planning for Coalition Warfare 1941–1942*, 2 vols. (Washington, DC, 1953–1959); and Ray S. Cline, *Washington Command Post: The Operations Division* (Washington, DC, 1951).

For the U.S. Army Air Forces and the coming of the war, see Robert Hessen, ed., *Berlin Alert: The Memoirs and Reports of Truman Smith* (Stanford, 1984); and Keith E. Eiler, ed., *Wedemeyer on War and Peace* (Stanford, 1987). For the outbreak of the war, see General H. H. Arnold, *Global Mission* (London, 1951). Finally, on the U.S. Navy, see Ernest J. King and Walter Muir Whitehill, *Fleet Admiral King: A Naval Record* (New York, 1976); Patrick Abbazia, *Mr. Roosevelt's Navy: The Private War of the U.S. Atlantic Fleet, 1939–1942* (Annapolis, 1975); and Thomas B. Buell, *Master of Sea Power: A Biography of Fleet Admiral Ernest J. King* (Boston and Toronto, 1980).

WASHINGTON AND THE WHITE HOUSE AT WAR

Numerous White House aides and servants left valuable recollections. These include Alonzo Fields, *My 21 Years in the White House* (Greenwich, CT, 1961); J. B. West, *Upstairs at the White House: My Life with the First Ladies* (New York, 1973); Irwin Hood (Ike) Hoover, *Forty-Two Years in the White House* (Westport, CT, 1974); Henrietta Nesbitt, *White House Diary* (Garden City, NY, 1948); Lillian Rogers Parks and Frances Spatz Leighton, *My Thirty Years Backstairs at the White House* (New York, 1961), and *The Roosevelts: A Family in Turmoil* (Englewood Cliffs, NJ, 1981); Edith Benham Helm, *The Captains and the Kings* (New York, 1954); and especially Grace Tully, *F.D.R.: My Boss* (Chicago, 1949).

Among the visitors to the White House in December 1941 were William M. Rigdon, *White House Sailor* (Garden City, NY, 1962); Jonathan Daniels, *Frontier on the Potomac* (New York, 1972); Mrs. Charles S. Hamlin, "An Old River Friend," *The New Republic* (April 15, 1946); and especially Louis Adamic, *Dinner at the White House* (New York and London, 1946). The setting itself is painstakingly described in William Seale, *The President's House: A History*, vol. 2 (Washington, DC, 1986). The capital at war is richly described in David Brinkley, *Washington Goes To War* (New York, 1988); also, in Scott Hart, *Washington at War: 1941–1945* (Englewood Cliffs, NJ, 1970).

THE SOVIET UNION

For the third leg of the Allied triad, the Soviet Union, the basic documents are in *Foreign Relations of the United States: Diplomatic Papers 1941*, vol. 1, *General: The Soviet Union* (Washington, DC, 1958). Basic recent works include Steven Merritt Miner, *Between Churchill and Stalin: The Soviet Union, Great Britain, and the Origins of the Grand Alliance* (Chapel Hill and London, 1988); Amos Perlmutter, *FDR & Stalin: A Not So Grand Alliance, 1943–1945* (Columbia, MO, and London, 1993); David Reynolds, et al, eds., *Allies at War: The Soviet, American, and British Experience, 1939–1945* (New York, 1994). On the intelligence side, see Bradley F. Smith, *Sharing Secrets with Stalin: How the Allies Traded Intelligence, 1941–1945* (Lawrence, KS, 1996). On Roosevelt's ambassadors to the Soviet Union, see Dennis J. Dunn, *Caught Between Roosevelt & Stalin: America's Ambassadors to Moscow* (Lexington, KY, 1998).

GERMANY

The basic documents concerning German reactions to and interactions with Roosevelt's prewar foreign policy are in Germany, Auswärtiges Amt, *Documents on German Foreign Policy 1918–1945*, Series D, vol. 8, *The War Years* (London, 1954).

For Hitler's reactions to Roosevelt's various diplomatic and naval moves, see the compilation of Hitler's speeches and decrees by Max Domarus, ed., *Hitler. Reden und Proklamationen 1932–1945*, vol. 2, *Untergang* (Munich, 1961). The authoritative edition of the Führer's so-called "secret conversations" is Werner Jochmann, ed., *Adolf Hitler. Monologe im Führer-Hauptquartier 1941–1944* (Munich, 1980). Confidential meetings with foreign leaders are reproduced in Andreas Hillgruber, ed., *Staatsmänner und Diplomaten bei Hitler. Vertrauliche Aufzeichnungen über Unterredungen mit Vertretern des Auslandes 1939–1941* (Frankfurt, 1967). The SS secret reports on the public mood are in Heinz Boberach, ed., *Meldungen aus dem Reich 1938–1945. Die geheimen Lageberichte des Sicherheitsdienstes der SS*, vols. 8 and 9 (Herrsching, 1984). Especially revealing are the newly published complete diaries of Hitler's propaganda minister: Elke Fröhlich, ed., *Die Tagebücher von Joseph Goebbels*, part 2, *Diktate 1941–1945*, vols. 1 and 3 (Munich, 1994 and 1996). Hitler's official Foreign Office translator also left his remembrances: Paul Schmidt, *Statist auf diplomatischer Bühne 1923–1945. Erlebnisse des Chefdolmetschers im Auswärtigen Amt mit den Staatsmännern Europas* (Bonn, 1950). Of special interest are the superbly edited memoirs of State Secretary Ernst von Weizsäcker: Leonidas E. Hill, ed., *Die Weizsäcker Papiere 1933–1950* (Frankfurt, Berlin, and Vienna, 1974).

The most important naval documents of the Third Reich pertaining to the Battle of the Atlantic have been edited by Michael Salewski, *Die deutsche Seekriegsleitung 1935–1945*, vol. 3, *Denkschriften und Lagebetrachtungen 1938–1944* (Frankfurt, 1973). An analysis is in Holger H. Herwig, *Politics of Frustration: The United States in German Naval Planning, 1889–1941* (Boston and Toronto, 1976); more recently, Norman J. W. Goda, *Tomorrow the World: Hitler, Northwest Africa, and the Path Toward America* (College Station, TX, 1998).

PRIMARY SOURCES: THE UNITED STATES

The Franklin D. Roosevelt Library and Archives at Hyde Park, New York, contain vast amounts of materials used for this project. For the president, they include: President's Official File Papers, President's Personal File 1933–45, President's Secretary File Papers, President's Safe Files, FDR: Reminiscences by Contemporaries, FDR Speech Files, Map Room Papers, Press Conferences Reports, and President's Book Collection. For Eleanor Roosevelt, there are the voluminous Eleanor Roosevelt Papers. Of special interest were the White House Correspondence/Personal Letters, the Speech and Articles Files, the "My Day" columns, and the Oral Histories files.

Hyde Park also houses the papers of numerous FDR aides and Cabinet members: Henry A. Wallace Papers (vice president), Harold Ickes Papers (Secretary of the Interior), Henry L. Stimson Papers (Secretary of War), Henry Morgenthau, Jr., Presidential Diaries (Secretary of the Treasury), Adolf A. Berle Diary, Sumner Welles Papers, Sam I. Rosenman Papers, Felix Frankfurter Papers, John G. Winant

Papers, Stephen Early Papers, William D. Hassett Papers, Joseph Lash Papers, and Henry L. Hopkins Papers, among others. The Library also has the Secret Service Records and the Federal Bureau of Investigation Files pertaining to Roosevelt and the White House.

Last but not least, there are countless papers of minor characters: Bernard Bellush Papers, Betty Hight Papers, Admiral John L. McCrae Papers, Lorena Hickok Papers, Lela Mae Stiles Papers, Margaret Suckley Papers, and the personal reminiscences of Mrs. Charles Hamlin (Huibertje Pruyn Hamlin).

The Manuscript Division of the Library of Congress in Washington, DC, also has a good collection of manuscripts by people who worked with FDR. These include, at the senior level, The Presidential Diaries of Henry Morgenthau, Jr. (Secretary of the Treasury), Cordell Hull Papers (Secretary of State), Diaries of Henry L. Stimson (Secretary of War), The Papers of Frank Knox (Secretary of the Navy), The Papers of Ernest Joseph King (Navy), and the Henry H. Arnold Papers (Army Air Forces). There are also numerous lesser papers: Hanson W. Baldwin papers, The Papers of Ruby Aurora Black, The Papers of Claude Charles Bloch, Benjamin V. Cohen Papers, Joseph E. Davies Papers, Ira Eaker Papers, Rudolph Forster Papers, The Papers of Julius August Furer, Charles S. Hamlin Papers, W. Averell Harriman Papers, The Papers of Charles A. Lockwood, Donald J. MacDonald Papers, John L. McCrea Papers, Henrietta Nesbitt Papers, Robert P. Patterson Papers, Carl Spaatz Papers, and John H. Towers Papers.

PRIMARY SOURCES: UNITED KINGDOM

The Public Record Office in Kew has an abundance of documents relevant to what transpired during ARCADIA. The Admiralty Papers were indispensable in providing the career history and personal letters of Sir Dudley Pound and other naval officials of the era. The logs of HMS *Duke of York* are also in the Admiralty Papers and, fortunately for historians, are meticulous in their recounting of the ship's activities in December 1941 and January 1942. The War Cabinet Papers contain all the telegrams dealing with Operation ARCADIA, as well as the records of most discussions and meetings that took place in Washington. The Prime Minister's Office: Correspondence and Papers to 1945, the Records of the Foreign Office and the War Office Papers, were also key to this study.

The Churchill Archives at Cambridge provided a wealth of information for this book. The holdings include the original copies of Churchill's correspondence with his contemporaries and family members, along with the Chartwell Estate Papers. The archive also holds the papers of many other important figures who figure in this story, including Churchill's private secretary, John Martin; Dudley Pound; E.I.C. Jacob; and Lord Halifax. Like the Churchill Archives, the Liddell Hart Centre for Military Archives at King's College, London, has a large collection of documents pertaining to Churchill and the Second World War. These include the Sir John Dill Papers, the Ismay Papers, and the Alanbrooke Papers. The Beaverbrook Papers are held by the House of Lords Record Office. The Imperial War Museum Department of Documents contains the papers of Sir Leslie Hollis and Royal Navy Volunteer Reservist R. A. Bennett-Levy's account of the trip to Washington aboard the *Duke of York*.

PRIMARY SOURCES: CANADA

The National Archives of Canada (NAC) holds the complete Diary of Canadian prime minister William Lyon Mackenzie King, which is also available, in full, on the NAC website.

ACKNOWLEDGMENTS

W E WERE FORTUNATE TO BE ABLE TO SECURE THE SERVICE OF Ms. Laurel Halladay and Ms. Stephanie Cousineau to help in the research for this book. Both are Ph.D. candidates in the Department of History at the University of Calgary and both have held prestigious competitive national scholarships. Their diligence in tracking down sources, their enterprise in mining archives in North America and the United Kingdom, and the intelligence they brought to the task is alone evidence of their great futures as historians in their own right. We owe them more than we can possibly say.

As always, our friend and agent, Ms. Linda McKnight, proved more than worthy of our trust. She suggested the topic and encouraged us to pursue it over several years. While we were at sea for three weeks in the spring of 2002—some 400 miles west of the French coast—helping James Cameron film his epic documentary on the German battleship *Bismarck*, Linda was but a far away voice on a noisy satellite phone. That voice was one of calm and reason, as it always is.

Our wives, Barrie Bercuson and Lorraine Herwig, read every word of this manuscript—several times. There was much lively discussion between them and us as they helped hone our views and polish our prose about two of the most famous men in history. They remain our toughest critics, our closest friends, and the loves of our lives. We dedicate this book to them.

INDEX